D1566687

It's a New Day

RELIGION AND AMERICAN CULTURE

Series Editors

David Edwin Harrell Jr.
Wayne Flynt
Edith L. Blumhofer

It's a New Day

Race and Gender in the Modern Charismatic Movement

Scott Billingsley

THE UNIVERSITY OF ALABAMA PRESS

Tuscaloosa

Typeface: ACaslon

∞
The paper on which this book is printed meets the minimum requirements of
American National Standard for Information Sciences-Permanence of Paper for
Printed Library Materials, ANSI Z39.48–1984.

Library of Congress Cataloging-in-Publication Data

Billingsley, Scott, 1968–
    It's a new day : race and gender in the modern charismatic movement / Scott
Billingsley.
        p.   cm. — (Religion and American culture)
    Includes bibliographical references and index.
    ISBN 978-0-8173-1606-8 (cloth : alk. paper) — ISBN 978-0-8173-8013-7 (electronic :
alk. paper) 1. Pentecostalism—United States—History. 2. Race relations—Religious
aspects—Pentecostal churches. 3. African American Pentecostals—History. 4. Sex
role—Religious aspects—Pentecostal churches. I. Title.
    BR1644.5.U6B55 2008
    277.3'08208—dc22

                                                                        2007035577

Contents

Illustrations

Acknowledgments

The support I received from my colleagues, friends, and family while writing this book was invaluable. Mark Roberts and his staff at Oral Roberts University's Holy Spirit Research Center, David Roebuck and Louis Morgan at Lee University's Dixon Pentecostal Research Center, and Tony Cooke and Owen Adams at the Rhema Bible Training Center not only assisted in my research but became valued friends in the process. Nor would this project have been possible without the cooperation of the evangelists themselves. Staff members from the following ministries accommodated my needs and answered my questions: Billye Brim Ministries; Keith Butler's Word of Faith International Christian Center; Kenneth Copeland Ministries; Creflo Dollar Ministries; Kenneth Hagin Ministries; Marilyn Hickey Ministries; Vicki Jamison-Peterson Ministries; Freda Lindsay's Christ for the Nations; Eddie Long's New Birth Missionary Baptist Church; Kate McVeigh Ministries; and Joyce Meyer Ministries.

Several organizations provided the financial assistance necessary for completing the research and writing of this project. The Milo Howard travel award, Graduate School, College of Liberal Arts, and Daniel F. Breeden Eminent Scholar fund at Auburn University, as well as the history department at the University of North Carolina at Pembroke, provided research and travel funds. Elizabeth Normandy, director of the Teaching and Learning Center at UNCP, graciously subsidized the cost of two photographs. Two fellowships—the Marguerite Scharnagel Scholarship and the Christian Scholarship Foundation's Graduate Fellowship Award—allowed me to devote two summers to writing. Housing expenses were offset by the hospitality of the Kevin and Christy Gardner and Steve and Holly Kirby families, who graciously opened their homes for extended stays while I was traveling. Tony Cooke also made housing arrangements for me at Rhema Bible Training Center.

David Edwin Harrell Jr. served as both mentor and friend while I was researching and writing this book. I greatly appreciate his insight, advice, and generosity. Auburn University history professors Donna Bohanan, Anthony Gene Carey, Wayne Flynt, Larry Gerber, and Jeff Jakeman also provided guidance, making sure I received the training necessary to become a well-rounded scholar. Portions of this book were presented at the annual meeting of the Southern Historical Association and the spring meeting of the American Society of Church History. At these meetings, the comments of Nancy Hardesty, Glenda Bridges, David Roebuck, and Dwain Waldrep were most helpful. Special debts of gratitude go to Jonathan Lawrence, for his supurb copyediting skills, and to Edith Blumhofer and Randall Stephens, for their excellent critiques of the manuscript. I am also indebted to the staff of The University of Alabama Press for guiding this book to completion.

David Carter, Jeff Frederick, Christian Gelzer, John Hardin, Charles Israel, Joe McCall, Steve Murray, Ken Noe, Jim Ross, and Mark Wilson offered friendship and moral support at various stages of research and writing, and my colleagues in the history department at the University of North Carolina at Pembroke were also encouraging as I revised the manuscript. I am especially grateful for the support of my family. The Billingsley, Betterton, Clower, and Greene clans were genuinely interested in the progress of my research. My wife, Kelly, was just glad that I finally finished; she was far more patient than any wife should have to be. Our daughters, Afton and Addie, made the final months of writing and editing a true joy.

It's a New Day

Introduction

Historian Peter Williams, in his survey of America's religions, observed that it "is tempting to characterize *every* era of American history as one of rapid social and cultural change."[1] The years following World War II mark such an era in which the lives of everyday Americans were transformed through dramatic social, political, demographic, economic, and technological changes. The rising suburban population, the growth of the middle class, and the introduction of new forms of mass media helped shape the landscape of American society through the end of the twentieth century. The civil rights and feminist movements of the 1950s, 1960s, and 1970s fostered some of the most notable changes, and these largely secular movements provided the backdrop for major transformations in American religion in the last quarter of the century.

The rise of female and African American evangelists in the independent charismatic movement has proven to be a remarkable story of the struggle for sexual and racial equality in modern American Christianity. This book identifies some of the major and minor figures in this movement, examines their rise to prominence, explores the people and institutions that influenced their ascent, and describes the major themes emphasized in their teaching. It is not my intent to provide comprehensive theological or sociological critiques of these ministers or their movement. I have simply tried to tell their stories and analyze their significance in modern American society. I argue that these ministers served as cultural mediators between the secular and religious worlds—religious entrepreneurs, if you will—taking socially and theologically liberal ideologies and adapting them to fit the sensibilities of conservative evangelical audiences.

Historians have long used sociological and anthropological models to provide theoretical frameworks for studying religious movements. Variations of the relative deprivation theory have provided the basis for many studies of the Pentecostal and charismatic movements, which Robert Mapes Anderson found persuasive in his classic study of the origins of Pentecostalism. He argued that early Pentecostals experienced anxiety caused by poverty and social marginalization. They were less able than the general population to cope with the changing world around them and therefore retreated from the larger society, finding solace in a new religious movement that emphasized religious ecstasy and the imminent Second Coming of Jesus.[2] Certainly the changes of post–World War II America also caused a great deal of anxiety for some people, but those same changes produced hope for others. In 1966 anthropologist Anthony F. C. Wallace argued that religion functioned to satisfy human needs and wants by helping to revitalize and stabilize societies in flux. He outlined how successful revitalization movements developed, and he demonstrated how religious leaders often served as cultural mediators who used religion to create new social orders and restore social equilibrium in a seemingly disorganized society.[3]

A quarter century later, sociologists Roger Finke and Rodney Stark advanced an economic model for interpreting the state of religion in America. Although their idea was not entirely original (observers of American religion had used such language since at least the eighteenth century), it sparked considerable debate among historians and sociologists when they challenged dominant interpretations of American religious history and argued that it should be analyzed through a market-oriented lens.[4] Building on this and other research, historian R. G. Robins, in his biography of Pentecostal leader A. J. Tomlinson, "focused on the intersection of religion, modernization, and the marketplace" to describe the rise of this religious entrepreneur. He explains how Tomlinson "preserved key elements of traditional spirituality by repackaging them as mass-consumable products capable of thriving in the modern world."[5] Sociologist Shayne Lee, in his study of charismatic evangelist T. D. Jakes, used an "economic approach that studies churches as companies competing to offer religious products for potential clients" when explaining "Jakes' mass appeal."[6] Despite its limitations, I have chosen to use this economic model because it can provide a better understanding of how the independent evangelists who emerged in the postwar era sought to capitalize on the social transformations occurring in secular society and create a new social order of racial and sexual equality in their churches.

The ministers examined in this book have been largely overlooked by historians, and few scholarly works have been written about them, even in fields other than history. Sociologists have been at the forefront of much of the existing scholarship. Milmon F. Harrison, in *Righteous Riches: The Word of Faith Movement in Contemporary African American Religion* (2005), offers the best sociological account of how the prosperity message affected modern black churches, and Shayne Lee's *T. D. Jakes: America's New Preacher* (2005) analyzes the life and ministry of a leading proponent of the prosperity message. Although this volume will cover some of the same territory that Harrison and Lee covered, I focus more on the historical context and less on the sociological and theological contexts. For much of my source material I rely on Pentecostal and charismatic periodicals such as *Charisma and Christian Life;* magazines, books, and other literature published by independent ministries; audio- and videotapes of sermons; newspaper articles; and personal interviews. Although I offer some critical analysis and interpretation, I have tried mainly to let these people speak for themselves and tell their story in their own words. This book seeks to fill a void in the literature by explaining how this new generation of charismatic leaders rose to prominence and interacted with other cultural phenomena in modern America.

Evangelicalism and the Charismatic Movement

Defining the terms used in this study is a difficult task, since they have many nuances and there is no consensus among either scholars or the participants about their meaning. Pentecostals and charismatics are most often identified by their belief in the charismata—the miraculous gifts of the Holy Spirit—especially glossolalia (speaking in tongues) and divine healing. The ecstatic experience of speaking in tongues is, according to Pentecostals and charismatics, the evidence of "being filled with the Holy Spirit" or "receiving the baptism of the Holy Spirit." I use the term *Pentecostal* when referring to those who belong to traditional Pentecostal denominations such as the Assemblies of God and the Church of God in Christ. I typically use *charismatic* when referring to those who believe in the charismata but are not members of an established denomination. I also use this term when referring to those who believe in the charismata and belong to non-Pentecostal denominations, such as Baptists and Episcopalians. I use the term *neo-Pentecostal* to identify mainline congregations that have adopted Pentecostal and charismatic theology and worship styles. Some of these churches remained in their traditional denominations while others became independent, effectively becoming charismatic churches.

The term *evangelical* is often used to describe a monolithic entity that espouses a certain set of conservative theological, political, and social beliefs. Historians of American religion have done much to dispel this myth and emphasize the diversity that exists within evangelicalism. George Marsden, Randall Balmer, and others have described the kaleidoscopic nature of evangelicalism and have shown how this designation serves as a broad umbrella encompassing many different types of Christians. Most scholars agree that, in general, evangelicals emphasize a grace-oriented theology, encourage some sort of conversion experience whereby an individual acknowledges his or her personal sin and accepts the atoning sacrifice of Jesus' death on the cross for their salvation, believe in authority of scripture over human tradition, have an evangelistic zeal to spread the Christian message, and try to lead a pious lifestyle.[7]

Beneath this umbrella are groups of Christians who have common histories, identities, cultural experiences, and tendencies but who otherwise may not have any formal connection with each other. In fact, sometimes these groups have disparaged each other over various doctrinal, social, or political issues. One of the more notable subsets within evangelicalism is fundamentalism. Fundamentalists became an identifiable group in the early twentieth century and took a militant stand against modernism, primarily over the issues of biblical inerrancy—particularly as it related to the theory of evolution, which was being taught in some public schools at the turn of the century—and the increasing influence of biblical criticism in churches and seminaries across the country. Secular modernists willingly accepted these new ideas, which, conservatives believed, directly contradicted biblical teaching and authority. Christian modernists adapted these ideas to fit into a Christian context whereby they could maintain their faith in God and the Bible and still acknowledge the role of science and higher criticism. Between 1910 and 1915 fundamentalists published a series of essays titled *The Fundamentals: A Testimony to the Truth,* explaining their doctrinal positions on these and other issues. In 1919 they also established the World's Christian Fundamentals Association, which further enhanced their status as a cohesive group committed to fundamentalist principles. They became one of the most conservative groups within American Protestantism, and, despite their setbacks after the Scopes trial of 1925, continued to build formal and informal networks, allowing them to maintain significant influence within evangelicalism for the remainder of the twentieth century.[8]

Pentecostals and charismatics represent two more subsets of evangelicalism. Although many evangelicals—including fundamentalists—did not accept them into their fold, the Pentecostal/charismatic theology and worldview fit neatly under the evangelical umbrella. Pentecostals and charismatics adhered to basic evangelical beliefs—salvation by grace, conversion experience, infallibility of scripture, emphasis on evangelism, and pious living—and had the same countercultural attitude that characterized evangelicalism for much of the twentieth century. Historian Matthew Sutton argues that the early-twentieth-century Pentecostal evangelist Aimee Semple McPherson, through her ecumenism and conservative theology, "paved the way for pentecostals to contribute to the fundamentalist movement and led pentecostals into the mainstream of American evangelicalism."[9] He maintains that Pentecostals were not outsiders looking in on the fundamentalist-modernist debates, as some scholars have suggested, but were equal participants in a broad and diverse stream of American fundamentalists:

> Pentecostals did have unique beliefs that characterized their movement and set them apart from other groups. But so did dispensationalists and conservative Presbyterians. While each group had its own room in the big house of fundamentalism, everyone—pentecostals, holiness, dispensationalists, and Presbyterians—lived under the same roof. But this has not been the image conveyed by scholars, who have typically overemphasized Pentecostals' doctrinal variations, privileging the rhetorical battles sporadically waged in theological journals and Bible colleges, even as they have underemphasized pentecostals' grassroots relationships with fundamentalists.[10]

McPherson's conservative theology and connection to other evangelicals placed her in the forefront of the fundamentalist-modernist debates, but, Sutton claims, she was rejected by the evangelical subculture (particularly the National Association of Evangelicals) because of her controversial actions and personality.

By midcentury, Randall Balmer contends, evangelicals had become ambivalent about secular society. They grew less suspicious of the secular world's values, attitudes, and standards of success. In the 1970s they emerged from their self-imposed exile to embrace the values of mainstream American society. "Even as many evangelicals retain the old rhetoric of opposition to the world," Balmer writes, "they are eager to appropriate many of that world's standards of success. This explains, for instance, the proliferation of prosperity theology in evangelical circles, the doctrine that God eagerly bestows the accouterments of middle-class materialism . . . upon the faithful."[11]

By century's end, Pentecostals and charismatics had been accepted by most evangelicals. Baptist evangelist James Robison noted that the "Washington for Jesus" rally held in April 1980 marked "one of the first times that mainline denominations joined hands with charismatics and Pentecostals and said, 'Let's stand up together.' That was significant. That was sort of a coming together of a lot of different groups."[12] Several charismatic and non-charismatic ministers used their radio and television broadcasts, mailing lists, and personal contacts to draw more than two hundred thousand evangelicals to the rally. John Gimenez, the pastor of a charismatic megachurch in Norfolk, Virginia, first suggested such a gathering. He was joined by charismatic leaders such as Pat Robertson, Jim Bakker, and Demos Shakarian along with non-charismatic evangelicals such as Adrian Rogers, Charles Stanley, and James Robison.[13]

Historian David Edwin Harrell Jr. explains the role that televangelists such as Christian Broadcasting Network founder and *The 700 Club* host Pat Robertson played in the acceptance of charismatics into the evangelical subculture and the convergence of evangelicalism into mainstream American society. "More than most pentecostals and charismatics," he argues, "Robertson was tied to a body of evangelical thought that historically preceded charismatic theology." He took the self-help, positive-attitude message that evangelicals such as Norman Vincent Peale made popular in the 1950s and "added an overtly miraculous dimension" that appealed to charismatics.[14] "Charismatic belief in the power of positive faith," Harrell writes, "was often difficult to distinguish from the positive thinking emphasis found in evangelical circles. It was their belief in miracles and the gifts of the Holy Spirit that most clearly separated pentecostals and charismatics from other evangelical Christians."[15] But, Harrell asserts, "for better or for worse, it is rhetoric that separates charismatics from other Christians, not practice. When faced with the imponderable, with decisions that transcend rational investigation, most Christians pray and consult the Scriptures and then try to make a spiritual choice." In other words, charismatic and non-charismatic evangelicals believe that God takes an active role in the modern world. But charismatics, unlike other evangelicals, claim to have more faith in God's willingness to provide a supernatural solution to the problems they face.[16] As these two groups began to acknowledge that their theological differences were not as great as they once seemed, non-charismatic evangelicals came to tolerate charismatic ideas about the miraculous. This acceptance by evangelicals allowed charismatics and Pentecostals to become an important part of the conservative political and social coalition that emerged in the 1970s and 1980s.[17]

Several features that characterized the charismatic movement from the 1970s through the 1990s help to explain why charismatics moved into the mainstream of American society and why this new breed of evangelists succeeded. An important organ for promoting the modern charismatic movement was *Charisma and Christian Life* magazine, which began to appear in 1975. This publication proved to be the best single source for gauging the mood of the charismatic movement as it addressed the important topics of the day—and by the 1970s racial and sexual equality had become hot topics in the charismatic movement. In his study of race and class in southern religious sects, Harrell notes how members of sectarian groups raised their education levels and socioeconomic status in the 1950s and 1960s and adopted moderate and liberal racial views in the 1970s. "Many of the 'new evangelicals,'" he writes, "proudly looked on this new social conscience as a symptom of the growing maturity and sophistication of their sects."[18] Echoing the observations of sociologists David Moberg and David Reimers, Harrell contends that "the racial views of southern sects . . . 'reflect the larger society'" and that "'churches are social institutions that are shaped by the culture in which they exist.'"[19] Evidence of this sociological phenomenon can be seen in *Charisma* magazine, which promoted racial and sexual equality from its inception. *Charisma*'s publisher and founder, Stephen Strang, worked to foster a sophisticated and respectable image for the charismatic movement as it made the transition from outsider to insider status in popular American culture. *Charisma* reported on and promoted a wide range of female and African American evangelists, helping them to become international icons among charismatics and evangelicals.

Another important feature of the charismatic movement was the use of technology. For centuries there has been an important interplay between new forms of mass communication and religious, intellectual, and social change, but globalization and the technological advances of the twentieth century made this interaction particularly poignant.[20] In the 1920s, evangelist Aimee Semple McPherson was one of the first preachers to use radio to promote her ministry and become a modern American celebrity. Charismatic evangelists Oral Roberts and Kathryn Kuhlman pioneered the effective use of television to build their empires in the 1950s and 1960s. But televangelism did not become a truly significant force in American society until religious networks emerged in the 1960s and 1970s.

The growth of the charismatic movement also contributed to the trend toward megachurches. In addition to their evangelistic crusades and television shows, many of these independent evangelists established churches that ranged in membership from two thousand to thirty thousand. According to Donald Matthews of the Chicago Theological Seminary, "Pastors are building these tremendously large churches in urban areas that are attracting a large number of black lower-middle and middle-class folks. They want to be involved in a church setting where both the intellectual and spiritual aspects of worship can be experienced."[21] In 1991 there were forty-five American churches that consistently had at least five thousand attendees each Sunday; ten years later there were more than four hundred such congregations, of which thirty-five were black.[22] Theologian Anthony B. Pinn observed that "a needs-based approach to ministry will dominate in churches with large numbers as well as those attempting to gain large numbers. The basic theological parameters will soften to accommodate this form of ministry." The churches will advocate "the acquisition of goods," and "[m]arketing and public relations companies will help churches develop the language and appeal necessary to increase their audience."[23] In other words, Pinn argued that successful religious entrepreneurs would adopt market strategies that would allow them to sell their wares in an open and competitive market.

Good entrepreneurs also understood the importance of finding a niche market and tailoring their message to a particular audience. Megachurches, according to missiologist Harvie Conn, had unique demographics. He characterized them as regional churches which drew their membership from a homogeneous racial or ethnic group that did not necessarily live in the same community: "A commonly shared ethnicity overcomes long distances and draws members from a wide geographical area for fellowship and nurture . . . creating their own urban centers out of the destination they can reach by car in a reasonable length of time."[24] Many megachurch pastors built their religious fiefdoms by espousing a message of hope and prosperity; by catering to the physical, emotional, and social needs of their constituents; and by providing a sense of community through Bible studies, social programs, and small cell groups.

Another hallmark of the burgeoning charismatic movement was strong leadership. All of the independent evangelists who rose to prominence in the twentieth century developed and articulated a particular vision for their ministry—and then they convinced their followers to carry out that vision. In his study of Christian fringe groups, historian Richard Kyle argues that "almost every major, successful, contemporary parachurch ministry is built around a single personality, who is able to attract a coterie of dedicated followers."[25] Each evangelist created a unique identity for his or her ministry that was "broad enough to appeal to a wide range of persons" yet specific enough to "offer a cohesive world view" that promoted unity among his or her followers.[26] With some, the emphasis was on prosperity; with others, it was on emotional healing; and a few even continued to focus on divine physical healing. Regardless of their core message, these men and women had the organizational skills, natural charisma, and vision necessary to build and sustain large ministries.

Although leadership styles varied widely, sociologist Scott Thumma's examination of megachurches and their pastors is instructive for understanding independent charismatic evangelists. Thumma maintains that a gifted spiritual leader with a recognized "calling" was essential for the success of most megachurches. "The character of these churches usually reflects the vision and personality of this one person," and as founder and senior pastor, "these persons occupy the singular, most prominent, high profile position in the congregation." Very often they had little or no formal religious training, relying on their "anointing by the Holy Spirit" to provide validation. They were typically astute businesspeople who worked hard, took chances when necessary, and learned how to delegate responsibility as their ministries grew. They became CEOs of multimillion-dollar corporations and adopted the institutional structures and leadership styles of corporate executives. Despite the existence of accountability procedures, such as executive boards and external auditors, most independent evangelists maintained highly centralized, sometimes dictatorial control over their ministries. These were clearly *their* ministries, which sometimes made the issue of succession difficult.[25] Family members played an important role in perpetuating charismatic ministries. Oral Roberts's son Richard and Kenneth E. Hagin's son, Kenneth Hagin Jr., successfully took the helm of their fathers' institutions, but other healing evangelists did not have heirs to continue their work. Although at the turn of the twenty-first century it was too early to tell who would take over the ministries under consideration here, there were clear signs that a few of these evangelists were grooming their offspring for a transfer of power.

The explosion of charismatic and neo-Pentecostal groups created quite a stir in the last quarter of the millennium. Although some twentieth-century scholars predicted the decline of religion in modern times, the evangelical subculture was prepared to become a dominant force in American Protestantism. By the 1980s Pentecostals and charismatics had gained the respect of the evangelical community and were able to participate as full partners in the resurgence of conservative Christianity. Most evangelists quit holding tent crusades and moved their meetings into posh hotels, large convention centers, major sports arenas, and megachurches. They placed less emphasis on divine healing and more on religious education—with much of that teaching focusing on prosperity and emotional healing. As one megachurch pastor freely admitted: "My assignment is to preach good news to the poor. . . . What is the good news to the poor? You don't have to stay poor. Get the anointing and God will equip you with discipline and will so you can move from poverty to prosperity—not billionaireship, not millionaireship, but you will have more than enough to meet the needs of your family."[28] This attitude dominated much of the charismatic movement at century's end, and it contributed greatly to the success of female and African American independent evangelists.

Outline of the Book

Chapter 1 examines the origins of Pentecostalism and the important leaders of the independent healing revival and charismatic movement after World War II. Postwar independent evangelists challenged traditional models of racial and gender roles by holding integrated services and giving women and African Americans important positions within their organizations. Asa A. Allen, a prominent healing revivalist in the 1950s and 1960s, increasingly appealed to poor blacks late in his career, and by the 1960s he advocated fully integrated services. He even took the bold step of speaking against segregation, and in 1961 he added a black singer named Gene Martin to his evangelistic team. By the late 1960s he was mentoring future black ministers, allowing them to live in his home and become part of his family. Although personal problems and public scandals followed Allen up to his death in 1970, his influence upon many independent ministers was evident in later decades.

Oral Roberts and Kenneth E. Hagin also exerted tremendous influence on the ministry-building techniques and theology of modern revivalists. They provided models for later ministries and promoted African American involvement and leadership in the charismatic movement. Roberts, probably the most famous independent charismatic leader of the twentieth century, provided a pattern for how to build a strong, self-sustaining empire. His success in promoting his revivals, raising money, selling books, and using radio and television as evangelistic tools made him a celebrity among Pentecostals. He instinctively knew when and how to expand his ministry, cultivate relationships with non-Pentecostals and wealthy businessmen, and refocus his message to make evangelism—instead of healing—the dominant theme of his revivals. A key to Roberts's success was his ability to maintain close ties with Pentecostals while at the same time reaching out to traditional churches.

Kenneth E. Hagin, less famous outside charismatic circles but equally important, provided the message—generally labeled the "Word of Faith" teaching—that most of the new ministers espoused. Although Hagin was not the first Pentecostal to embrace the principles of what came to be called the "prosperity message" or "faith message," he was widely credited with making it popular. He sold millions of books and sermon tapes, and his Rhema Bible Training Center, which he established in the mid-1970s, instilled this message into thousands of pastors and evangelists worldwide.

Two twentieth-century female evangelists provided models for later female ministers to follow. Aimee Semple McPherson, one of the most prominent evangelists of early Pentecostalism, succeeded in large part by using modern forms of entertainment to transmit her fundamentalist message. Later female evangelists effectively used these techniques to build their own successful ministries. Kathryn Kuhlman built a large healing ministry during the 1960s and was the first female healing evangelist to have a national television audience. Popular periodicals such as *People* and *Christianity Today* recognized her as one of the most prominent faith healers and female preachers in the United States in the 1970s. Like McPherson, Kuhlman also influenced a generation of charismatic evangelists, both male and female.

Other women in the post–World War II period made substantial contributions as well. Chapter 2 examines the role that the wives of prominent male evangelists played in promoting the charismatic revival. Daisy Washburn Osborn, wife of Oklahoma evangelist T. L. Osborn, played an important role as organizer, administrator, teacher, and preacher in their ministry after 1948. Always an important part of her husband's operation, she became an outspoken advocate of women's rights toward the end of her life. Several other women played critical roles in the development of large independent ministries. Freda Lindsay, wife of Pentecostal evangelist Gordon Lindsay, supported her husband in his role as pastor, evangelist, and promoter of the healing revival until his death in 1973. She assumed control of their Dallas-based ministry, Christ for the Nations International (CFNI), after he died. A respected editor, publisher, CEO, and religious leader, Lindsay used her sharp business acumen to make CFNI one of the most influential charismatic institutions in the world. Gloria Copeland, wife of television evangelist Kenneth Copeland, also played supporting roles in the early years of her husband's ministry, but eventually she became an important public figure in her own right. She succeeded in gaining notoriety as a co-evangelist partly because she, along with her husband, effectively used cutting-edge technology, such as cable and satellite television, to promote the prosperity message to a receptive audience.

Chapter 3 discusses the rise of female ministers, such as Marilyn Hickey and Joyce Meyer, during the last quarter of the twentieth century. Hickey was one of the first female evangelists to become popular when a new generation of charismatic leaders began to emerge in the 1970s. Although physical healing and the prosperity message were important themes in her teaching, her primary appeal was as a conventional Bible teacher. Her devotional guides, Bible reading programs, and radio and television teaching series were quite popular. Hickey espoused conservative views about the role of women in the home, but she believed that God used female leaders in the church. She encouraged female ministers to strike a healthy balance between their roles as mothers and wives with their role as pastor or evangelist. By the mid-1990s Joyce Meyer had become the most popular female evangelist in America, her message of emotional healing appealing to a broad cross section of evangelical women and men. She also maintained a traditional view of male spiritual leadership in the home, but she clearly embraced modern notions of sexual equality in the church. The extraordinary success of these women, coupled with the influence of Oral Roberts and Kenneth Hagin, inspired other women to launch ministries of their own. Although these lesser-known figures did not have the broad exposure that Hickey and Meyer had, they were important to the dramatic growth of the charismatic movement and its influence on modern American religion.

Chapters 4 and 5 examine the growing prominence of black charismatic ministries in recent years. In the 1950s and 1960s African Americans began to take visible roles in some healing ministries; they were often musicians who greatly influenced the changing music and worship styles of the charismatic movement. White revivalists trained some of these young evangelists, while others established successful independent ministries on their own. Probably the most important African American charismatic evangelist in the late twentieth century was Frederick K. C. Price. The first black preacher to become popular in the new generation of charismatic leaders, Price influenced others to start their own ministries. Like Marilyn Hickey, he began his ministry in the mid-1970s and rose to prominence during the 1980s. Price, whose Crenshaw Christian Center was located in a poor area of downtown Los Angeles, initially emphasized Kenneth Hagin's prosperity message. In the early 1990s, however, he had a personal conflict with the Hagin family and began to focus more of his teaching on racism in the church.

Although the neo-Pentecostal movement of the 1960s and early 1970s occurred mainly in white churches, a second wave of charismatic renewal swept through black churches in the 1980s and 1990s. Many of the new black leaders promoted social and political activism, engaged in community outreach, and provided leadership training and life skills to African Americans, especially young men. Several of the new black charismatic leaders came from Baptist or Church of God in Christ backgrounds and worked to forge ties with some mainline Protestant and black Pentecostal denominations, but the Word of Faith movement had the most visible impact on these new leaders. The emergence of large, independent megachurches and successful television ministries was indicative of the tremendous growth and popularity of the charismatic movement among African Americans.

T. D. Jakes and Creflo Dollar were two of the most prominent African American evangelists in the 1990s. Jakes began his ministry in 1982 but did not gain national recognition until the early 1990s. In 1996 he established the Potter's House, a multiracial, nondenominational charismatic church in Dallas, whose membership soared to thirty thousand within five years. His message of emotional healing, racial unity, and spiritual renewal was popular among charismatics and non-charismatics alike. Dollar started his World Changers Church International in Atlanta in 1986, beginning with only eight people. His congregation grew to over twenty thousand members by century's end, and he became an internationally known author, conference speaker, and television and radio evangelist. Kenneth Hagin and Kenneth Copeland influenced Dollar early in his career, and he emphasized the Word of Faith message advanced by these two ministers.

In one way or another, all of these evangelists addressed issues of gender and race, but their messages were generally designed to defuse rather than ignite tensions. They fit well anthropological and sociological models of religious leaders who mediated powerful secular ideologies into traditional religious formats. Each of these leaders used religious symbols, myths, and ideological rituals to reconcile new intellectual currents to traditional religious beliefs. They helped to develop a new conservative social milieu that adapted the core beliefs of independent charismatic theology to modern social concerns. As a result, they modified individual and group behavior, moods, attitudes, and values so that an acceptable level of social stability could be maintained. The new charismatic ministers reinterpreted and domesticated the ideas of modern feminists and civil rights activists, and they provided religious rituals and symbols that accommodated new values and made radical reforms palatable to a largely conservative audience.

1
Origins and Pioneers

At the dawn of the twentieth century, Agnes Ozman, a young student at the Bethel Bible School in Topeka, Kansas, became the first modern Pentecostal when, according to historian Vinson Synan, she "received a startling manifestation of the gift of tongues." Synan records the recollections of this event by the school's founder, Charles Fox Parham: "I laid my hands upon her and prayed. . . . I had scarcely completed three dozen sentences when a glory fell upon her, a halo seemed to surround her head and face, and she began speaking the Chinese language and was unable to speak English for three days." Parham began his ministerial career as a supply pastor for the Methodist Episcopal Church in Kansas, but after 1895 he adopted an anti-denominational position and emphasized the Holiness doctrine of faith healing. By 1900 he had been exposed to New Englanders who practiced glossolalia, believing it was one of several gifts of the Holy Spirit given to Christians after their conversion experience. Parham and his students ultimately concluded, however, that speaking in tongues was *the* scriptural evidence of the baptism with the Holy Spirit.[1]

Most historians have traced the theological and social roots of Pentecostalism to the Holiness movement, which separated from mainline Methodism in the late nineteenth century.[2] As many Methodists moved into the American mainstream and adopted middle-class lifestyles, the poorer rural and working-class Methodists believed their co-religionists had become far too accommodating of secular culture and denominational structures. The poor Methodists emphasized personal holiness and refrained from "worldly" activities such as drinking, smoking, and card-playing. Their belief in a "second blessing" of sanctification, or moral purification, set them apart from many evangelicals who simply espoused an initial conversion experience, whereby a person received "forgiveness of sins through faith in the propitiatory death of Jesus" on the cross.[3] This second blessing was evidence of the indwelling of the Holy Spirit in a person's life and could have been an instantaneous occurrence or a lifelong process of moral regeneration. Pentecostals added a third act of grace, maintaining that while conversion and sanctification were required, the true evidence of baptism with the Holy Spirit was the gift of speaking in tongues, as described in the New Testament.[4]

Although American Pentecostalism at the turn of the century was an amorphous movement that emerged in different places and at different times, it became an internationally recognized phenomenon in 1906. William Seymour, an African American minister, learned about Holy Spirit baptism and the evidence of tongues from Charles Parham in Houston in 1905. Seymour traveled to California the following year, where he began holding revival services in an old warehouse-turned-church building on Azusa Street in downtown Los Angeles. The three-year revival garnered a great deal of attention in both the religious and secular press. The *Los Angeles Times* ran a front-page story about the revival shortly after it began in April 1906:

> Breathing strange utterances and mouthing a creed which it seems no sane mortal could understand, the newest religious sect has started in Los Angeles. Meetings are held in a tumble-down shack on Azusa Street . . . and devotees of the weird doctrine practice the most fanatical rites, preach the wildest theories and work themselves into a state of mad excitement in their peculiar zeal. Colored people and a sprinkling of whites compose the congregation, and night is made hideous in the neighborhood by the howlings of the worshippers who spend hours swaying forth and back in a nerve-racking attitude of prayer and supplication.[5]

Religious periodicals such as Seymour's newsletter *The Apostolic Faith*, which had a circulation of about fifty thousand readers by 1909, also helped spread the Pentecostal fervor throughout the country and around the world.[6] Early accounts of racial and sexual equality at the Azusa revival led later Pentecostal and charismatic leaders to tout the egalitarian nature of the movement in its embryonic stage.[7]

As the movement moved into its second decade, the delicate nature of integrated religious groups—especially in the South—became apparent and Pentecostal denominations divided along racial lines. Charles H. Mason's Church of God in Christ, based in Memphis, was the first legally chartered Pentecostal denomination that provided ministerial credentials to both black and white preachers. Although the church was predominantly black, Mason did not tolerate "the separation of Christians on the basis of race." As Synan notes, "for many years Mason's church was the most integrated denomination in the United States." But most whites left the Church of God in Christ after the all-white Assemblies of God was formed in Hot Springs, Arkansas, in 1914.[8]

Two years later the Assemblies of God divided over the doctrinal issue of the nature of God. One faction accepted the traditional trinitarian view that God was three persons in one—the Father, the Son, and the Holy Spirit—and that sanctification and baptism in the Holy Spirit occurred sometime after the conversion experience. A minority faction, labeled "oneness" Pentecostals, maintained that "everything (salvation, sanctification, and baptism in the Holy Spirit with tongues) was received in the waters of baptism by immersion in the 'name of Jesus'" only.[9] Oneness Pentecostals found a haven in the Pentecostal Assemblies of the World, a loosely organized group that came to be led by Garfield T. Haywood, the African American pastor of a large, racially integrated congregation in Indianapolis. But white ministers separated from the Pentecostal Assemblies in 1924 and formed the United Pentecostal Church, effectively ending classical Pentecostalism's interracial character for much of the century.[10] Although Pentecostals faced a number of divisive issues that "led to seemingly endless schisms in the small churches," they also allowed several independent charismatic figures to rise above the fray and minister to the whole movement. These men and women "were the legitimate ancestors of the charismatic revivalists of the post–World War II period" who served as models for later independent ministers.[11]

From the beginning, women played crucial roles in the Pentecostal and charismatic movements. An authority on gender issues in Pentecostalism, Susan C. Hyatt, asserts that "women have always found greater freedom in Spirit-oriented renewal movements," where their legitimacy has typically been based on their skill and ability as leaders, not on institutional sanction.[12] John Wesley's acceptance of female preachers in the early nineteenth century bled over into the Holiness and Pentecostal movements of later years. Phoebe Palmer became a famous advocate of the Holiness movement in the mid-1800s as she inspired other women to enter public ministry. Catherine Mumford Booth (co-founder of the Salvation Army), Amanda Berry Smith (an accomplished evangelist and singer), and Hannah Whittal Smith (a women's suffrage and temperance activist) all had roots in the Holiness movement and helped lay the foundation for the rise of modern Pentecostalism. Carrie Judd Montgomery and Maria Woodworth-Etter conducted huge healing revivals in the late nineteenth and early twentieth centuries, and both joined the Pentecostal movement as it coalesced into organized denominations.[13]

Aimee Semple McPherson

One of the most prominent independent evangelists of the 1920s and 1930s was Aimee Semple McPherson. She not only influenced succeeding generations of ministers but also demonstrated how to use modern technology and popular forms of entertainment to transmit her fundamentalist message to modern American society.[14] After being widowed, separated from her second husband, bearing two children, and launching her own evangelistic career, she moved to Los Angeles in 1918 and immediately started a revival meeting. Despite the national and international influence of the Azusa Street mission, biographer Edith Blumhofer notes, "Pentecostalism had never really become a cultural force in the city. Aimee's arrival changed that: within a few years, thanks largely to her efforts, Pentecostalism took its place among the city's enduring religious currents." Los Angelenos accepted McPherson because she was different from the Pentecostal men who regularly squabbled with each other over doctrinal issues or personality conflicts. She, according to Blumhofer, was "dedicated, talented, energetic, and, most important of all, uninvolved in the infighting of recent years. They saw in her a leader with a fresh vision behind whom they could rally. She offered direction and a dream."[15]

Her appeal, however, was not restricted to Pentecostals. Between 1919 and 1922 McPherson amassed a sizable following of evangelical Christians who came to her meetings to receive healing or inspiration, witness the manifestations of the Holy Spirit, or experience the excitement that her ministry generated. She established a national reputation for demonstrating God's power in the here and now, which strengthened Pentecostalism in the United States and Canada, and her ecumenical appeal created a sense of unity among evangelical Christians throughout North America.[16] Her sermons were simple and direct, her "mood was upbeat, confident, friendly, and affirming," and she showed how a timeless God continued to work in the lives of modern Americans.[17] Her message was full of stark contrasts where people could clearly choose between right and wrong, God and Satan, which, Blumhofer contends, "coincided neatly with the ebullient cultural mood of the postwar years." In an effort to appeal to a broad ecumenical audience, she used Hebrews 13:8, which states that "Jesus Christ is the same yesterday and today and forever, to express her core message that Jesus was unchanging.[18] She emphasized love and forgiveness and offered her listeners hope of eternal life, unlike earlier evangelists who tried to convince people of their sinfulness by focusing on guilt and fear of eternal condemnation.[19]

McPherson's apocalyptic worldview shaped her message and ministry, which fit well in the premillennial fervor that characterized early-twentieth-century evangelical subcultures. There was a sense of urgency in her message that Christ's return was imminent and that she must spread that message to the world as quickly as possible. The return of the miraculous gifts of the Holy Spirit to the modern church proved that the last days had arrived and the Second Coming was at hand.[20] Part of her appeal was derived from the way she wove her own life story into her crusade message, which became an effective tool in helping her audience better understand the rapidly changing world in which they lived. Personal testimony was an integral part of the Pentecostal and charismatic experiences throughout the twentieth century, and most evangelists made it a central part of their ministries.[21] McPherson preached "that old-time religion," but she presented it in a thoroughly modern way using illustrated sermons that became increasingly elaborate.[22] She also received positive coverage in the secular press, which contributed to her rising popularity at home and abroad in the early 1920s.[23] One biographer attributes much of her success to her charismatic personality, which allowed her to manipulate her audience. "A crowd is not moved by logic or subtlety," observes Daniel Epstein. "A crowd is not moved by noble ideals, purity of purpose, or by the everlasting truth. The crowd of humankind is moved by raw passion."[24]

McPherson's popularity did not last forever, however, as scandals plagued her career after 1925. That year she was accused of having an affair with Kenneth Ormiston, a married man who managed her KFSG radio station at Angelus Temple. He was forced to resign from the ministry, and McPherson traveled to Israel in 1926 in an effort to curtail the mounting gossip. On May 18, 1926, McPherson, who had returned from her trip abroad, mysteriously disappeared from Ocean Park Beach in southern California. She was allegedly kidnapped and held prisoner for a month in the desert of northern Mexico until she escaped and turned up in the border town of Douglas, Arizona. She returned to Los Angeles on June 26 as more than one hundred thousand well-wishers met her at the train station and lined the streets to welcome her home. Los Angeles district attorney Asa Keyes and local investigative reporters, however, were skeptical of McPherson's story and launched a campaign to discredit her. In the fall of 1926 Keyes charged McPherson and her mother with perjury, contending that they had lied to a grand jury about the kidnapping incident. He maintained that McPherson and Ormiston had arranged a tryst at a lovers' hideaway and that the kidnapping story was a cover-up for this affair. Unable to prove his theory, Keyes dropped the perjury charges in January 1927, but McPherson was never fully vindicated in the court of public opinion as reporters continued to highlight the scandal in the secular press. Thereafter, press coverage of her was decidedly less sympathetic than it had been before 1926, and although her ministry continued to succeed, she was not as popular among evangelical Christians as she had been in her early career.[25]

Despite the attention given to these events, she left an enduring legacy through the institutions she established.[26] The Angelus Temple, which she hoped would function as the hub for her Echo Park Evangelistic Association, provided a place for Los Angelenos—many of whom were midwesterners displaced by the Great Depression—and tourists to hear her conservative gospel message. She considered herself an "evangelist-in-residence" and liked the fact that Hollywood, a growing symbol of American success, was located nearby.[27] The Hollywood culture allowed her to get fresh ideas and experiment with daring new ways to spread the gospel. Her location also provided an "uprooted constituency" of conservative migrants who struggled to reconcile their traditional midwestern values with the rapidly changing modern world. McPherson, with her old-time gospel message and dramatic, innovative presentation, was a master at bridging that gap.[28]

Shortly after opening Angelus Temple, McPherson started a training institute for aspiring evangelists and missionaries, which later became the Lighthouse of International Foursquare Evangelism (LIFE) Bible College. This institution influenced thousands of Christians in the twentieth century, including Freda Lindsay and other leaders of the post–World War II charismatic movement.[29] In 1924 McPherson's KFSG radio station went on the air and introduced a new dimension to her ministry. "Radio," Blumhofer contends, "enabled Sister to come into the homes of her followers at any time of the day or night, greatly augmenting her influence."[30] She pioneered the use of radio as an evangelistic tool, hiring a talented radio engineer away from a local commercial station to build and run her modern broadcasting studio on the third floor of Angelus Temple. His engineering expertise and her natural instincts made KFSG a huge success, and McPherson's voice became one of the most recognizable on American radio.[31] She had a deep concern for the needy, often mobilizing her followers to provide food, clothing, shelter, and other relief for victims of natural disasters. Battered, abused, and pregnant women also sought help at Angelus Temple, where McPherson readily offered physical assistance as well as spiritual and emotional comfort.[32] In 1927 the Angelus Temple commissary began dispensing food, clothing, and other goods to anyone who needed help, regardless of race or ethnicity. During the Great Depression the demands on the commissary increased dramatically; the staff provided physical and spiritual comfort as best they could, but they struggled to keep up with the heavy demand for supplies, sending the Temple into debt.[33]

After being plagued by difficulties in the 1920s and 1930s, McPherson spent the final years of her career maintaining her institutions. In the late 1930s she stopped planning evangelistic crusades and gave more attention to the Lighthouse churches, which were part of her Foursquare Gospel Association. The steady growth of her churches and the large number of graduates from LIFE Bible College were indicative of the strong following she had at the end of her life. She did not garner the national attention that characterized her early ministry, but she was able to leave a substantial legacy when she died. At her death in 1944 Angelus Temple had more than four hundred branch churches in North America, twenty-two thousand members, two hundred foreign missions, and over three thousand graduates of LIFE Bible College. She tried to maintain the nondenominational character of her ministry, but after she died her successor and son, Rolf McPherson, began to treat the ministry for what it really was, an established denomination.[34]

Aimee Semple McPherson became a cultural icon in the 1920s and 1930s because she was a practical, simple, ordinary person who related well to like-minded Americans. She had a genuine concern for the socially marginalized, and she used her innate creativity to take whatever resources were at her disposal and achieve her goals.[35] McPherson co-opted modern forms of entertainment to deliver her fundamentalist message, and in the process she became a celebrity to a group of conservative Christians who could not identify with other modern, worldly celebrities. Her fundamentalist doctrine resonated with a large segment of Americans who feared the effects of liberal theology and modernist thought on their society. Her warm, sincere personality, dramatic instincts, ecumenical nature, and compelling message influenced the style and teachings of future evangelists.[36]

But more than that, as historian Harvey Cox notes, McPherson "was the first of what would later develop into a series of full-fledged Pentecostal media stars." He maintains that she was successful not only because she was talented, motivated, and dedicated but also because she ignored the official theology that forbade women to take prominent leadership roles in the church. Pentecostalism, despite its restrictions on women preachers, "provided a space where gifted women could play dramatically important roles" through their testimonies and their recognition as independent evangelists, missionaries, healers, teachers, prophets, writers, and editors. McPherson was able to push the limits of Pentecostalism's cultural separatism through her theatrics and to use the prevailing culture to advance her message, all the while criticizing that culture. Her success paved the way for future Pentecostal, charismatic, and evangelical women to succeed in public ministry.[37]

Healing and Charismatic Revivals

By midcentury the Pentecostal movement was in need of renewal, and the healing revival that began in 1947 provided a freshness and sense of unity that Pentecostals had not experienced since the heady days of the Azusa Street revivals. There was a long tradition of belief in divine healing throughout Christian history, particularly among Catholics, but the modern emphasis on supernatural healing was rooted in the late-nineteenth-century Holiness movement and inherited by its Pentecostal descendants. Although speaking in tongues was considered the evidence of Holy Spirit baptism, divine healing was just as important to the movement in its early years. The Pentecostals' basic theological assumption regarding divine healing was "the belief that physical healing, in addition to the forgiveness of sins, was premised by the death and resurrection of Jesus."[38]

A number of famous healing evangelists flourished during the interwar period, but the "heyday of healing revivalism in America came in the two decades following World War II." Huge independent ministries and parachurch organizations emerged, drawing attention to this strange cultural phenomenon, giving rise to a new type of celebrity—the televangelist—and leading to important changes in the fabric of American religion and society. These independent healing evangelists created a distinctive rhetorical genre, demonstrated a remarkable knack for raising money, proved to be shrewd businesspeople, and challenged traditional sexual, social, and racial customs.[39]

In the 1960s the healing revival spawned the charismatic movement, which claimed nearly half a billion adherents worldwide by the year 2000.[40] Some of the old healers gained new sources of support as they achieved a greater level of sophistication and respectability in the larger Christian world. Many classical Pentecostals criticized the charismatic movement for being too worldly and not espousing a distinct blessing of sanctification.[41] But the impressive growth of this "second wave" of Pentecostalism in mainline churches marked the dawn of a new era in American religious history. Christians in all denominations accepted the legitimacy of the gifts of the Holy Spirit; parachurch organizations such as the Full Gospel Business Men's Fellowship International (FGBMFI) became the "propagator[s] of a new gospel of wealth, health, and glossolalia"; and a new type of minister emerged whose organizational and teaching skills were often more important than his or her speaking ability.[42]

From the 1970s through the 1990s this new generation of leaders did much to draw charismatics and Pentecostals into the mainstream of American religion. The diverse charismatic movement meshed well with conservative evangelicals, who emerged from their subculture in the 1970s to become an important force in modern American society and politics. Their informal networks, formal institutions, and mastery of mass communication allowed charismatics to spread their beliefs efficiently and effectively among non-Pentecostals. Television proved to be their best tool, and the rise of prominent religious networks, such as Pat Robertson's Christian Broadcasting Network (CBN), Paul and Jan Crouch's Trinity Broadcasting Network (TBN), and, more recently, Morris Cerullo's Inspiration Network (INSP), demonstrated the importance of this medium to the success of the evangelists and the movement.[43]

The first of these networks was Robertson's CBN, founded in 1960. The fledgling network used its radio programs to advertise its television shows, and for several years it struggled to stay afloat. By the late 1960s it was receiving solid financial backing through its innovative fund-raising methods, and it had found dynamic personalities, such as Jim and Tammy Bakker, who were able to connect with viewers in ways that virtually guaranteed long-term success. CBN began *The 700 Club*, a talk show patterned after *The Tonight Show Starring Johnny Carson*, which proved to be hugely successful and exposed a larger audience to charismatic worship styles and teaching. CBN's foray into cable television and its use of satellite technology allowed it to expand rapidly in the 1970s and 1980s, and Robertson's decision in 1981 to air "family style" entertainment instead of strictly religious programs gave him a much broader audience. Robertson also used his network as a teaching tool. According to biographer David Harrell, "Robertson was determined to use television as a tool for instruction, not allowing the message to be overshadowed by the medium. He took . . . his viewers through extensive technical discussions of theory and current events," conducted interviews, provided commentary, and "became the instructor of millions of politically unsophisticated Americans who shared his religious commitment."[44] Although most independent charismatic evangelists did not address the political issues that Robertson did, many followed his lead in using their airtime for teaching. Fred Price, founder and pastor of Crenshaw Christian Center in Los Angeles, was probably the most adamant about devoting the majority of his television program to teaching, typically spending fifty-six minutes of his hour-long show instructing his audience.[45]

Other Christian networks began to flourish in the 1980s and 1990s. Paul and Jan Crouch's TBN was quite successful and contributed a great deal to the rising popularity of black and female charismatic evangelists in the late twentieth century. Although the Crouches claimed they were not in the business of showcasing new talent, a few ministers—including Fred Price and T. D. Jakes—got their start on TBN. Paul Crouch initially served as an associate pastor for the Assemblies of God denomination and worked part-time at a local South Dakota television station before starting his own Christian television station in southern California in 1973. After a series of setbacks, including a fallout with one of their co-hosts, a fire, and various legal and financial crises, the Crouches finally got TBN on a sure financial footing in the late 1970s. In 1977 it became the first twenty-four-hour Christian television station in the United States; in less than ten years it was able to purchase the maximum number of television stations allowed by the Federal Communications Commission and was seen on more than two hundred cable systems nationwide. In 1980 RCA reportedly offered TBN space on its new communications satellite at the bargain rate of $34,000 per month, which gave the Crouches unprecedented exposure and changed the nature of the network. They soon bought one of the first mobile satellite transmitters manufactured—which they dubbed "The Holy Beamer"—and began airing live broadcasts of Billy Graham crusades, Kenneth Copeland camp meetings, and Full Gospel Business Men's conventions.

By the late 1980s, TBN claimed that its market value was at $500 million and that it was virtually debt free. In 1997 a New York brokerage firm, representing an anonymous investor, reportedly offered the Crouches $1.9 billion for the network. (Robertson, incidentally, later sold CBN to Rupert Murdoch's Fox network for the same amount.) In 1995 the Nielsen rating company estimated that it was the most-watched religious network in America, and TBN claimed to be seen on thirty-five hundred cable affiliates, five hundred broadcast stations worldwide, and in 28 million households.[46]

Other networks followed suit, but few had the Crouches' staying power. Jim Bakker founded the PTL Network in 1974, but it suffered from his personal and financial scandals in the late 1980s. In 1990 the seasoned healing evangelist Morris Cerullo purchased PTL for a reported $7 million. A year later he sold most of the corporation to a group of Malaysian investors but retained control of the PTL Network and renamed it the Inspiration Network, which had gained considerable popularity by the end of the decade. At the turn of the century, TBN, INSP, and the secular Black Entertainment Television (BET) network continued to provide most of the publicity for modern independent evangelists.[47] The men and women who used these media outlets developed formulas for success that became standard for most ministers. They generally devoted fifteen to twenty minutes of air time to teaching—often showing a segment of one of their crusade sermons—and the remainder of their thirty-minute slot promoting books, tapes, and conventions or otherwise soliciting funds. Television exposure was essential to their success; without it they could not sell their books and tapes, advertise their conventions, or build a substantial partner base. Partners were regular contributors to these ministries and were the cornerstone of their financial support. Although direct mailing continued to be a vital fund-raising tool, television offered the broadest exposure. Religious networks also benefited from their relationship with televangelists. Viewers not only tuned in to see their favorite preachers but also partnered with the networks, keeping them on the air and making them important tools for spreading the charismatic revival.

Oral Roberts

Granville Oral Roberts, without question the most famous televangelist of the twentieth century, provided a model for other charismatic ministers who built their own self-sustaining empires. His innovative use of mass media and his success in promoting revivals, raising money, and establishing lasting institutions not only made him a celebrity among Pentecostals but also earned him the respect of American evangelicals. He instinctively knew when and how to expand his ministry, cultivate relationships with neo-Pentecostals and wealthy businessmen, and refocus his message to appeal to a broader audience. A key to his success was his ability to maintain close ties with Pentecostals while at the same time reaching out to traditional churches that were taking part in the charismatic renewal. Roberts was a talented, pragmatic man whose organizational skills and willingness to take risks left an indelible impression on the charismatic movement.

After claiming to have been healed of tuberculosis and a speech impediment at a tent revival in 1935, the young Roberts spent the next few years as an impoverished preacher for several small Pentecostal holiness churches in Oklahoma. In 1947 he resigned his pastorate in Enid, Oklahoma, and began his career as a healing evangelist, reporting his first major healing in the fall of that year. He also started publishing his first magazine, *Healing Waters*, which became "his primary system of communication with his followers" for the remainder of his career. In early issues he touted the success of his healing campaigns, promoted the sale of his first book (*If You Need Healing—Do These Things!*), advertised his radio program, and asked for partners to support him financially. The following year he created a nontaxable religious corporation and hired a small staff—composed of five stenographers, himself, his brother, and his wife, Evelyn—to run the ministry from his home in Tulsa. When Lee Braxton, a successful banker and businessman, visited the ministry headquarters he advised Roberts to build an office and run his operation in a more professional manner. Roberts knew Braxton was right "and resolved to develop an efficient organization," becoming both evangelist and businessman.[48]

Roberts's selection of a talented crusade team also boded well for the success of his ministry, which witnessed impressive growth during the late 1940s and early 1950s. His correspondence and magazine circulation increased dramatically; Roberts moved at least three times in the 1950s to bigger and better office buildings; and his tent revivals drew larger crowds each year. By the mid-1950s he was filling his new 12,500-seat tent, and his radio program was heard on over three hundred stations. His most important leap of faith in those early years, however, was his foray into television. Despite the seemingly insurmountable costs, he garnered the necessary financial support to start a weekly program—featuring his healing services—that was seen in about a hundred minor and three major U.S. markets.[49] These early administrative decisions were crucial to his success, but his keen business sense and willingness to take risks also paved the way for future ministers. Texas evangelist Kenneth Copeland served as Roberts's copilot and chauffeur, and he studied the techniques of the famed healing evangelist. "March of 1967 was a turning point in my life," Copeland recalled thirty years later. "I was learning so much at ORU [Oral Roberts University] traveling with Brother Roberts, going to classes during the day and listening to

Brother [Kenneth] Hagin's tapes at night. I was watching Brother Roberts do by faith what I was hearing Brother Hagin teach."[50]

The moderate Roberts at first identified with the larger healing revival, but the outrageous claims and questionable tactics that eventually plagued the movement caused him to remain aloof from "less gifted and frequently less responsible" evangelists.[51] He maintained cordial relations with full-gospel churches during the 1950s, but he made a conscious effort to reach out to all denominations, regardless of their position on the modern manifestation of the miraculous gifts of the Holy Spirit. As his biographer David Harrell noted in 1975, "Roberts' work became more ecumenical with time," which eventually led to friction with Pentecostal churches.[52]

Financial success also brought Roberts considerable criticism. While he seldom opened his financial records for public inspection, he was generally forthcoming about his personal income and that of the ministry. Despite charges of chicanery by his critics, there was never any solid evidence of impropriety on his part. Early on, he established policies that he believed would ensure financial integrity and reflect his desire not to put too much emphasis on money. Most of his personal wealth came from book royalties and the large "love offerings" that were taken at his meetings. According to Harrell, much of the ministry's "financial success depended mainly on his ability to attract and mobilize a growing group of successful charismatic businessmen."[53] The FGBMFI, founded by Demos Shakarian, provided important support for Roberts and other charismatic evangelists from the 1950s through the 1970s.[54]

Roberts's ability to connect with his partners and make them feel like he had a personal relationship with each of them was crucial to his success. His ecumenism and religious tolerance allowed him to develop a broad base of support, which helped bridge the gap between charismatics and evangelicals. This lesson was not lost on succeeding generations of evangelists. Early in his career Kenneth Copeland learned the importance of maintaining regular contact with his supporters. One day Roberts reportedly invited Copeland to his home and told him, "'I'm going to ask you to make one of the most serious commitments you've ever made in your life,' he explained. 'I want you to commit to God that every 30 days for the rest of your life you will pray in the Holy Ghost until *you* have something anointed to write to your Partners, just the way Paul wrote to his.' . . . From that time until now," Copeland assured his partners, "I've written a letter every month to my friends who are in partnership with me. They aren't money-raising letters. I don't write them for that reason. *God* is my source, and *He* meets all my needs. I write the letters because I want to bless my Partners. . . . As a result, those letters have changed lives—my Partners' and *mine*. Thanks to God, and to the Holy Spirit working through the Apostle Paul and Brother Roberts, we have all been blessed!"[55] Despite Copeland's assertions to the contrary, those "blessings" were manifested in financial contributions to his ministry. Roberts instructed his protégé on how to build a self-sustaining ministry, and Copeland used these techniques to build his own religious empire.

Roberts also profited from his controversial seed-faith teaching, which he pioneered in the 1950s but did not fully develop until the 1970s.[56] He argued that God intended for Christians to have material wealth and physical health; they were not supposed to live impoverished lives, barely scraping by and longing for their heavenly reward. The way to access these benefits, he maintained, was to follow a simple threefold principle: First, know that "God is your source." If Christians relied solely on God to supply their material needs he would give them far more than they could ever ask. Second, "Give that it may be given to you"; the key to receiving, he argued, was in giving. If one made a financial investment in a ministry, then God would make a return on that investment that would far exceed the original amount. Third, he told his supporters to "Expect a miracle." Christians had always been taught to give, but they had never been told to expect anything in return. Harrell asserts that this "theology was the financial message which allowed the huge expansion of the Roberts ministry in the late 1970s." Scores of charismatic evangelists and pastors latched on to the prosperity message and made it the focus of their teaching. As more Pentecostals and charismatics—especially African Americans—moved into the middle class, they associated their financial success with these principles. By the end of the twentieth century, the prosperity message had come to dominate the ministries of many independent evangelists and provided a broad base of financial support.[57]

Although Roberts transformed his message over the years, healing remained at the core of his ministry. It was a positive and practical message "aimed at activating the faith of the supplicant."[58] He taught that God's healing came from within people and that having a point of contact would release their faith and allow them to receive their miraculous blessing. He sent thousands of prayer cloths to supporters to serve as points of contact, and scores of other ministers followed his lead. Denver evangelist Marilyn Hickey, for instance, regularly sent prayer cloths, packets of oil, packets of cornmeal, and brown lunch sacks, among other things, to serve as points of contact so her supporters could receive their physical or emotional healing and financial breakthrough.[59] Roberts's primary point of contact was his "God-anointed hands." He believed that the sensation he felt in his right hand when he touched people in his healing lines was God's healing power flowing through him. He never claimed to have a miraculous touch, only that his hand was a point of contact for believers to release their faith and receive their healing.[60]

In the late 1950s Roberts shifted his focus to evangelism. Despite his Pentecostal roots, he had always resisted denominational control and reached out to traditional churches; his ecumenical impulse found an outlet in the burgeoning charismatic revival of the 1960s. "More than all other charismatic evangelists combined," writes Harrell, "Roberts put his mark on the neopentecostal movement which grew out of the healing revival."[61] Once again, he made a series of administrative decisions that were crucial to his success and, ultimately, to his legacy.[62] In 1962 he began construction of Oral Roberts University (ORU). In keeping with his emphasis on evangelism, he initially planned to establish a "University of Evangelism" that would train students from diverse religious backgrounds in the art of soul winning. Ultimately, Roberts decided to open a liberal arts institution that educated "the whole man—body, mind, and spirit."[63] His emphasis on wholeness and health dominated his thinking in later years and led to his experiment in combining faith and medicine at the City of Faith Medical Center he opened in the 1980s.[64] ORU proved to be a huge success, receiving accreditation from the North Central Association of Colleges and Secondary Schools in 1971, becoming a respectable liberal arts university that catered to students from a wide variety of Christian backgrounds but especially to charismatics, and attracting a large number of minority students, particularly black Pentecostals.[65] Citing a 1994 U.S. Department of Education study, the *Journal of Blacks in Higher Education* reported that of the one hundred institutions in the Coalition for Christian Colleges and Universities, ORU had the highest percentage of African American students—19 percent of its total enrollment.[66]

Harrell observed that Roberts's "antennae constantly scanned the landscape to identify anyone on the horizon who might further his mission."[67] In the early 1970s Roberts recognized the talent of a black ORU student named Carlton Pearson and promoted him as a leader among African Americans in the charismatic renewal. In 1977 Roberts told Pearson that "The next great outpouring of the Holy Spirit, and the mighty healing power of God, is to be upon black people, and you're to be one of the major leaders in it. It's the black race's hour to look up to their true Source—God—and expect an outpouring of His grace and gifts as they've never known before as a race of people."[68] As a member of various ORU singing groups, Pearson played an important role in advertising the interracial nature of the Roberts ministry. He went on to establish a successful career as a pastor and evangelist, which Roberts enthusiastically supported until the turn of the century.[69] Roberts's vision and pragmatism were borne out in his administrative skills, the creation of lasting institutions, and his ability to recognize and promote talented individuals. He hired the right people to accomplish his goals, and he expected a strong work ethic and sense of loyalty in his employees.

Another important move was his innovative use of television in the late 1960s. In 1967 Roberts announced he was canceling his weekly television program after thirteen years because he thought it had become an outdated method. Two years later he announced his return to television in a series of prime-time specials that featured a chic new format, were professionally produced, and were chock full of notable figures from the religious, political, and entertainment worlds. The new shows were a huge success, and Roberts reported that his ministry received thousands of new supporters as a result. Most of his new followers did not come from the Pentecostal ranks, however, and "many of his old pentecostal friends were scandalized by the new specials."[70] Ralph Carmichael, a pioneer in the Christian music industry, helped Roberts develop a new kind of singing group, called the World Action Singers, made up of sixteen men and women from the ORU student body. Their choreographed movements to a new genre of gospel music drew both praise and criticism from viewers. Many Pentecostals believed Roberts had sold out to secularism and allowed his ministry to become too worldly, but he gained the attention of a new clientele of non-Christians and non-charismatics who were often put off by the old-fashioned-gospel-hour approach of classical Pentecostalism. Roberts later claimed that this new format gave rise to the praise-and-worship style that characterized the public assemblies of many charismatic, independent evangelical—and eventually mainline—churches.[71] By century's end, many American churches offered "contemporary" worship services that offered a more relaxed atmosphere, boasted "relevant" sermons, and featured the praise choruses that had been a part of Pentecostal and charismatic services for years.

Much has been written about Oral Roberts, critiquing the man, his ministry, and his message, but Harrell's biography is by far the most comprehensive account. In his 1995 autobiography Roberts even echoed many of Harrell's assessments about himself. In a word, Oral Roberts was pragmatic.

He often made sudden, dramatic changes in his ministry, but they were almost always methodological and not theological in nature. If he sensed that something was no longer effective, he immediately made an adjustment. He was acutely aware of the changing nature of his ministry and the healing and charismatic revivals in which he participated. The changes "were always in the window dressing," Harrell asserts, "the words and tools that allowed him to teach old truths to new people." Roberts often had to convince his old followers to stay with him while he reached out to new audiences.[72]

Roberts's greatest contribution was his ability to explain and popularize the central beliefs of the Pentecostal movement. He emphasized the miraculous—especially divine healing—and the hope that came with believing in a good God. His upbeat message resonated not only with the poor and downtrodden but also with middle-class Americans who were struggling to adjust to dramatic social changes in postwar America. He reached across denominational divides and had little patience for religious intolerance. His willingness to listen to dissenting views and accept people as Christians if they had a personal faith in Jesus contributed greatly to the ecumenical nature of his ministry. This openness allowed him to tap into an entirely new clientele with the burgeoning neo-Pentecostal movement.[73]

Kathryn Kuhlman

Roberts's contemporary Kathryn Kuhlman inherited Aimee Semple McPherson's mantle as the best-known female preacher in the world. Just as "winsome and flamboyant" as her predecessor, Kuhlman used her rhetorical skills and star status to attract huge crowds to her services.[74] She built a large healing ministry during the 1960s and was the first female healing evangelist to have a national television audience. Popular periodicals such as *People* and *Christianity Today* recognized her as one of the most prominent faith healers and preachers in America in the 1970s. She influenced an entire generation of charismatic ministers—both male and female—who used her style and techniques to build their own successful careers in the late twentieth century.[75]

Calling themselves "God's Girls," Kuhlman and her associate Helen Gulliford began their independent ministry in Boise, Idaho, in 1928, preaching in small towns and country churches throughout the state. They lived hand to mouth, often sleeping in turkey houses and haystacks, accepting whatever money or food people gave them in those difficult early years of the Great Depression.[76] In 1933 they left Idaho for Colorado, where they opened the Denver Revival Tabernacle in an abandoned warehouse. The duo never established churches on their evangelistic tours, partly because Kuhlman, although she accepted female evangelists, believed pastorates should be held by men. The Denver Tabernacle was an evangelistic center where nonbelievers could learn about the gospel before joining an established church. The depression had taken its toll on many Denver churches. Denver residents were starving for spiritual nourishment, and Kuhlman presented a positive, upbeat message that reflected God's greatness, love, and power during hard times.[77]

Her success in Denver was overshadowed by her scandalous marriage to evangelist Burroughs Waltrip in 1938, whom she had met three years earlier when he was preaching a revival at the Denver Revival Tabernacle. He had a wife and two young sons living in Austin when their romance began. He summarily divorced his wife, claiming she had deserted him, and began building an elaborate revival center in Mason City, Iowa, called Radio Chapel. Kuhlman's followers at the Denver Tabernacle recognized the perilous nature of their relationship and tried to convince her to end it, but she refused to heed their warnings. When the couple finally married in the fall of 1938, her followers lost faith in her ability to provide spiritual leadership and the Tabernacle soon failed. Helen Gulliford began ministering to another church in Denver, and Kuhlman joined her husband in Iowa. Radio Chapel did not succeed either, and by January 1940 the Waltrips, unable to make the mortgage payments, left town and sold the $75,000 building for $50,000. The couple conducted joint and separate meetings throughout the nation until 1946, when Kuhlman finally left Waltrip in Los Angeles and never saw him again. He divorced her the following year after she had established a new ministry in Pennsylvania. Their divorce remained secret until 1952 when journalists in Akron, Ohio, trying to discredit Kuhlman's ministry in that city, reported the story. By that time, however, her ministry was so well established that the revelation did not affect her popularity.[78]

In the 1940s Kuhlman began building an international reputation as a faith healer—a term she did not like—and eventually became the most popular female evangelist in America.[79] In the summer of 1946 she started a regular radio broadcast in western Pennsylvania.[80] She had used radio in Denver to promote her ministry, but her *Heart to Heart* program, which aired every day from Oil City, Pennsylvania, made her an icon among Pentecostals and evangelicals everywhere. At the time, McPherson had been the only other female preacher to have much success with this medium.[81] Kuhlman's popularity cut across denominational and theological barriers, and she was able to garner a following among a new group of evangelicals led by men such as Billy Graham.

Although Kuhlman had always believed in divine healing, it was not a central part of her ministry in the early years. But in 1947 she stopped forming traditional healing lines and began praying for mass healings in her services, making her unique among faith healers.[82] Her ministry grew quickly after 1947, and the public response to her teaching on faith healing was overwhelming. She expanded her radio ministry and began holding regular meetings in larger venues to accommodate the growing crowds. In the summer of 1948 she held a meeting at Carnegie Hall in Pittsburgh; two years later she moved her base of operations to the Steel City. Much of her publicity came by word of mouth, her radio program, and newspaper and magazine advertisements. She refused, however, to associate herself with Gordon Lindsay's magazine *The Voice of Healing,* the primary organ of the burgeoning healing revival that featured evangelists such as A. A. Allen, William Branham, and T. L. Osborn. In fact, she was appalled by the antics of some of the more radical faith healers and hated being associated with them.[83] Kuhlman's popular appeal was enhanced in 1950 when the popular magazine *Redbook* featured her ministry. *Redbook* editors reportedly documented and verified the healings they investigated, providing Kuhlman with the credibility that eluded other evangelists. People flocked to her meetings to hear her sermons and experience divine healing. Those who could not travel to see her wrote letters and sent telegrams asking her to pray for their physical well-being.[84]

By the 1960s Kuhlman had firmly established herself as an important figure in the charismatic movement. Content with her success in the Northeast, she seldom ventured beyond the geographical boundaries of Ohio, West Virginia, and Maryland, but in 1965 Ralph Wilkerson, a pastor on the West Coast, convinced her to hold one meeting in Pasadena, California. It was so successful that she started holding monthly healing services at the Shrine Auditorium in Los Angeles and scheduling revivals in cities across the nation. She challenged racial taboos in some regions by allowing a black singer, Jimmie McDonald, to open her services.[85] She also published several best-selling books during the last fifteen years of her ministry, including *I Believe in Miracles, God Can Do It Again,* and *Nothing Is Impossible with God.* Furthermore, she added a regular television ministry, *I Believe in Miracles,* to her already highly successful radio show. She hired Dick Ross, a Hollywood producer who had worked with Billy Graham and Oral Roberts, to produce and direct the program, and the CBS network ran the half-hour show for nearly ten years. Her ministry experienced remarkable growth from the television publicity; she increased the number of miracle services she conducted around the world, keeping an almost frenetic pace the last decade of her life. The only lasting institution Kuhlman created, however, was the Kathryn Kuhlman Foundation, which continued to air her radio broadcasts, distribute her literature, and support various charities and foreign mission programs after her death in 1976. It finally closed six years later, but her legacy lived on in the lore of the late-twentieth-century charismatic revival.[86]

Despite health problems and personal scandal at the end of her life, Kuhlman maintained a good reputation as a leader in the charismatic movement.[87] She had a tremendous amount of energy, a strong work ethic, an unmatched devotion to her ministry, and an uncanny ability to make people feel loved and accepted. She was not sophisticated, but she could identify with the rich, the famous, and the educated professionals who often came to her services. Her homey, down-to-earth nature allowed her to communicate just as easily with the blue-collar steelworkers in Pittsburgh and the social outcasts who came to her for spiritual, emotional, and physical healing. Like McPherson, Kuhlman had many associates but few truly close friends, and she was never able to fully reconcile the success she had in her public life with the failures of her private life. Unlike some of the women who followed them, McPherson and Kuhlman did not have spouses who supported their public ministries, and they ultimately chose public acclaim over traditional family life. Both of these women, however, provide examples of the skill, hard work, and determination it took for women to succeed in a male-dominated profession and become widely acclaimed role models for later female evangelists.

A. A. Allen

Another evangelist whose healing ministry spanned the healing revival of the 1950s and the charismatic revival of the 1960s was Asa A. Allen. While Roberts and Kuhlman led the moderate wing of the healing movement and ultimately appealed to a broader, more respectable middle-class audience, Allen led the radical wing of the movement, which continued to make extravagant miraculous claims and be shrouded in controversy. He appealed to those who were often labeled socially marginalized: racial minorities, the poor, and the undereducated flocked to his tent meetings until his mysterious death in 1970. His openness, innovativeness, and persistence allowed him to succeed as an old-fashioned healing evangelist when other ministers were packing up their tents and leaving the sawdust trail for pastorates that provided more security and stability.[88]

Born into poverty in 1911, this Arkansas native was raised in an unstable home; by his early twenties he was a drunkard and emotionally unstable. Allen converted to Pentecostalism during the depression, and in the late 1930s and early 1940s he worked as a full-time revivalist for the Assemblies of God denomination. In 1947 he took a pastorate in Corpus Christi, Texas, but after attending an Oral Roberts campaign two years later he quit his job and started holding his own healing revivals.[89] His "native shrewdness, unparalleled showmanship, and startling miraculous claims" all contributed to his success, and by the 1960s he had one of the largest tents in the world, a magazine that boasted two hundred thousand subscriptions after its first year, radio and television programs, and a sprawling thirteen-hundred-acre headquarters in the Arizona desert that housed his Bible college, media production facilities, a publishing house, and a healing pool. Despite his occasional legal troubles, constant media criticism, and eventual alienation from the Assemblies of God and other Pentecostal ministers, Allen maintained a loyal following.[90]

Pentecostalism in general and the healing revival in particular were known for attracting social outcasts. Over time—and for a number of reasons—these movements became more sophisticated and began drawing a different clientele. Allen, however, continued to appeal to the marginalized segments of American society.[91] In 1969 he told *Look* magazine, "The real move to God today is among the colored people. . . . The Scripture says the common people received Him gladly, referring to Jesus. But the religious leaders were the ones who killed Him. The colored people right now are the common people."[92]

Photographs of Allen's revivals suggest that large numbers of African Americans were attending his meetings by the fall of 1956. In 1958 Allen held an integrated service in Little Rock, Arkansas, and in 1960 he held the first completely integrated service in Atlanta. Although he may have exaggerated some of his claims, Allen was clearly one of the first healing evangelists to completely disregard racial taboos and regularly hold integrated services in the South. He also made "racial liberalism an effective theological plank in his ministry" and openly challenged segregation in his preaching.[93] He argued that white racism was rooted in pride and tied to upward mobility in modern American society. "Most of the white people in America are so bound with pride that they are no longer common people," he contended. "They don't want this old time religion." He called for white preachers to accept blacks as equals in their churches just as he accepted blacks as equals in his revivals.[94] Maintaining that God considered segregation in the church and secular society to be a "boil" and "sore evil," Allen predicted that God would soon curse America and deliver the church from this wickedness.[95]

In the 1960s Allen actively sought to bring blacks to his ministry. He introduced gospel rock music to his meetings (a practice that later ministries adopted) and hired Gene Martin, a talented African American singer, to lead his services. Martin, an Atlanta native born in 1939, had gained a modest reputation as a gospel singer in Georgia before joining Allen's crusade team in 1961. He remained with Allen throughout the 1960s and continued with Allen's successor, Don Stewart, into the early 1970s. Stewart later noted that Allen "was ten years ahead of his time. . . . He brought a little bit of the black beat in, and now it is the thing with the Jesus kids." His innovation and willingness to take such risks allowed him to continue his old-fashioned healing campaigns when other evangelists were failing and giving up.[96]

Although Allen never had a large number of blacks on his staff, he mentored several young men who went on to establish their own ministries. He also influenced white ministers to reach out to African Americans and start their own integrated ministries. H. L. Wood, a white pastor in Seattle, praised Allen for his work in the "civil rights program. God has the answer to the battles between races!" he proclaimed. "At the Northwest Evangelistic Center . . . [w]e have an interracial group. . . . We have the Caucasian race, the Negro race, the Oriental race, the Mexican! We haven't reached out for this. God has just brought them in. . . . All kinds of organizations, movements, and leaders are trying to solve the problems between the races in this nation. I'll tell you that there is only one thing that will bring the answer. It's the love of God, and the supernatural move of God in revival such as we witness in the ministry of Brother A. A. Allen!"[97]

F. H. Thomas, a black Baptist minister in California, became convinced of the holiness message that Allen preached and decided to drop his Baptist affiliation and adopt a full-gospel message and worship style. "I smoked cigarettes and drank whiskey, and went to card parties," he confessed. "There was no gospel I had sat under, to stop me from doing those kinds of things. I thought I was doing my best, and people in my church were following me in that mess." After being converted to Pentecostalism, he and his family received the Holy Spirit: "I thank God for Brother Allen. I'm thankful I sat under his ministry, and when I saw signs and wonders, God stirred my heart!"[98]

Allen also appealed to the sense of financial desperation that many of his followers felt. As the healing revival gave way to the charismatic revival most evangelists struggled to maintain their ministries, but Allen found ways to shore up support and continue holding old-fashioned tent campaigns through the 1960s. He was an outstanding fund-raiser and "one of the first in the revival to gain support by appealing to the financial dreams of his followers."[99] Although Roberts had introduced his seed-faith teaching in the early 1950s, it never became a central part of his ministry. By the early 1960s, however, Allen had made the prosperity message the focus of his teaching, and "testimonies of financial blessings came to outweigh reports of healing in *Miracle Magazine*."[100] He argued: "Health and wealth come from the Lord. Sickness and disease are the curses of the devil. God gives men power to receive health and wealth. The devil brings the curses of sickness and poverty upon those who do not believe and obey God! *You are given the power of choice!* Jesus came to destroy the works of the devil . . . and the devil works on many people with the double curse of sickness and poverty! If you will claim the promises of God, He will lift that curse of poverty and let the blessings of prosperity come upon you."[101]

This message proved to be the key ingredient in spreading the charismatic movement during the last quarter of the twentieth century. An emerging new black middle class was beginning to see the fruits of their hard work and, many believed, the financial reward for their persistent faith. But it was not A. A. Allen who made this teaching popular; a respected but lesser-known figure advanced the prosperity message and made it central to the modern charismatic movement.

Kenneth E. Hagin

Kenneth E. Hagin, less famous than Roberts, Kuhlman, and Allen outside charismatic circles but equally important, provided the theological and philosophical foundation for most of the new ministers, generally labeled the "Word of Faith" teaching. Although not the first Pentecostal to embrace the principles of the prosperity message, Hagin was widely credited with fully developing the teaching and popularizing it. The Word of Faith philosophy became one of the most important—and most criticized—hallmarks of the modern charismatic movement.

Born in 1917, Hagin began his preaching career in 1934 as the pastor for a small community church near his hometown of McKinney, Texas. Because he believed in divine healing, he associated himself with full-gospel Christians in the area. He was skeptical of speaking in tongues, but after studying the Bible he became convinced that glossolalia was a legitimate supernatural experience for modern Christians, and he was "baptized in the Holy Spirit" in April 1937. A year later he was ordained an Assemblies of God pastor. In his ministry he emphasized divine healing, and in 1947 he joined the ranks of traveling evangelists. Despite having modest success during the 1950s, at the height of the healing revival in America, he did not conduct major crusades like Roberts and Allen. Hagin was a soft-spoken, unassuming minister who had "a homey and humorous Texas" preaching style. He avoided publicity and was not interested in building a large empire to bolster his ego. Even after he achieved greater success in the 1970s and 1980s he led a modest yet comfortable lifestyle, and, despite criticism of his theology, he maintained a reputation as an honest and sincere man.[102]

As early as 1950 Hagin recognized that his place in the healing and charismatic revivals would be that of teacher. Although divine healing remained an important part of his ministry, in 1962 he gave up his ministerial papers in the Assemblies of God, formed his own evangelistic association, and began to focus on his calling. He received numerous invitations to hold meetings around the country in the 1960s, and he became a popular speaker with the FGBMFI. He and other new leaders brought to the charismatic revival much-needed teaching skills that had not been present in the healing revival of the 1950s. These teachers helped to stabilize the neo-Pentecostal movement and provided a sense of respectability that it previously lacked.[103]

Radio and print media were central to Hagin's outreach in the 1960s. Freda Lindsay of the Voice of Healing ministry persuaded him to publish his first book in 1960, and she and her staff edited his books for several years thereafter. In the mid-1960s Gordon Lindsay asked Hagin to teach on his radio show in Dallas, offering additional exposure. Hagin moved his ministry headquarters from Garland, Texas, to Tulsa in 1966, expanded his tape ministry, and began his own radio program, *Faith Seminar of the Air*. In 1968 he started sending a regular newsletter to his supporters, which later became *The Word of Faith* magazine. His popularity grew after 1967, but he kept his ministry small; in 1973 he had only nineteen full-time employees. He continued to conduct meetings and seminars in hotels and churches around the country, and in the summer of 1973 he held his first annual Campmeeting at a Tulsa church with over four hundred people in attendance. The 1976 Campmeeting had become so large that it was held at the

Tulsa Convention Center, and by 1982 his crowds had reportedly grown to as many as twenty-four thousand people. At the turn of the millennium the Campmeeting's popularity had declined somewhat, with attendance dipping to about twelve thousand in 1998 and only eight thousand in 2000, but it was still popular among the Word of Faith faithful. He branched out into television in 1976 with *The Faith That Lives*, but his mainstay continued to be radio broadcasts, sales of sermon tapes, and print media. By 1981 he and his son, Kenneth Hagin Jr., had written eighty-five books, and their magazine reportedly went to 160,000 homes. By century's end Kenneth Hagin Ministries had grown considerably. The ministry claimed that his radio show was heard on more than 300 daily American broadcasts and in 120 countries. Hagin and his son reportedly had written about 130 books and sold roughly 60 million copies, *The Word of Faith* magazine had a circulation of over half a million, and the ministry distributed more than fifty-eight thousand tapes each month. The staff had also grown to nearly three hundred employees.[104] Probably the most enduring aspect of Hagin's ministry was the founding of Rhema Bible Training Center in 1974, which allowed his ministry to solidify, institutionalize, and spread his faith message all over the world.

The Word of Faith movement garnered considerable attention at century's end and became a lightning rod for controversy. When the scandals of the healing revival ebbed after the 1950s and the charismatic movement attained respectability among mainstream American Christians in the 1960s, Hagin's teaching about divine prosperity became a focal point for proponents and critics of the neo-Pentecostal revival. The basic tenets of the faith message—sometimes called the "prosperity message" or "positive confession"—were that Christians should study the Bible to determine God's will for their lives, verbally confess God's promise for a particular need, and believe that God had already provided a solution to their problem. Faithful Christians, the argument continued, recognized that they were entitled not only to eternal life in the hereafter but also to "divine health" and prosperity in the present as part of the blessing they received through Jesus' death on the cross. Although Hagin continued to believe in miraculous healings, he also taught that Christians who practiced his principles of positive confession would never again experience sickness. This emphasis on "divine health" became a hallmark of the Word of Faith movement.[105]

Hagin generally tried to avoid polemics and often did not respond to his critics, who were certainly not in short supply.[106] He claimed to maintain a moderate position theologically, seeking to avoid "some of the extreme positions taken by some in the faith movement."[107] His son defended this position: "Neither Dad nor I have ever taught that being a Christian means you'll never have any problems. The devil will always try to hinder you but you have authority over the devil through the Word of God. . . . I get so tired of Rhema students who talk about houses and Cadillacs. . . . Thank God, God has provided us prosperity. But the Church doesn't exist for Christian prosperity. The Church of the Lord Jesus Christ exists for those who are locked in the chains of Satan himself."[108]

Despite these assertions of moderation, the prosperity message lent itself to overindulgence. Critics generally focused on the potential, and real, excesses of this theology and its proponents. Charles Farah, a professor at ORU in the early 1980s, characterized the faith message as "a kind of heavenly butler, [which] twists true Biblical faith into an almost magic formula."[109] Michael Horton, evangelical theologian and editor of *The Agony of Deceit*, commented on the cultural implications of this doctrine: "It is appropriate that a prosperity gospel be born in the hedonistic, self-centered, get-rich-quick milieu of modern American society. We are, by nature, pagan. Either our religion will transform us or we will transform our religion to suit our sympathies."[110] In *A Different Gospel: A Historical and Biblical Analysis of the Modern Faith Movement*, Dan R. McConnell contends that, because the faith message is rooted in New Age metaphysics, it is occultic and therefore satanic. Furthermore, he charges that Hagin plagiarized much of this theology from a turn-of-the-century evangelist named E. W. Kenyon. Kenyon drew from a variety of contemporary ideas, including New Thought metaphysics and the holiness tradition of Higher Christian Life, to develop his faith theology.[111] The charges of plagiarism, which were well founded, did not seem to diminish Hagin's appeal. His generally good reputation, modest lifestyle, and affable personality allowed him to rise above most controversies surrounding the Word of Faith movement. As a result, he was able to influence and promote some of its most important proponents, many of whom were black or female.

Although positive confession had deep roots in the Holiness and Pentecostal traditions of the nineteenth and early twentieth centuries, Kenneth Hagin was commonly regarded as the father of the Word of Faith movement in the late twentieth century. In a sympathetic but fair critique of this ideology, Derek E. Vreeland noted: "The theological systems of the various word of faith ministries, churches and faith teachers lack precise similarity. The faith theology of Hagin differs somewhat from the theology of

[Kenneth] Copeland, etc. This presents a methodological problem in identifying what is 'word of faith theology.' The most efficient analysis and reconstruction of word of faith theology proper is to concentrate on the theology of Kenneth Hagin in particular. The various faith ministries may lack systematic cohesion, but a common denominator can be found in the influence of Hagin."[112] Kenneth Copeland, Buddy Harrison, and John Osteen were but a few of the prominent ministers whom Hagin influenced in the 1960s and 1970s. In turn, these men spawned their own theological offspring. Copeland mentored one of the most renowned black ministers, Atlanta pastor and evangelist Creflo Dollar. Harrison, who was also Hagin's son-in-law, had a profound impact on the charismatic movement through the Harrison House publishing company, which he founded in 1975. Many of the major charismatic evangelists in the last quarter of the twentieth century used Harrison House to promote their books and ministries. John Osteen's son, Joel, became a prominent pastor, evangelist, and author at the turn of the twenty-first century. In 2005 his Lakewood Church in Houston had a reported weekly attendance of twenty-eight thousand, his weekly television broadcast could be seen on numerous networks in the United States and abroad, and his book *Your Best Life Now* quickly became a national best-seller.[113]

In 1990 *Charisma* magazine noted that the Word of Faith teaching was prominent in "most of the new independent black churches, many of which were founded by graduates of Hagin's Rhema Bible Training Center." But these graduates' interpretation of Hagin's message often went beyond an emphasis on individual prosperity and focused on prosperity for black communities. Independent ministers used the faith message to attract African Americans to their churches, offered them hope for the future, and built up their individual and communal self-esteem. "I think that for any black pastor," one minister remarked, "one of the main emphases must be to help believers recognize that they are somebody, they are the righteousness of God, and they don't have to feel inferior. So I teach people how to dream again, how to believe in themselves, how to hope again because of the Word of God."[114]

If Kenneth E. Hagin was the father of the modern faith movement, then his spiritual son among African Americans was Frederick K. C. Price. Price and his wife, Betty, had been Christians for several years, but they struggled financially and with their faith until he claimed to have received the gift of the Holy Spirit in 1970. Shortly after he was introduced to Hagin's Word of Faith theology, Price became completely enthralled with this new teaching.

After reading three of his books, he met Hagin in Albuquerque and asked his crusade manager if this experienced evangelist would preach at his small church in Inglewood, California, in 1972.[115] A dozen years later Price joked: "I am Brother Hagin's black child . . . and I am proud to be. One of the most beautiful things about his ministry is that it has a world outreach. It also has reached the black community here in the United States. I think it's beautiful what God has done in a very quiet way through this man, his faithfulness, his love, and his generosity of heart in sharing the Word of God. I took that Word of God and in 10 years we've grown from 300 people to 13,230 people at Crenshaw Christian Center in Inglewood, California."[116] Betty Price provided a glimpse into the racial implications of their relationship with Hagin: "I remember when we came here [to Campmeeting] in 1973, there was not another black person in the conference. . . . And our hearts went out to our black people. It's like Israel—my heart's desire is that *my* people be saved and *my* people get the Word." Through their television ministry and pastorate of Crenshaw Christian Center, this desire to minister to African Americans came to pass. "It's a church of all races," explained Betty Price, "but, naturally, with our being black, we draw more black people." She also noted that they preferred to address the spiritual problems of their Los Angeles community directly rather than relying on community action or legislation to correct social ills.[117]

Fred Price's involvement in Watts, his influence on other Word of Faith ministers, and his popular television teaching ministry made him an important figure in the charismatic movement in his own right. In the late 1970s he touched the life of football legend Rosie Grier, who joined Price's church and became a proponent of positive confession.[118] Price maintained a close relationship with Hagin's ministry until a controversy over race erupted in the early 1990s that drove a wedge between the two families.[119]

African Americans continued to support Hagin, and several prominent black ministers continued to speak at Campmeetings and other functions sponsored by Kenneth Hagin Ministries. Keith Butler, a 1978 graduate of Rhema Bible Training Center, established the Word of Faith Christian Center in Southfield, Michigan, which in 1979 claimed about 150 members. By the end of the century his congregation had more than eighteen thousand members, he had a dozen satellite churches located in the United States and the Virgin Islands, and he had thriving radio, television, and crusade ministries. In 1997 he received a special offering at Hagin's Winter Bible Seminar for Rhema Bible Training Center's new media center, and he testified to the influence that the Word of Faith teaching had on his per-

sonal and professional life. "My wife and I started our church in a little rec-
reation center with ten people," he remarked. "When we'd come to Tulsa for
Campmeeting or other meetings, we'd always bring a special offering from
our church, and we would increase the amount of the offering every year.
Every time we sowed seed into the special offering, God would give us a
miracle, such as a building or equipment that we needed."[120]

Another Word of Faith preacher who gained notoriety in the 1990s was
Louisiana native Leroy Thompson. Thompson preached in the Baptist
Church until he accepted the charismata in 1983 and went to California to
study positive confession theology with Fred Price for three years. Price introduced him to Hagin in the mid-1980s, and Thompson began attending
Hagin's meetings. He was invited to speak briefly at Campmeeting 1993,
and Hagin invited him back as a featured speaker the following year. He
continued to work closely with Hagin throughout the 1990s as he built a
large television ministry, pastored a congregation of almost two thousand
members, and was a featured speaker at many large crusades held by himself and other prominent Word of Faith ministers.[121]

Hagin's contributions to the modern charismatic movement were im-
measurable. His propagation of the Word of Faith teaching through his
books, tapes, magazine, radio and television programs, meetings, and training center made him an important leader in one of the fastest-growing religious phenomena in modern American history. The keys to his success
were his prosperity message, which offered hope to anyone who wanted a
more fulfilling life, and his stable institutions, which produced thousands of
people propounding that message. Several women, such as Vicki Jamison-
Peterson and Kate McVeigh, established thriving, if rather small, Word of
Faith ministries, while other women, such as Gloria Copeland and Taffi
Dollar, joined their husbands in building huge empires that were rooted
in Word of Faith theology. Regardless of their ministries' size and scope,
these women found a niche where they could become successful evangelists, pastors, and businesspeople in a religious culture that traditionally offered limited opportunities to female leaders. The most impressive growth
of the Word of Faith movement, however, came through African American
preachers. Fred Price, Creflo Dollar, and Keith Butler were but a few of
Hagin's disciples who carried the prosperity message to African American
communities throughout the United States and abroad. They crafted this
message to meet the needs of poor and middle-class blacks who were struggling to find their place in the post–civil rights era, and in the process they
created for themselves lucrative and influential religious empires.

Conclusion

The men and women who established ministries and took to the airwaves in the late twentieth century were indebted to the pioneers of the healing and charismatic revivals of the postwar era. These pioneers challenged racial and sexual taboos, provided ministry-building techniques, developed and popularized a cogent message, and generally laid the foundation upon which later generations of evangelists built. The new breed of ministers was also a product of the civil rights and feminist movements of the postwar era, which caused Americans to rethink their traditional notions about the place of women and minorities in society as African Americans and women began to move into the mainstream of American life. These innovators capitalized on the crucial roles that women and blacks had always played in the Pentecostal and charismatic movements, and they recognized the enormous possibilities of catering to a conservative audience that had been influenced by the progressive changes in American society.

2

A New Life for Women

From the 1940s through the 1990s, itinerant evangelists Daisy and T. L. Osborn spoke at conferences, conventions, and churches all over the world, promoting sexual equality and leadership roles for women in the church. Daisy became wildly popular among the laity in many countries, but some clergymen were appalled by her unorthodox message of female empowerment, which, they believed, threatened their hegemony. She recalled an incident after one Australian crusade where the pastor for an Assemblies of God church invited the congregation's elders and their wives onto the stage and asked the women to take a public oath of submission to their husbands. The pastor then asked his wife to come onstage and take the same oath. When she refused, the pastor insisted that all of the audio- and videotapes of Osborn's lessons be brought to the podium, presumably to be confiscated or destroyed. She later exclaimed that this "was the BEST publicity I got in Australia!!" A year later she ordained ten female pastors in that country; at the next conference she ordained fifty women.[1]

Just as Aimee Semple McPherson and Kathryn Kuhlman influenced a generation of ministers, another group of women also made their mark on the burgeoning charismatic movement. These were the spouses of prominent evangelists who often worked behind the scenes—as well as in the public eye—to make their husbands' ministries successful. Much of what they did was administrative or domestic in nature, but they also assumed leadership roles within their ministries and became prominent in their own right. They served as cultural mediators—religious entrepreneurs— marketing secular ideas about sexual equality to an increasingly receptive audience, and presenting those ideas in traditional conservative language. Their stories reflect the changes that occurred in modern American culture regarding family dynamics and women's roles in society. Daisy Osborn, Freda Lindsay, and Gloria Copeland somehow managed to live up to the modern "superwoman" ideal, keeping one foot in their conservative, traditional religious world while forging ahead to become successful leaders in the charismatic world.[2]

Despite some important changes in American society, the plight of women remained difficult after the passage of the Nineteenth Amendment in 1920 until the publication of Betty Friedan's *The Feminine Mystique* in 1963. In the 1920s and 1930s more women were working outside the home, attitudes about sex and procreation were changing, and there was a growing interest in and acceptance of modern birth control, but women remained largely dependent upon men for their financial well-being and still had relatively little political influence. After World War II women continued to work outside the home—some to make ends meet, others to maintain their middle-class lifestyle—but the social pressures to be a good housewife and mother caused a great deal of stress for many women. They were encouraged to be the keepers of hearth and home, allowing their husbands to be the primary breadwinners. Friedan sought to dispel the myth that all women found fulfillment in their roles as housewives and mothers; many, she argued, longed for rewarding experiences outside the home and family. More recently, feminist historians have demonstrated how, despite their lack of organization and institutional power, women in the 1950s and 1960s *did* manage to contribute to society in productive ways and on their own terms, especially through religious institutions.[3]

In her analysis of the Women's Aglow Fellowship International, a charismatic parachurch organization that emphasized prayer, emotional healing, and personal transformation, Marie Griffith describes the broader development of female participation in modern American evangelicalism. She rejects "the cultural stereotypes commonly depicting conservative Christian women as meek followers of the men who run their churches, puppets duped by the leaders of the religious right, or, more threateningly, militant antifeminists in the tradition of Phyllis Schlafly and Beverly LeHaye." She shows how women "carved out spaces for themselves" within their patriarchal religious structures and "resisted those structures in subtle and unexpected ways." These women were constantly renegotiating the boundaries of power and authority and reshaping their personal identities through the healing and transformative power of prayer. They expanded their roles from the traditional domestic sphere "to encompass a more general nurturing role in society" as well as accepting the increasingly public role of women in religious and secular culture.[4]

In *Godly Women: Fundamentalism and Female Power,* ethnographer Brenda E. Brasher maintains that there was a sacred canopy of beliefs that covered and drew together the people of fundamentalist congregations, but there was also a sacred wall that separated the men from the women under that canopy into two separate and distinct spheres. She argues that the women beneath that divided canopy found in fundamentalist Christianity a sense of empowerment in their churches and marital relationships. When she began her study, Brasher wanted to find out how "fundamentalist women could be powerful people in a religious cosmos generally conceded to be organized around their disempowerment." She discovered that "to Christian fundamentalist women, the restrictive religious identity they embrace improves their ability to direct the course of their lives and empowers them in their relationships with others." She was surprised to learn that these women believed that the submissive roles they held in their churches and families were ordained by God—not men—and that the relationship with their husbands was one of mutual submission. Furthermore, Brasher contends that the all-women's ministries, parachurch organizations, and social networks formed within fundamentalist churches gave women "a valuable source of religious alterity and institutional power. For when fundamentalist women want to exercise power, want to change their congregation in any way, these groups provide them with an organizational base from which to operate."[5]

Religion scholar Julie Ingersoll takes exception to the interpretations of Griffith and Brasher, contending that they provide an incomplete picture of the struggles that evangelical women have faced. She admits that some women felt a sense of empowerment through submission and the separate spheres that shaped Christian fundamentalism, but she asserts that many women faced staunch resistance when they sought gender equality in their churches and parachurch organizations, causing some to leave the evangelical movement.[6] Her study presumes "that religious traditions are cultural systems that are always in a process of change" and that scholars should focus on the people who participate in that process, how it occurs, what the costs are, and who bears the burden of those costs.[7] She argues that "gender is a central organizing principle and a core symbolic system in this [the evangelical] subculture." Furthermore, she contends that interpreting and controlling that system is an organic, constant "process of construction" that requires considerable negotiation on the part of all participants in the system. Finally, she maintains that conflict is the key characteristic of the symbolizing system.[8] This threefold thesis shapes her "sociological study of conservative women who challenge gender norms within their religious traditions." She examines the difficulties they experienced and "the significance of the conflict over gender for the development and character of culture."[9]

Ingersoll also uses three theories—cultural production theory, conflict theory, and the gender theory that Judith Butler outlined in *Gender Trouble: Feminism and the Subversion of Identity* (1990)—to inform her analysis of the conflicts and negotiations that occur during cultural production. She focuses on the "conflicting voices in the conservative Christian world" to explain how gender "is the product of ongoing cultural work characterized by negotiation, compromise, and even conflict."[10] Hearing these conflicting voices, she maintains, allows one to better understand how culture "is explicitly produced" and does not simply serve as a "backdrop against which life occurs."[11] She draws these three theories together to show that gender is not simply imposed on a less powerful group by a more powerful one but "is evolving and malleable" and is created by a diverse group of people, institutions, and other resources in an ongoing and ever-changing process.[12] She contends that traditionalists within the evangelical subculture had the greatest influence on popular evangelical thought, thus creating and sustaining a gendered dualism whereby men and women operated in separate spheres.[13]

The women in the present study exhibit qualities of both of these interpretations of conservative evangelical women. On the one hand, they created spaces within their separate spheres where they exercised a certain amount of influence over the charismatic movement. Although men dominated many of the churches and organizations within this subset of evangelicalism, there existed a long tradition of female involvement and leadership. It was, to some extent, natural for these women to participate in their husbands' ministries or to develop their own independent ministries. On the other hand, as was seen in the incident at the beginning of this chapter, there was a great deal of resistance and negotiation by the male leaders, the female evangelists, and the women to whom they preached. I argue that the evangelists under consideration here were leaders in the negotiating process and helped shape the views of many Pentecostals and charismatics. Although they continued to espouse traditional views about submission to male authority, in practice they undermined those views—sometimes in subtle ways, sometimes in more obvious ways—to construct new ideas about gender equality in the charismatic world. At the same time, as Brasher, Ingersoll, and other scholars admit, many evangelicals more readily accepted sexual equality in their subculture as it became more acceptable in the larger secular society.[14]

The gradual acceptance in the 1960s and 1970s of women working outside the home challenged the Victorian notion that men were the sole breadwinners and that women should be only housewives and mothers. Ideally, this shift in working patterns moved women from a subordinate position in the family and society to one of equality with their husbands; the hierarchical family structure was supposedly replaced with an egalitarian "wife-companion" model. In reality, elements of the hierarchical model persisted, and working women were expected to effectively juggle their household duties while building and maintaining successful careers.[15] Many female ministers met the challenge of being both housewife and career evangelist. Most had supportive spouses and extended family members who encouraged their career aspirations and helped with raising their children and running their ministries. The early female ministers successfully promoted sexual equality in the church, which made it easier for later female evangelists to build their careers. By century's end, conservative Christians had adopted much of the secular culture's views about women's roles in society, and most audiences accepted female evangelists as a matter of course.

Daisy Osborn

David Harrell asserted in 1975 that T. L. and Daisy Osborn were among the most influential figures in the modern charismatic movement.[16] They gained notoriety as overseas evangelists in the post–World War II era by holding crusades throughout the world, establishing indigenous churches, and training native leaders to pastor churches or become highly successful evangelists themselves. Unlike leaders in many Western denominations, they did not try to "colonize" a region by maintaining strict control over the mission churches. Their message emphasized redemptive salvation for all, regardless of race, sex, or social status, and they promoted sexual equality in the church through their crusades, audio- and videotapes, tracts, books, and *Faith Digest* magazine. Native pastors and evangelists, such as Nigeria's Benson and Margaret Idahosa, mimicked the Osborns' ministerial style and adapted their message of Christian equality to their own culture. They also reflected a shift in secular culture in their teaching. Daisy Osborn claimed to oppose modern feminism, but she successfully adapted and used the feminist movement to promote her own religious agenda. She called modern feminists "Satan's seed" and was "categorically opposed to everything they teach, [and] everything they say." But she also acknowledged the sway feminists had on the charismatic movement, and she lauded the progressive changes that secular influences had on conservative churches in the last quarter of the twentieth century.[17]

Daisy Osborn played an important role as organizer, administrator, and preacher in the couple's ministry after 1948. Their foreign audiences generally accepted her as an equal partner with her husband, but by 1980 the duo discovered that some of their co-religionists in the United States were resistant to the sexual equality that characterized their ministry. During the 1980s and 1990s Daisy used her influence and popularity to promote sexual equality in American charismatic and Pentecostal churches. She remained popular until she died of respiratory failure in Tulsa on May 27, 1995.[18]

The tenth of eleven children, Daisy Osborn was raised in an impoverished migrant farm family in California. They were derisively called "fruit tramps" because they moved about the state, following the many harvest seasons of California's fruit crops. Under the influence of an older sister, Daisy had a conversion experience at the age of twelve and remained a faithful Christian throughout her lifetime.[19] She was accustomed to seeing men and women work together in the home and the church, and her childhood was filled with strong male and female role models. Her parents made family decisions together, she was exposed to both male and female preachers and Bible school teachers, and she always assumed that men and women were equal.[20]

Poor teenage girls had few career options in the years just before World War II. Daisy did not have enough money to attend college, and "nice girls" did not leave home and live alone in those days. When she was sixteen years old she met T. L. Osborn at a revival service in Almo, California, while he was serving as a musician and youth minister for Pentecostal evangelist Ernest Dillard. They married the following year, and the newlyweds moved to the Kiamichi Mountains in eastern Oklahoma to be missionaries. After a few unhappy months in "those backward mountains," the Osborns returned to the West Coast. They started a church in Portland when Daisy was nineteen, but the next year they moved to Lucknow, India, to be missionaries for the Pentecostal Church of God (Joplin, Missouri). They were not very successful as foreign missionaries, however; after only ten months they returned to the United States.[21]

The Osborns pastored a church in Oregon for a short time and then, once again, "felt called" to evangelize the world. "It was during these days that I sought God concerning specific direction for my own life," Daisy later stated. "The Lord made me to realize that I had to make a major choice myself." She decided to give up the "comfortable" lifestyle of a stay-at-home mother while her husband traveled around the world as an evangelist. "I could exercise faith and act on God's word, I could preach and teach the gospel, I could cast out devils, I could have power and authority over sicknesses and over demons; or I could remain at home, lead a quiet life and be a happy Christian mother," she recalled. "The Lord let me know that if I wanted to share in gospel ministry to the world, then it would be my own choice."[22] Although many conservative Christians taught that a woman's place was in the home, Daisy chose to minister alongside her husband as his "team-mate in ministry." "[M]y husband and I have walked together, prayed, fasted and read together, taught and preached together, enjoying the supreme privilege of leading broken, bleeding and suffering humanity to the feet of Jesus." But she also tried to make life on the road as normal as possible for their family by staying in houses instead of hotels whenever possible and by homeschooling their children.[23]

Her role as co-evangelist allowed Daisy to participate in all aspects of their ministry. She spoke at evangelistic meetings; published tracts, books, and other literature; produced audiotapes of sermons; filmed their crusades; and trained native preachers—both women and men—to be missionaries in their home countries. She also oversaw the administrative operations of the ministry, served as personnel manager, planned crusades, and chaired their nonprofit organization, the Osborn Foundation (OSFO) International. She never liked being called a "woman preacher," but she often warmed up the crowd at a crusade with a rousing thirty-minute sermon before her husband delivered the keynote address. Sometimes, in his absence, she would be the featured speaker.[24]

Most overseas audiences accepted Daisy's public role in their ministry, but some foreign and domestic church leaders disapproved of her actions. In 1980 the Osborns decided to curtail their overseas campaigns and work more in the United States, but they quickly discovered that because they had spent so much of their lives abroad they were unfamiliar with American culture. At one of their first stateside speaking engagements, Daisy was not allowed to sit onstage with her husband. She was seated in the front row of the audience, and the host pastor introduced her as T. L. Osborn's "lovely wife." Incensed at this snub, she decided not to attend any meetings where she was not specifically invited. Event organizers were surprised when her husband showed up without her, since they assumed she would accompany him and support his ministry. "He was the only one invited to speak those first two years that we were home," she recalled. "He would arrive. They'd say, 'Well *where's* your wife?' (They never seemed to know my name.) And he'd say, 'Well, she didn't come.' They'd say, 'We expected she would.' And then they'd name some wives—important wives—who always came. He said, 'Well, did you *invite* her?'" After a couple of years organizers began to invite Daisy too, but she would only go if she was scheduled to speak. She did not want to "go and then *sit!*"[25]

There was a division of labor in the Osborn ministry, but it was not gender specific. They assumed roles that best suited their talents, skills, and interests. T. L. enjoyed preaching and teaching and had no interest in the business affairs of their ministry. Daisy had studied finance and business and enjoyed tending to the administrative details that ensured a smooth operation. Despite her acceptance by most foreign audiences, male pastors in other countries were often reluctant to take orders from a woman. Daisy, according to her own testimony, discovered that if she first got the approval and cooperation of a country's high government officials, then the local pastors would honor her requests as well.[26] In the early 1960s, for example, she went to Nigeria to prepare for a crusade. Local clergy met her at the airport and presented her with a schedule of activities that had nothing to do with preparing for an evangelistic campaign. Osborn decided to accomplish her goals through government channels instead of the traditional religious hierarchy: "I was graciously accepted in my official capacity as President of OSFO International, and my being a woman did not cause even the Head of State to bat an eye. With the cooperation and blessing of the governor, the tribal king and the village chiefs, we were able to leave no stone unturned, and the gospel invasion was carried out victoriously."[27] Osborn understood that local leaders took their cues—and received favors—from their political superiors, and she knew how to "work the system" to her advantage. But she also recognized her influence on women, and this was where she had the greatest impact on the charismatic revival.

In a 1991 interview with David Harrell, Daisy recalled how she began ministering to women in 1973 when a women's group in Indonesia invited her to speak to them. She began studying the issue of sexual equality and noticed that many Pentecostal and charismatic preachers taught that a woman's only role in the church "was to be supportive of her husband!" She had always supported her husband's ministry, but he had also been supportive of her. In 1982 she expanded her women's ministry and sponsored the first

International Women's Conference, which proved to be a huge success. By 1985 she kept a full speaking schedule at conferences, conventions, and large churches in the United States and abroad. She held another International Women's Conference in 1988, and her husband taught workshops for men on "How to Assist a Woman in Ministry." A third conference was held, which focused on the theme of biblical equality, and audio- and videotapes of these workshops were sold in huge quantities all over the world. As was the case with most independent ministries, the distribution of tapes, books, tracts, and study guides was imperative to the success of her ministry.[28]

Daisy's daughter, LaDonna, who became vice-president and CEO of OSFO International after her mother's death, noted that her "prolific ministry of teaching, preaching, writing, [and] recording," as well as her organizational skills and natural business sense, helped "women of the world to discover their dignity and their destiny in God's plan of redemption."[29] Her husband fully supported her ministry, and he attributed her meteoric success to her teaching style. The years she spent homeschooling their children, he claimed, taught her to present organized and structured lessons. Daisy also understood the conservative nature of her audience and presented her message of sexual equality in a nonthreatening way. She generally found it easier to teach in a classroom setting than to preach to thousands, and she believed that classroom teaching was "her territory" because there were "some things you can say in a class setting that you don't say from a pulpit preaching."[30]

Daisy Osborn taught that women had to reject the social restrictions that traditional American society placed on them in order to attain sexual equality in the home and church. "Women of faith and of vision," she argued, "can exercise their right of choice and release themselves from the traditional limits imposed by a male-dominated clergy system, and reach far beyond the confines of restricted sanctuaries."[31] They also needed to develop a positive self-image. She encouraged women to discover and explore the unique and innate abilities that God gave them as individuals and not to rely on the affirmation of other people for their self-worth. Osborn rejected the traditional notion that men should be held accountable for the actions of their wives. "T. L. Osborn, my dedicated, soulwinning husband will not answer for me," she noted in *Five Choices for Women Who Win*. "I will stand alone before the King [on the Judgment Day] as an individual. My husband's deeds will not make points for me. My record will stand on its own. I have an individual responsibility, and so do you." She taught that women could choose their own influences and develop their personal faith by reject-

ing the "demeaning, bigoted, religious voices" of traditional Christian theologians and "sermonizers."[32]

The best way to acquire a positive attitude, Daisy believed, was through
education. Women were given the same abilities as men, but they had never
been taught how to use their talents and intelligence. After they married
and had children, she argued, they should educate themselves and develop
the skills necessary for becoming independent, confident leaders in their
homes and churches. "Don't sit home and watch *soap operas*," she exhorted
in *Five Choices*. "Your kids, you've taken 'em to school—what're you gonna
do with those hours? I say, become a student! You got twenty years for your
kids—you got twenty years that your husband's gonna pick up the tab and
you can get an education! Keep learning! *Free* education! You'll never have
it again in your life." Both Osborns believed that denying women their individuality and the freedom to develop and use their abilities in public ministry was tantamount to psychological abuse.[33]

Daisy was one of the first charismatic women to openly call for emotional
healing not only for women who had suffered psychological abuse but also
for those who had experienced physical and sexual abuse. She maintained
that female pastors could address certain issues better than men could and
that women struggling with these issues would respond more readily to female ministers. Once, at a large women's conference in Ohio, she asked
the audience of preachers' wives and other upstanding Christian women
to come forward if they had been battered or were addicted to drugs or alcohol. The response was overwhelming. "One third of that audience answered that call," she reported.[34] The emphasis on emotional healing, always a popular message in Pentecostal and charismatic circles, would later
catapult evangelists such as Joyce Meyer and T. D. Jakes to phenomenal
popularity in the 1990s, but it was Daisy Osborn who helped make this a
particularly important topic for women in the modern charismatic movement.

Her ministry provided a model for other women ministers to follow in
the 1980s and 1990s, and Daisy taught women how to assume leadership
roles in their denominations. Her message was not based on the notion that
women should replace men in church leadership positions. "I don't think
we should teach a message that encourages women to become all that they
can be at the expense of men," she explained. Both sexes should realize that
men and women were equally valuable to God because he had given them
both a sense of self-worth.[35] She preached a traditional gospel message that
humans were redeemed by the grace of God, that God offered salvation to

men and women alike, and that men and women held equal status in God's kingdom. "My life's passion for many years," she maintained, "has been to help women and girls—and people worldwide, to discover their individual dignity, their identity, their destiny, and their equality in God's redemptive plan."[36] Women were not limited to keeping house, raising children, and supporting their husbands' ministries. They had the same rights and responsibilities as men did to minister to and share the gospel with other people.[37] Daisy also argued that women were entitled to material prosperity and that it was not "God's plan for the daughters of His family to be dependent upon men for their material needs in order to keep them humble, submissive and subservient." According to Proverbs 31, she believed, women could be good wives, good mothers, and good businesspeople. They should not be expected to give up their careers—or their career aspirations—just because they got married and had children. Furthermore, they should not become "general unpaid maid[s] or servant[s]" to the men they married. They should instead educate themselves and use their training to become successful Christian businesswomen and ministers, as well as good wives and mothers.[38]

Much of Daisy's success lay in her ability to assess the needs and mood of her audience and communicate her radical message in a palatable manner. Her lack of formal training in theology and pedagogy appealed to her audience, which was often skeptical of ministers and scholars with advanced degrees. Even though many Pentecostals and charismatics had attained higher levels of education in the post–World War II era, they still considered a "word from God" and life experiences to be more valuable than a college education or seminary training. Paradoxically, Daisy understood that formal education was important for achieving success in modern society, and she encouraged her audiences to take advantage of every opportunity to further their education. Throughout her ministry she emphasized the importance of individual responsibility, personal dignity and action, and a strong sense of self-worth among the dispossessed. She encouraged people to be overcomers, to not allow their difficult circumstances to determine their position in life, and to reject traditional cultural stereotypes. Unwilling to adjust her personal views to accommodate the cultural shifts going on around her, she perceptively capitalized on the opportunity to take her message of sexual equality to a new and increasingly receptive audience. More than any other woman in the charismatic movement, Daisy Osborn provided the intellectual justification for late-twentieth-century women to join the ranks of independent evangelists.

Freda Lindsay

Osborn's contemporary Freda Lindsay supported her husband, Gordon, in his role as pastor, evangelist, and promoter of the healing revival until his death in 1973, when their ministry's board of directors voted unanimously to give her control of the organization. She became a respected editor, publisher, author, CEO, and religious leader in her own right, using her business acumen and shrewd managerial skills to make Christ for the Nations International one of the most influential charismatic institutions in the world. Her position, first as a behind-the-scenes administrator and adviser to her husband and later as a public figure leading her own organization, typified the role many spouses played in the modern charismatic movement. Lindsay provided a model for other women to follow as co-evangelists with their husbands or in building their own ministries.

"More than any single man," wrote David Harrell, "Gordon Lindsay brought system and unity to the healing revival. Lindsay contributed to the revival an orderly mind, a keen business sense, boundless energy, badly needed literary skills, and an ecumenical spirit. He very correctly surmised that the revival needed a coordinator and publicist much more than another evangelist." In 1924, when he was only eighteen years old, Gordon became a traveling Pentecostal preacher. He itinerated or pastored small Pentecostal churches until 1947, when healing evangelist William Branham asked him to manage his crusades. On April 1, 1948, Lindsay "opened wide the door of revival when he edited the first issue of *The Voice of Healing*," a magazine that promoted the leading healing ministries until the late 1950s. He established a loose fellowship of independent revivalists in 1950, also called The Voice of Healing, through which he coordinated and publicized the burgeoning charismatic movement and tried to maintain good relations between the evangelists and the Pentecostal denominations.[39]

Gordon Lindsay, a peacemaker, promoter, coordinator, and "shrewd manager and financier," became one of the most respected leaders in the charismatic movement, but he was unable to preserve his ministerial alliance. He was also unable to control the excesses of the independent evangelists and maintain harmony between them and the established denominations, from which they gained financial support and with which they often competed for adherents. In the early 1960s he "abandoned his role as publicist for the revival" and focused his attention on international evangelism. He started a native-church program that provided money to foreign congregations to build church buildings, which remained quite successful years after his death. A prolific writer and respected teacher, he started a Bible training school in Dallas and distributed millions of copies of his books all over the world in dozens of languages. At the time of his death on April 1, 1973, exactly twenty-five years after he launched *The Voice of Healing*, he had changed the name of his magazine and organization to Christ for the Nations International. He left his ministry with a strong institutional base, with solid financial support, and in the very capable hands of his wife of thirty-five years.[40]

Freda Lindsay was born in a sod house in 1914 in Burstall, Saskatchewan, Canada, to German immigrants Gottfred and Kaity Schimpf. The Schimpfs eventually moved their fourteen-member family into a ten-room house and had a prosperous wheat farm during World War I. Freda's mother did not care for the harsh Canadian winters, so the family sold their farm and bought an apple orchard in Oregon City, Oregon, in 1919. They experienced difficult times after moving to the United States. The apple orchard was a financial disaster, and they were unable to collect the money owed them for the sale of their wheat farm and equipment in Canada. Although they had been a nominally religious family, during this time of hardship they accepted the Pentecostal message. Their pastor in Oregon City tried to adopt Freda when she was six years old to alleviate the financial burden on her parents, but her mother, determined to keep their family together, refused his offer. Her father found a low-paying job at a lumber mill, but his daily wage of $3.10 was hardly enough to feed such a large family.[41]

Freda's hardscrabble life of picking berries and vegetables in the summertime to supplement her family's income taught her the value of hard work and instilled in her a desire to receive a formal education. But her father did not believe that women needed an education to fulfill their roles as wives and mothers. According to Freda, "he was strongly opposed to his daughter going to more than the required grammar school." Her mother, therefore, secretly agreed to convince him to let Freda go to high school if she promised to find a job. Freda secured a three-dollar-a-week job during her freshman year doing housework for a nearby family and was allowed to attend high school during the day. The following year she worked for another family for fifteen dollars per month plus room, board, and clothing. She graduated from Jefferson High School in Portland and was given a partial scholarship for college. She was unable to attend college after graduation, but she did receive a better-paying job. "As fall came," she wrote in her memoir, "and I watched some of my classmates go off to college while I worked as a domestic in a home for $30 a month, I felt completely frustrated. Life didn't seem worth living. And I was plagued with serious and dark thoughts that robbed me of my peace. It was now the fall of 1932." But those dark thoughts subsided when she rededicated her life to God and met a certain itinerant preacher.[42]

In October 1932 Freda's sister invited her to a revival meeting where Gordon Lindsay was preaching. The two had been acquainted since childhood, and their families attended the same full-gospel mission in Oregon, but they had never been especially close friends. After all, he was eight years her senior and had left home to preach at age eighteen. She responded to the altar call at the end of his sermon and heard a "still, small voice" tell her that she would marry this evangelist if she would remain a faithful Christian. During the next few years she saw her future husband only once a year when he came home to visit his family. Continuing to believe that she would indeed marry this man, she began preparing herself to become a minister's wife. She enrolled in a local Foursquare Bible School and received formal Bible training for three hours every weeknight, all the while working at a department store during the day. She recounted that her meager daily wage was not enough for her to ride the train to school or buy supper, so she usually walked two miles to school and ate supper around 11 P.M. when she returned home. Aside from her busy work and school schedule, she also sang in the church choir, served on its communion board, helped with church youth meetings, and delivered speeches at the local rescue mission, downtown street meetings, and jail ministry. In 1936 Gordon walked into her workplace and invited her to dinner. "It was a beautiful night," she recalled, "and one for which I had been waiting four years." A few days later he returned to the Deep South to continue his evangelistic career.[43]

Their courtship lasted just over a year and was carried out mainly through correspondence, since Gordon was preaching throughout the South and she continued to work and go to school in Oregon. His views about women's roles in the ministry were progressive for the time, but they still fit within the confines of fundamentalist theology. "I'll be happy indeed," he wrote shortly before their wedding, "when the time comes that you can take part with me in 'our' work."[44] In another letter he told her, "Women are and should be equal to men. Man does not want either a superior or an inferior helpmate. Men and women are not competitors but should be an inspiration one to another in the battle of life."[45] Each was concerned about interfering with the other's personal ministry if they got married too soon. When she suggested that they "wait a year or so" because she might hinder his work, he dismissed the notion completely: "The idea is preposterous and unreasonable! Why darling, your presence will prove a great blessing, not only to me, but to the church."[46] He also wanted to make clear to her pastor in Oregon, Harold Jefferies, that, while he supported her work in Jefferies's church, he needed her help in his ministry as well:

> I know your kindness to her has been a great blessing in her life. She is not the type to push herself forward and, therefore, her promotion (as president of the young people) was due to merits alone, and your ability to judge human nature. I trust your mutual friendship may ever be sustained. . . . I realize the opportunity that lies before her in your movement. . . . It would bring poignant regret if I were ever to learn that she felt her future career were in any way hampered by myself. . . . It is my earnest desire that Freda may get the very best out of life, and that she may be able to realize opportunities that come her way. . . . As for Freda, you of course understand that *she was saved and received the baptism under the ministry of your correspondent.*[47]

The couple married on November 14, 1937, and settled in California, where Gordon had agreed to pastor a small church.[48]

Freda quickly adjusted to her new role as a pastor's wife. "I found myself doing a lot of things for which I really was not qualified," she remarked.[49] She led the congregational singing, performed solos, preached, taught the young people's classes, directed the choir, visited current and prospective members in their homes, and sometimes even served as janitor. After only two months at that congregation she decided she should finish her Bible school training, so Gordon once again went on the road as an itinerant evangelist and she enrolled in Aimee Semple McPherson's LIFE Bible College in Los Angeles. Some family members did not approve of their decision to separate so soon after being married, but Freda insisted that she "had always been a stickler for finishing whatever I started." She never regretted completing her education, and, as she wrote in her memoir, the "beautiful part about it was that I had Gordon's full approval, without which I would never have gone."[50] Freda's drive and determination served her well throughout her life, especially when she took over the ministry after Gordon's death.

The Lindsays considered themselves equal partners in their ministry, and they worked as a team. Freda balanced the duties of being a pastor's wife with the responsibilities of motherhood, and her limitless energy and determination allowed her to do both quite well. She was also her husband's best critic, and Gordon recognized her talents and encouraged her to use them in their work. "One night after speaking on the baptism in the Holy Spirit, when he came home from the service, I mentioned to Gordon several areas where he should have been more clear," she wrote. "I felt that he could have been more effective had he included some simple instructions at the close, and I suggested what he should have said." He replied that perhaps she should teach on this subject and that he would announce it the next Sunday. Freda was reluctant to take on this assignment, but he insisted. She was surprised at the positive response she got from the congregation after her lesson, and "[f]rom then on, Gordon would almost never pray with an individual to receive the baptism in the Holy Spirit, but would refer them to me. We worked as a team. He would make up for my deficiencies, and I would try to help where he lacked. There was never a spirit of rivalry, never a spirit of jealousy." This spirit of teamwork, camaraderie, and mutual support was typical of the relationship that the women in this study had with their spouses. Their husbands viewed them as partners and co-evangelists—not as subordinates—and encouraged them to take public roles in their ministries.[51]

By the late 1940s the Lindsays had settled into a comfortable pastorate in Ashland, Oregon, where Freda hoped they would spend the rest of their career. Those hopes were dashed, however, when Jack Moore, a good friend from Shreveport, Louisiana, invited them to a revival service in Sacramento, California, conducted by an independent Baptist minister named William Branham. Branham was one of the early giants in the healing revival that began in 1948, and much of his later success was attributed to Gordon's managerial skills and promotional efforts. Gordon took a year's leave of absence from their Ashland congregation to manage Branham's crusades, and Freda was left to oversee the church and care for their three children. As she reported, Gordon found Branham to be "a very simple brother in many respects . . . utterly incapable of coping with the cunning and shrewdness that he meets on every side. He has definitely turned over the management of the campaigns to Brother Jack Moore and myself."[52] But Gordon also recognized the evangelistic potential of promoting the healing campaigns of Branham and other full-gospel ministers, so he resigned his pastorate to advance the revival full-time. In 1948 the Lindsays moved to Shreveport and started *The Voice of Healing* magazine, which promoted up-and-coming evangelists such as A. A. Allen and T. L. Osborn.[53]

The Lindsays had an important influence on many of these ministers, and they encouraged their wives to become active in the healing campaigns. T. L. and Daisy Osborn, inspired by a Branham service they attended in

Portland, asked Gordon to help them start their own evangelistic ministry. Later, when the Osborns had a difficult time attracting large crowds to one of their meetings in Reading, Pennsylvania, Gordon suggested that they might have more healings if they would put the people with the most faith at the front of the healing lines. Then, when these people "received their healing," those at the back of the line—who were a bit more skeptical— would be encouraged to believe and they, too, would be "healed." Noticing that Daisy "seems to be an alert, observant, spiritually-sensitive woman," Gordon recommended that "[w]hen the people come forward for prayer, why not have her mill through the crowd and talk a few moments individually to the ones to whom the Lord leads her? Then let her select those who she feels have the faith for their healing and put them at the head of the line." Freda recalled that when the Osborns "acted on this suggestion . . . it was like an atomic chain reaction: Scores were healed successively." The crowds increased each night thereafter, and by the end of the revival there was a reported attendance of about five thousand people.[54]

During those early, heady years of the healing revival the Lindsays lived out of a travel trailer—even when they went "home" to Shreveport—and Freda participated in nearly every aspect of the ministry, in addition to taking care of their children. She tried hard to let her husband focus solely on promoting and managing the campaigns, and "[r]arely did I ask him to give me any assistance with regard to our home or business matters which I could possibly take care of myself."[55] They decided not to send their children to public school so they could travel as a family. Lindsay not only home-schooled their children but she noted that she attended two crusade meetings each day, directed the congregational singing, sang solos, edited the magazine, washed clothes, cooked meals, and drove their truck and travel trailer from city to city.[56] This nomadic lifestyle was hard on the family, and they had their share of parental concerns when their children were in their teens and early twenties.[57] They also realized that Shreveport was not large enough to handle the huge volume of mail they received and sent, so they moved to Dallas in 1952 and established a headquarters from which they could orchestrate the expanding healing revival.[58]

As the healing revival gave way to the charismatic revival of the late 1950s and 1960s, the Lindsays saw the need to adapt their ministry as well. At least one prominent evangelist that *The Voice of Healing* had promoted early in his career "told Gordon that he really didn't have a ministry anyway; that he had always just hung on the coattails of other preachers; that, in short, he was just a leech."[59] But the Lindsays were well aware of their influence on the movement, and as early as 1955 they began to consider other ways they could help to spread the revival. In November 1961 they announced the start of their native-church program, through which the Voice of Healing ministry gave missionaries $250 to erect a church building. The native Christians had to buy the land and supply the labor, but the $250 would cover the cost of materials. In 1967 the Voice of Healing's board of directors changed the name of the organization to Christ for the Nations International (CFNI), which better reflected the ministry's new character and mission. By the end of the twentieth century CFNI had reportedly built more than ten thousand churches worldwide.[60]

During this period Freda saw her role in their ministry slowly evolve from that of a behind-the-scenes administrative supporter to a spiritual leader within the charismatic movement. She had always handled "most of the business affairs of Christ For The Nations," she later wrote, "leaving him [Gordon] free to speak in conventions and seminars, to write his many books, to serve as editor of our monthly magazine, and to oversee the worldwide foreign missions program."[61] She generally took notes at the meetings they attended and read them back to him while they traveled; he then wrote the reports for the magazine. One day he asked *her* to write the report on the latest convention. When she objected, he insisted that she do it, and from that time forward she "had a 'steady job' of reporting the conventions" for *The Voice of Healing*. She also began writing articles for other magazines and even contributed essays to some of Gordon's books.[62]

In addition to her roles as reporter and author, Freda learned to manage their print shop. Their son Gilbert majored in business at Baylor University and returned home to run the print shop after graduation. In the late 1960s he joined the National Guard and was sent to Missouri for six months of training. Instead of hiring an interim manager, Gordon prevailed upon Freda to take the job herself. She resisted, "telling him I was already 50 years old and that most people do not start a new career at 50—especially a career in printing, which is so technical and involved. Besides," she noted, "I already had all I could do in helping Gordon with his books, the magazine, traveling with him and assisting in the public meetings we held." Once again, he insisted and she finally gave in. With Gordon's encouragement, Freda became familiar with nearly every aspect of the ministry.[63]

Freda was also a shrewd businessperson and maintained a strong sense of purpose about her ministry. She was attentive to detail and could be matter-of-fact and blunt when necessary. "[Y]ou have to be strong to run an organization like this," she told *Charisma* magazine in 1984, "and I'm not afraid to make difficult decisions." One of the first questions she would ask a male applicant for a job at CFNI was, "Will you have difficulty taking directions from a woman?" She considered that very important. "After all, I'm boss and I don't mind letting them know that. . . . [W]hen a major decision has to be made, I'm not afraid to make it and to stand by it. . . . We're not a ladies' aid society that meets for socials."[64]

On several occasions Freda demonstrated her willingness to make important decisions. Shortly before the Lindsays opened the Bible training center in 1970, a small piece of property adjacent to their Dallas headquarters became available. The owner knew they wanted to buy the property and believed he had them, in Freda's words, "over a barrel," so he raised the asking price to an exorbitant fifteen thousand dollars. She reminded the owner that their existing property surrounded him on all four sides and that "he might have to get to his land by helicopter, for we would just build the new institute around him." According to Freda, CFNI eventually bought the land for the fair market price of three thousand dollars.[65] She also helped negotiate the terms for much of the land on which CFNI was built, and she acquired several apartment buildings, a nearby motel, and a Sheraton hotel across the street to be used as student housing. In 1972 she traded her own home for some apartments near the ministry headquarters and moved into them within a few days of closing the deal.[66]

When Gordon died on the stage of the unfinished chapel at the three-year-old Bible institute, CFNI had accumulated a considerable amount of debt and did not have enough tuition-paying students to make its monthly mortgage payments. To make matters worse, Freda's personal secretary entered the hospital and was diagnosed with terminal cancer, and her brother died unexpectedly one week after her husband's death.[67] Freda struggled to maintain her composure in the midst of all these crises, but one morning, shortly after her husband's funeral, she found that she did not have the physical strength to get out of bed and go to work. She lay back down and called her daughter, Carole, into the room and told her that the load was too great for her to bear. The ministry was too large, and she did not know how they would complete and pay for the construction on the Bible institute. But, bolstered by her family, friends, and CFNI's board of directors, she continued to raise money and manage the daily operations of the ministry.[68]

Nine years before Gordon's death, charismatic minister John Osteen had predicted that Freda would one day have her own ministry. He claimed that although her ministry had been submerged into her husband's, she would eventually become a spiritual leader in her own right. "I did not immediately see myself launching out," she remarked years later, "as I felt my ministry was being a helpmate to Gordon." But the responsibilities she had in supporting her husband's ministry trained her well to lead one of the most influential charismatic institutions of the twentieth century.[69] Other charismatic leaders, such as Kenneth Hagin, Demos Shakarian, and Jimmy Swaggart, expressed their confidence in her ability to lead CFNI; Hagin and Swaggart even helped raise money to pay off the institute's debt. Freda was also pleasantly surprised to find that her husband, who had been writing furiously for several years, was three years ahead of schedule on his book writing. She continued to publish one of his books each month to help pay for the school, and in 1998 there were a reported 60 million copies of his books in print in seventy-nine languages.[70]

Freda took control of CFNI at the height of the feminist movement in the United States. Although she did not support its agenda, through her actions she advocated sexual equality and inspired other conservative Pentecostal and charismatic women to become leaders in their communities and churches. Many people recognized her talents even when her husband was alive, but others were skeptical that she could maintain such a large organization after his death.[71] She proved that she could not only maintain their ministry but even expand its influence. Brenda Brasher, in her study of evangelical women, noted that women between the ages of twenty-one and thirty typically did not believe that men had inherently superior leadership qualities over women. Although they accepted male leadership in their churches, they did not believe that men had a God-given right to exercise authority over women in their communities. A generation of women and men that attended CFNI or followed this ministry from the 1970s onward saw in Freda an example of a strong female leader in a traditionally male-dominated context. Many women in that generation—who were influenced by the changes in secular society—internalized those subtle messages of female empowerment.[72]

Gloria Copeland

Unlike Daisy Osborn, who emphasized sexual equality in her teaching, and Freda Lindsay, who came to prominence after her husband's death, Texas evangelist Gloria Copeland gained notoriety alongside her husband by emphasizing the same prosperity message that characterized his teaching. She, too, provided modern women with a model for juggling the responsibilities of wife, mother, and evangelist, and her popularity rivaled that of some of the most prominent leaders—both male and female—in the charismatic movement. Copeland, born Gloria Neece and raised in a small town near Little Rock, Arkansas, received very little religious training as a child. Her family was critical of the healing revival of the 1950s, and she recalled how her grandmother refused to believe that Oral Roberts actually healed people.[73] Little did she know that Gloria would one day have her own healing and teaching ministry and take her cues from Oral Roberts himself. Her circuitous journey into the charismatic world began on October 8, 1961, when her parents introduced her to a young commercial pilot and part-time nightclub singer from Texas named Kenneth Copeland. They felt an immediate attraction for each other and began dating two months later, when she was nineteen and he was twenty-five. He proposed on their first date and she impulsively accepted, thinking all along that she could back out later. They married on April 13, 1962, and borrowed a hundred dollars to honeymoon in the resort town of Hot Springs, Arkansas.[74]

Their life together was anything but marital bliss in those early years. According to their personal testimonies, the Copelands had entered into a promising new business with some friends in the summer of 1962; within three weeks the business failed. They had rented a nice house and hoped to buy furniture for it shortly thereafter, but instead they struggled to pay their bills and find new jobs. Gloria noted that they "had a stunning metal coffee table that Ken had made in high school shop," a small black-and-white television set, a coffee pot, a rented rollaway bed, and two borrowed lawn chairs.[75] Their three-bedroom house, she recalled, did not even have a stove or refrigerator. Her mother-in-law gave them potatoes, which Gloria cooked in the coffeepot, and as soon as the weather turned cold enough she set a cardboard box on the porch to use as a makeshift icebox.[76]

She despondently started reading her Bible, searching for some respite from their hardship. She found a passage in Matthew's Gospel where Jesus explained to his disciples that they should not worry about food or clothing because God would provide those things to people who follow his teaching. After reading these verses she realized that God cared about her needs and would provide for them if she would only be a faithful Christian. She also began to think that acquiring earthly possessions might not be the road to true happiness in life. "At the time," she noted, "I thought that material goods were about all that there was to life. It seemed that if you were married to a man that you loved, then financial prosperity should bring happiness."[77] But material goods, she soon decided, were just an added benefit of becoming a Christian, not the source of true contentment. In 1962 she dedicated her life to God; two weeks later, she claimed, the Copelands had jobs, a new car, a new apartment, and new furniture. She put God first in her life, asked for the things she needed, and was reportedly freed "from the kingdom of darkness and from the dire circumstances to which we had been bound."[78] From her perspective, the material benefits of being a Christian were obvious. These events heavily influenced her ministry and message in later years.

While Gloria was coming to terms with her newfound faith, her husband also experienced a religious enlightenment. He was raised a Baptist but showed no interest in religion for several years. Shortly after they moved into their new apartment, he told her that he wanted to start "preaching or making talks about the Lord."[79] She was surprised at his sudden interest in spiritual matters and noticed that their lives began to change after their conversion experiences. She reported that they both received the "gift of the Holy Spirit" three months after their conversions, but for "five years we plodded along spiritually without knowing how to use our faith."[80] They read the Bible, went to church, and were relatively happy, but they changed jobs frequently and never seemed to be as successful as they would have liked. They discussed attending Oral Roberts University in Tulsa but were not sure they could survive financially with their existing debt and a growing family.[81] When they finally moved to Tulsa in the fall of 1966 they were twenty-four thousand dollars in debt and saw little hope of getting ahead in life.[82] Gloria recounted how she would stand "in the check-out line at the grocery store, praying in the spirit, and believing God that I had enough money to pay for the groceries in my basket. Whatever I had in my purse at the time was all we had!"[83] But their outlook—and circumstances—began to change when they were introduced to the teachings of Kenneth Hagin and Oral Roberts.

Kenneth Copeland entered Oral Roberts University when he was thirty years old and was quickly given a job with Roberts's evangelistic team as his personal copilot and chauffeur. He also worked in the invalid tent at the healing revivals and learned how to apply the teachings and techniques of this "famed healing evangelist."[84] While the Copelands may have learned the techniques of healing evangelism from Oral Roberts, Hagin's Word of Faith doctrine first influenced their theology in 1967. Through seminars and teaching tapes Hagin taught them how to verbalize what they wanted from God, find a Bible verse to confirm their desires, and believe that God would give them whatever they asked for. Gloria noted: "In the past we had mentally agreed that the Word was true but did not know to act on it *before* we saw results. We were not believing that we received *when we prayed.* We only believed that we received when the answer came."[85] The Copelands wanted to learn more about this teaching, but they did not have enough money to buy Hagin's sermon tapes. When Kenneth offered to trade his car title for a set of audiotapes, Buddy Harrison, Hagin's son-in-law and crusade manager, gave him the tapes and told him to pay for them when he had the money. Years later Harrison told Kenneth that he would have given the tapes to him just to get that car out of his parking lot. "I *saw* that car!" Harrison joked. "I thought, *My goodness, I don't want the title to that car! We teach prosperity. What if somebody sees that thing parked in front of our office?*"[86] The year 1967 was a turning point for the Copelands: Hagin's Word of Faith teaching and Roberts's ministry-building techniques helped catapult them into the national spotlight.[87]

Initially, Gloria played the role of a traditional supportive wife and mother who stayed home with the children and kept house. Through her personal study, however, she prepared herself for a public role in their ministry. By the early 1970s she and the children were traveling with her husband and helping with administrative tasks such as taking pictures and counting the offering. "I was the photographer. I was the accountant. I carried the offering—what little there was—around in my purse," she recalled in 1997.[88] By 1974 she was assisting him with the healing lines and appearing onstage with him during services.[89] Her first articles in the ministry publication, *Believer's Voice of Victory,* were short promotional announcements, but she eventually came to write regular articles for the magazine.[90] She also wrote a book, *God's Will for You,* which was published in 1973.[91] In 1976 she spoke for the first time at a prosperity seminar in Tulsa, where she testified about how God's laws of divine prosperity had worked in their lives and how God had revealed those laws to her early in their ministry.[92] She wrote extensively in the late 1970s on the subject of divine prosperity, the importance of Bible study, and Bible teachings on the home, marriage, and family.[93]

Gloria came into her own as a public figure when she started conducting healing schools in the fall of 1979. Much of the Copelands' teaching during the 1970s had focused on prosperity, but there was a move within charismatic circles to return to the emphasis on healing that had characterized the movement in the 1950s.[94] In the summer of 1979 Gloria reluctantly decided to take a much more public role in their ministry. "I did not want to have a speaking ministry," she admitted. "I was not comfortable on the platform. I had no aspirations to be there! I had always helped and supported Kenneth in the background and really that's where I wanted to stay." When she told her husband about the "calling" she felt God had placed on her heart, he was immediately supportive; in September 1979 she held her first healing school in Atlanta.[95] By the early 1980s she had taken over the morning sessions and was listed as a co-host of their crusades. Her healing-school sessions were aired on the *Believer's Voice of Victory* television program and could be purchased on videotape. She even had speaking engagements that were separate from her husband's.[96]

Gloria's popularity grew throughout the 1980s, and in 1994 she received the Christian Woman of the Year Award. The Christian Woman of the Year Association was founded in 1983 to honor evangelical women leaders whose "activities, attributes, and accomplishments reflect a life of devotion to God, to the principles of His Word and to meeting the needs of people." Other notable evangelical women who had won this award included radio personality James Dobson's wife, Shirley; Oral Roberts's wife, Evelyn; Pat Robertson's wife, Dede; Billy Graham's wife, Ruth; and Dan Quayle's wife, Marilyn. The association's founder, Carolyn Evans, praised Gloria for her righteous living, faithful service to others, and superior leadership. She lauded her ability to successfully balance the challenges of public ministry with the rigors of motherhood and homemaking. "During her many ministerial activities," Evans noted, "Gloria has successfully been a homemaker and a mother. Her life is truly a continual inspiration for us to be all we can be as Christian women."[97] According to Evans, Gloria embodied the "super-woman" ideal to which many evangelical women aspired as they moved into public ministerial roles. This award also demonstrates the level of acceptance by mainstream evangelicals that charismatics and Pentecostals had achieved by the 1990s. No longer considered outsiders looking in, they were active participants and leaders in the evangelical subculture.

Gloria also had an important part in cultivating the relationship between their ministry and financial backers. Throughout their career the Copelands wrote their partners each month, insisting to their supporters that the letters were designed to bless them spiritually, not beg for money.[98] Despite efforts to avoid cajoling their supporters for cash, the Copelands were not afraid to invite people to "sow a seed" into the kingdom of God by partnering with them. They assured the readers of *Believer's Voice of Victory* that God would "bless them abundantly" if they contributed to Kenneth Copeland Ministries (KCM) and that they would receive "heavenly credit" for every person who was "saved, healed, or delivered" from dire circumstances through their ministry. "There may be those of you who are led to join with us in our Radio Outreach to North America," Kenneth implored in 1978, "so I want to allow you the opportunity to do so. . . . While I am on the front lines ministering to the people, my partners share the same rewards that I do. In God's eyes, it is as if you yourself were traveling around the country, preaching and teaching His Word."[99]

These low-pressure fund-raising tactics worked well through the 1970s, but the Copelands became more aggressive in the 1980s after buying property on Eagle Mountain Lake near Fort Worth to build a new headquarters. In 1983 Gloria realized that many people who received *Believer's Voice of Victory* were not regular contributors to the ministry. Given the slow progress KCM was making in raising funds for construction, she set out to encourage readers to do their part in supporting this work financially. "There are many of you who have been partners and have stood so faithfully with us for years," she wrote. "You have been faithful to *do your part* and you have enabled us to do all we've accomplished so far. . . . Those of you who give consistently are the financial backbone of what we do each month. Believe me, you have made the difference." But there were others who benefited from the ministry but had not supported the work. "I know that there are many of you who have had your lives changed by hearing this ministry and other ministries on tape, radio or television or meetings," she continued. "Many have been healed, saved and delivered through these outreaches, yet you have never given to help send these ministries to someone else. The Bible teaches that if you have partaken of spiritual things, it is your duty to minister of carnal things." She was appalled to discover that of the estimated 650,000 households that received *Believer's Voice of Victory* in 1982 only 181,000 gave money to the ministry. "I could not believe it," she exclaimed. "A few people are carrying the load . . . while the many, even in the Body of Christ, DO NOTHING. Brother and Sister, this ought not be so. No wonder it takes so long for ministries to get their job done." She called for a special "parts" offering so that all could do "their part" to help finance the construction of the headquarters.[100]

The appeals apparently worked. KCM moved into its new International Headquarters in 1986—reportedly without having to borrow money for its construction—and the ministry continued to grow.[101] One cannot overestimate the importance of these regular financial supporters to this and other ministries. The money these organizations made through merchandise sales and special offerings at conventions was significant, but the bulk of their financial support came from the partners who sent regular contributions. Although both Copelands participated in the fund-raising, Gloria's efforts during the financial crunch of the mid-1980s helped KCM reach its goals, finish the buildings, and expand the ministry to one of the largest and most successful charismatic ministries of the 1990s.[102]

The Copelands also received their share of public criticism and controversy. Aside from the critiques of their prosperity theology, which nearly all of the evangelists in this study faced, the Copelands' ministry came under considerable scrutiny after three people were killed on their private airstrip in the fall of 1997. The first incident was a helicopter crash on September 17 involving two Tarrant County, Texas, sheriff's deputies. The crash focused attention on the relationship between the Copelands and Tarrant County sheriff David Williams, who served as the Copelands' director of security in the early 1980s. The deputies were conducting aerial surveillance in connection with a car theft investigation when their helicopter crashed on the Copelands' property shortly after taking off from a Forth Worth airport. The National Transportation Safety Board concluded that the helicopter went down because the pilot failed to keep the aircraft's rotor blades spinning fast enough to keep it aloft. Sheriff Williams, who already had a strained relationship with county commissioners, was criticized for his unwillingness to divulge information about the helicopter program. Commissioners also wanted to know why the helicopter crashed on the Copelands' property, which was occasionally used by the sheriff's department for training exercises.[103] Barry Tubbs, a spokesman for KCM, assured reporters that their relationship with the sheriff's department was appropriate: "Because we are a . . . [tax-exempt] organization, we are not allowed to participate in campaigns. We pray for David, but we don't get any special privileges over and above anybody else."[104] Some observers were skeptical, claiming that the department provided security at some KCM events in return for use of ministry facilities.

Two other incidents occurred on September 28 when several people were injured and one girl was killed at the Copelands' eighth annual Eagle Mountain Motorcycle Rally. Around 6 P.M. an adult and a teenager riding a motorcycle collided with an eight-year-old and an eleven-year-old driving a go-cart. According to newspaper reports, the vehicles were racing down a runway at the Copelands' private airport. All four people were injured, with the youngest child suffering the most serious injuries and undergoing surgery at Cook Children's Medical Center in Fort Worth. Two hours later another collision occurred on the same runway between a motorcycle and a twelve-year-old girl. According to published reports, a motorcyclist and his passenger were traveling down the runway at speeds over seventy miles per hour—with some witnesses claiming they were going over ninety miles per hour—when the motorcycle struck the young girl as she crossed the runway on in-line skates. The driver of the motorcycle was arrested on suspicion of intoxication manslaughter. Local authorities found small amounts of alcohol, marijuana, and a tranquilizer in his bloodstream, but the district attorney's office refused to charge the man—or even send the case to a grand jury—because he was, under Texas law, not legally drunk.[105]

The Copelands were heavily criticized when it was revealed that officers with the sheriff department's reserve unit had, over a two-year period, repeatedly warned KCM staff that motorcycle racing on the runways was a serious safety concern. The *Fort Worth Star-Telegram* reported that reserve officers who provided security for the event had raised concerns with their superiors about the "dangerous amusement." KCM officials denied sanctioning these races and claimed that their staff had warned rally-goers to stay off the runways and had placed barricades around the area. Reserve officers charged that every time they raised these safety concerns, they were told that Kenneth Copeland wanted to keep the runways open for the motorcyclists to use.[106] In March 1998 the family of the slain girl filed a claim against the local authorities, charging that reserve officers had improperly used "patrol vehicles, radar guns for clocking the speed of motorcycles [racing down the runways], starter pistols and barricades."[107] In June the family filed a wrongful-death lawsuit against KCM, the motorcyclist who hit her, and the county sheriff's department. According to newspaper accounts, the suit charged that KCM did not provide a safe environment and that it had an improper relationship with the sheriff's department. It alleged "that the Copeland compound was used to store Sheriff's Department equipment and hold Sheriff's Department social functions and awards banquets, and that the grounds have been used for driver and helicopter training, in return for providing security at the rally."[108]

The Copelands canceled their 1998 motorcycle rally but insisted that this had nothing to do with the events of the previous year, the pending lawsuit, or the negative publicity that was generated. Citing a ministry spokesperson and an issue of the *Believer's Voice of Victory*, the *Fort Worth Star-Telegram* reported that God had told Kenneth Copeland on April 2, 1998, to cancel the rally: "On the way in, the word of the Lord came to me and said, Cancel the '98 motorcycle rally. At this point in time, I have no direct explanation from God as to why. I believe that sometime in the future he will reveal it to me," Copeland stated.[109] The rally was not held again until May 2002, when Texas evangelist Jerry Savelle, along with the Copelands and New

Orleans evangelist Jesse Duplantis, hosted the Thunder Over Texas Motor-cycle Rally at the Texas Motor Speedway near Fort Worth.[110] These three ministries continued to host these rallies each year in more controlled en-vironments and with business sponsors, such as Krispy Kreme Doughnuts, Starbucks Coffee, Christian Motorsports Illustrated, and Covenant Rac-ing, a Christian motorcycle road racing team.[111] Although these incidents produced some negative publicity in the local press, they did not seem to af-fect the Copelands' popularity or the success of their ministry.

Conclusion

Daisy Osborn, Freda Lindsay, and Gloria Copeland transcended traditional gender roles in their personal and professional lives. They embraced the "superwoman" ideal, modeling for women how to have it all by being good wives, mothers, businesspeople, and public leaders. In their personal testi-monies they emphasized their humble beginnings and the role that their faith in God played in their ministerial success, but they were also shrewd professionals who capitalized on the cultural shifts and changing attitudes regarding women's roles in society. They insisted that they preferred to shun publicity and stay behind the scenes, but their actions proved otherwise. Their husbands supported their public roles and encouraged them to use their talents and skills to enhance their ministries. Although these women expressed opposition to modern feminism, they clearly believed that men and women should receive equal treatment in the church and society. As conservative Pentecostals and charismatics became more receptive to the notion of sexual equality, they challenged some traditional beliefs about women's roles in society.[112] As cultural mediators, they demonstrated how conservative women could challenge traditional views of male dominance, participate in the public life of the church, and remain faithful to their reli-gious heritage. As religious entrepreneurs, they "sold" these ideas to a gen-eration of evangelicals that was already moving into and embracing the secular ideology of mainstream American society.

3

The Total Woman

In 1984, Lindsay Roberts, daughter-in-law of Oral Roberts, began serving as co-host for her husband's television program, *Richard Roberts: On the Air!*[1] She insisted that she did not feel comfortable with these public roles and that her maternal instincts were far superior to her speaking abilities: "When I started doing a daily television show with Richard, I used to get up in the morning and throw up. Lindsay Roberts is not comfortable in front of a crowd with a microphone. That's not me. You give me a baby and I can rock it to sleep as fast as any woman in the world, but to stand up in front of a group of people is not me. But sometimes you just have to get courage and do what God calls you to do."[2] Despite the early success of female evangelists such as Aimee Semple McPherson, Kathryn Kuhlman, Daisy Osborn, Freda Lindsay, and Gloria Copeland, charismatic and Pentecostal women in the 1980s still claimed to be ambivalent about taking public ministerial positions. They struggled to reconcile the traditional image of a meek, quiet, and submissive wife to the assertive, vocal, and public image of the emerging "total woman." Although they publicly claimed to be reluctant to step into these roles, many of these women demonstrated an amazing proclivity for public ministry.

The social turmoil of the early 1970s and the disorganization of the charismatic movement opened the door for women to become ministry leaders. Historian Ruth Rosen demonstrates that modern feminism fragmented in the 1970s, was co-opted by a number of constituencies, and became palatable to many different groups in mainstream American society. At the same time, the charismatic movement was undergoing similar changes as many male evangelists made the transition from the glory days of the healing revival to the more cerebral environment of the charismatic revival.[3] As attitudes regarding women in both secular and religious culture shifted, a few charismatics saw an opportunity to benefit from the feminist movement without having to abandon their traditional beliefs. These women soon began launching their own careers as independent evangelists. With the encouragement of Stephen Strang's *Charisma* magazine and the precedent of trailblazers such as McPherson, Kuhlman, Osborn, Lindsay, and Copeland, they began challenging the patriarchal social order of the charismatic movement. A few started their own ministries while others accepted public roles in their husbands' organizations. They had different emphases and experienced varying degrees of success, but all were determined to spread their message in much the same way their male counterparts had. They used the ministry-building techniques pioneered by Oral Roberts, and nearly all of them embraced Kenneth Hagin's Word of Faith message, which emphasized prosperity and divine healing. These women became part of a new generation of ministers who pushed the charismatic movement further into mainstream American culture, successfully marketed secular ideas about women's roles in society to a conservative Christian audience, and broadened the horizons of evangelical women.

Marilyn Hickey

Marilyn Hickey, the wife of Assemblies of God pastor Wallace Hickey in Denver, began her Life for Laymen teaching ministry (later renamed Marilyn Hickey Ministries) in the 1970s and was one of the first female evangelists to become popular as a new generation of charismatic leaders began to emerge. Hickey was influenced by William Branham and the healing revival of the 1950s, and her training and talent as an educator prepared her perfectly for the charismatic revival of the 1960s and 1970s. She brought a level of respectability and stability that the charismatic movement needed in order to move into the evangelical mainstream. Her devotional guides, Bible reading programs, and radio and television teaching series were popular for at least a quarter century. She espoused traditional Pentecostal views about the submissive role of women in the home, but she also believed that God called women to lead the church. She encouraged female ministers to balance their roles as mothers and wives with their roles as pastor or evangelist. She adopted the prevailing feminist notion that women could not only manage a household but also pursue a career outside the home. Most importantly, she created solid institutions and groomed her daughter, Sarah Bowling, to carry her ministry into the twenty-first century.

Hickey studied foreign languages in college and received her bachelor's degree from the University of Northern Colorado in 1953. Upon graduation she became a public school teacher in Pueblo, Colorado, and met a conservative Pentecostal salesman named Wallace Hickey. The young schoolteacher was at first not very interested in the restrictive Christian lifestyle that placed church attendance over dancing and moviegoing, but she grew fond of Wally and learned to tolerate his lifestyle. After they married in December 1954, Wally decided to become an evangelist, holding revivals throughout Colorado and neighboring states. In 1960 he was appointed pastor of a small Assemblies of God church in Denver, and Marilyn dutifully— but reluctantly—played the role of a pastor's wife. She later recalled, however, that she did not intend to spend all her time singing, playing the organ, and teaching Sunday school. According to autobiographical accounts, she immersed herself in intense Bible study, and the couple forged ties with up-and-coming charismatic leaders such as Kenneth Hagin, Kenneth Copeland, and the leader of the Full Gospel Business Men's Fellowship International, Demos Shakarian. Despite bouts with depression and a family history of mental illness, in the late 1960s Hickey began the long process of establishing her own ministry.[4]

Marilyn claimed to have "read, memorized, researched, and compiled detailed notebooks about all sorts of Biblical subjects." She studied Greek and Hebrew and applied the skills she gained as an educator to her own Bible study. In 1969 she started a home Bible study for young couples that eventually grew to twenty-two separate cottage meetings scattered throughout the Denver area. She built her study program on the notion that anyone should be able to read and understand the Bible without having to rely on a select group of specially trained clergy for interpretation. Her target audience was average Christians who had no formal theological training, and she called her ministry Life for Laymen. This was also the name of her first weekly local radio program; the sixty-dollar monthly broadcasting fee was paid for by her Bible study groups. *Life for Laymen* quickly expanded to a fifteen-minute national program, and in 1974 she moved on to local television. What began as a small teaching ministry operated from her kitchen table became a respected international ministry within just a few years.[5]

In 1976 Marilyn officially organized her own ministry and moved onto the increasingly crowded stage of charismatic evangelists. As she gained notoriety, invitations from all over the country began to pour in, asking her to speak at churches, seminars, and conferences. Even NBC's talk-show host Tom Snyder invited a panel of female preachers, which included Hickey,

Frances Hunter, and Ruth Carter Stapleton, to appear on the *Tomorrow Show*. The publicity generated by her local television program increased dramatically in 1977 when, according to ministry reports, a manager at Denver's public television station asked Hickey to host a thirteen-week teaching series on the Old Testament called *The Bible, The Source*. The show was so successful that it was syndicated and seen on scores of educational stations throughout the country. In the early 1980s she appeared regularly on Jim Bakker's *PTL Club* and Paul and Jan Crouch's Trinity Broadcasting Network. In 1986 she produced a one-hour documentary on miraculous healing, co-hosted and narrated by *The Love Boat* captain Gavin McLeod, football legend Rosie Grier, 1950s crooner Pat Boone, and former Harlem Globetrotter Meadowlark Lemon. Later that year she replaced her weekly television show with a half-hour daily program called *Today with Marilyn* on the PTL network and *Best Day of Your Life* on TBN. She believed this moved her closer to fulfilling her goal of spreading the gospel throughout the world. It also boosted her visibility, making her one of the most prominent charismatic evangelists of the day.[6]

In 1987 Marilyn informed her supporters that television would become her primary media tool: "Over the last year, I have found that the response to daily television is just overwhelming; and, because I want to be a good steward of God's money, I'm making television my number-one priority. I have recently cancelled some radio stations because I believe that money could be better invested in my second daily air time on the Inspirational Network."[7] Ironically, she made this decision just as the improprieties of some prominent televangelists were gaining national attention, and she was forced to spend a great deal of time and energy defending her record and soliciting funds for her program. Hickey worried that the secular media were trying to discredit all religious broadcasting because they discovered a few corrupt individuals. "By using the widespread news reports of scandal and financial extravagance by a few," she charged, "these adversaries are trying to convince the general public that all Christian broadcasters are charlatans who are building personal financial empires. Of course these charges are wildly exaggerated, and the truth is that *very few* Christian broadcasters have been careless with donors' funds." She went on to assert that her "ministry is *not guilty* of any of the extravagances of the few and will continue to maintain financial integrity." Her *Outpouring* magazine printed an annual breakdown of her ministry's media budget, which included $940,051 for her regular television programs, $180,000 for a television special, and $986,177 for radio. Her total radio and television budget added up to just over $2 million. "As you can see by these figures," she continued, "the TV and radio costs are substantial—and the bills come every month. Although this ministry's income—like that of other media ministries—has been down the past several months, I am determined to maintain a spotless testimony by paying every bill on time."[8] Throughout the 1980s, she continued to encourage her followers to support her ministry financially and keep her on the air. She knew that television exposure was the key to her success, and she did not want the scandals of a few evangelists to ruin her ministry. At the end of the century she estimated that her program was aired to more than 280 million homes in almost fifty countries via several cable and satellite networks, local stations, and the internet.[9]

As her reputation as a Bible teacher grew, Hickey focused much of her ministry on women. She held local and national women's conventions, organized conferences for pastors' wives, and in 1987 started a national prayer group—the Women's Christian Army. Some of her early national women's conventions were held in Tulsa, Denver, Washington, D.C., and Anaheim and featured well-known women such as Gloria Copeland, Freda Lindsay, and Daisy Osborn. These conferences were designed to encourage and empower Christian women to be good wives and mothers and to pursue their professional dreams—as long as their husbands approved.[10] When questioned about her ability to maintain a strong marriage, have a stable family life, and be a full-time evangelist, Marilyn responded: "I first want you to know that my husband is tremendously supportive; and, yes, I am submissive to him. In fact, if my husband were to tell me tomorrow, 'I don't want you to travel anymore,' I would cease to travel because I know that he clearly hears the voice of the Spirit." She believed that women should hold leadership roles as deacons, evangelists, prophets, teachers, and preachers and that God was raising up a new generation of women to fill those positions in the church. But she encouraged women not to be "too pushy" by demanding full equality immediately. "Don't harass men if they don't appoint you to serve in a certain position," she counseled. "Just pray and be assured that God knows how to convict their hearts. Let God turn them in the direction that He desires. Remember, promotion comes from the Lord. We don't have to beat our way in, for God will open the doors for us, and no man will be able to shut them."[11] Her subtle approach was consistent with that of other charismatic women who advocated sexual equality in the church. She did not want to alienate her conservative support base, but she believed strongly that women could—and should—hold public leadership roles. Her emphasis on the subjective nature of "God's calling" and her attentiveness to the "voice of the Spirit" was also standard fare for Pentecostals and charismatics. It was relatively easy for Hickey to justify her ministerial career, because she could claim that she was called by God to do this work and that her success was evidence of that calling.

Hickey developed a strong international ministry early in her career, and by the end of the century it had become the cornerstone of her success. Prompted by an eschatological belief that the Middle East must be evangelized before the Second Coming of Christ, she began her international ministry in Egypt in 1982. In the mid-1980s she preached in Latin America, Eastern Europe, and Africa.[12] She often coupled her overseas evangelistic efforts with humanitarian outreach by providing money, food, and other necessities to underdeveloped countries.[13]

These forays increased Hickey's visibility at home and abroad and provided bases for later crusades. *Outpouring* and *Charisma* noted that in 1988 and 1989 she preached and distributed religious literature in Japan and Eastern Europe.[14] In the 1990s she reportedly smuggled three thousand Bibles and seventy-five thousand religious tracts into the People's Republic of China.[15] In 1995, according to *Charisma,* she was one of the first Christian women to preach publicly in Pakistan. Roughly twelve hundred church leaders attended her daily training seminars, and she claimed that as many as twenty thousand people attended the nightly crusade meetings. By 1999 she reportedly devoted 50 percent of her time to her international ministry. She and her daughter, Sarah Bowling, traveled the globe, conducting healing and evangelistic services and building their reputation among Pentecostals and charismatics worldwide.[16]

Although she was a member of the Assemblies of God denomination, Marilyn was very influential among evangelicals and independent charismatics. She was a founding member of the International Charismatic Bible Ministries; she served on the board of directors for David Yonggi Cho's Yoido Full Gospel Church, one of the largest churches in the world; she chaired the board of regents at Oral Roberts University; and she regularly contributed articles to *Charisma.* Hickey was also named Christian Woman of the Year in 1989, an award given to outstanding evangelical women.[17] Marilyn Hickey Ministries' magazine, *Outpouring,* boasted a circulation of two hundred thousand in the late 1980s and was used as a fund-raising tool and primary means of communication with her financial supporters. At century's end her ministry reported that she had produced nearly fifteen hundred teaching cassettes, videotapes, and compact discs and had published more than one hundred books and booklets. Her promotional literature claimed that Marilyn Hickey Ministries employed almost 350 people in its Denver office, and her husband's church, located in the same facility, had between three thousand and four thousand members.[18] In 1981 Marilyn started a small Bible school called Word to the World College, which provided a measure of institutional stability for her ministry.[19]

Marilyn Hickey Ministries was a family business. Although Marilyn's husband was not involved with the daily affairs of the ministry, he served on her board of directors, provided pastoral oversight through his church, and, most importantly, wholeheartedly supported his wife's ministry and encouraged her to succeed. Her son-in-law, Reece Bowling, served as executive vice-president of the organization and as assistant publisher of *Outpouring*. Highlighting the female character of this ministry, Marilyn's daughter, Sarah, was poised to succeed her mother in ministry. As a child, Sarah accompanied her mother on many of her missionary trips and evangelistic crusades. After graduating from Oral Roberts University in 1990 and teaching school, she joined the ministry's staff in 1995 and became a co-evangelist, speaking at her mother's domestic and foreign conventions, holding her own "Jump Start Your Heart" conferences, and co-hosting their daily television show, *Today with Marilyn and Sarah*. In 2006, Sarah and Reece served as senior pastors at her father's church, the Orchard Road Christian Center.[20]

Although her following was never as large as some other charismatic evangelists', Marilyn succeeded where many other women failed. She established a solid ministry at a time when many conservative Christians opposed women preachers; she employed the same techniques and preached the same prosperity message that proved successful for other ministers; and she created institutions and a line of succession that ensured the longevity of her ministry. Despite critics labeling her the "fairy godmother of the Word of Faith movement" and the "mistress of mail-order madness," she avoided controversy at a time when many televangelists were dogged by scandals. Like other ministers, she was criticized by the secular press, by ministry watchdog groups, and by other evangelicals for promoting the prosperity gospel. Although she did not consciously advocate consumerism, many up-and-coming charismatics sought biblical justification for embracing the materialism of modern American society and used the prosperity message toward that end. Hickey also provided a model for modern women to follow by demonstrating how female evangelists could succeed in a male-dominated profession.[21]

Joyce Meyer

In the 1990s, no female evangelist attained greater success than Joyce Meyer. Although she did not gain national prominence until 1993, Meyer had begun her ministry nearly two decades earlier. Firmly rooted in the charismatic movement, she had strong ties to the Word of Faith movement. Her message of emotional healing appealed to a broad cross-section of evangelical women, and her message of practical Christian living resonated with a generation of conservative women struggling to adjust to a post-feminist era.[22] In 1998, *Charisma* reported that "Joyce Meyer's popularity reflects a rising women's movement in Christianity, which has increased support for female speakers." In an interview with *Charisma*, Pentecostal historian Vinson Synan observed: "I think she's speaking to modern women in a way men can't. . . . She's a teacher more than anything else. I think she is modeling a woman as teacher—rather than as evangelist."[23] Her grace-oriented message, coupled with her own vulnerability and practicality, were keys to her popularity. Although she taught the principles of Hagin's prosperity gospel, she publicly insisted that Christians did not want to hear only the message of prosperity, divine health, and success that many Word of Faith preachers emphasized. Instead, she argued, they wanted to relate to someone who had experienced hard times and could empathize with their emotional pain. She taught women that they could overcome those difficulties, be content with their lives, and find joy in living the Christian life. At her conventions she asserted that the prosperity message had been overemphasized in the charismatic community and maintained that it should be balanced with instruction on humility and self-denial. Her emphasis on emotional healing—instead of prosperity—set her apart from many other charismatic evangelists and broadened her support base to include a wide range of evangelicals, both charismatic and non-charismatic. But her critics charged that her prosperity message and her lifestyle substantiated the accusations of charlatanism leveled against her.[24]

Meyer's emphasis on emotional healing grew out of her own struggles as a child and young adult which made it hard for her to maintain stable relationships early in her life. Born into a blue-collar family on June 4, 1943, Meyer claimed she was sexually and emotionally abused by her alcoholic father. She left home at age eighteen and married the first man who would stay with her. Their marriage was unstable as she and her husband separated and reconciled many times before finally divorcing five years later. He eventually went to prison, and she moved in with her parents to raise her nine-month-old son. She admitted that her bad experiences with men left her bitter, feeling rejected and full of self-pity. But within a month after her divorce she met twenty-six-year-old Dave Meyer, and after only five dates he asked her to marry him. They wed in January 1967.[25]

In the early 1970s the Meyers were active in their Lutheran church, but they felt that traditional religion lacked spiritual depth and meaning. In 1976 Joyce decided to become an evangelist; she quit her job—cutting the family income in half—and began teaching home Bible studies, which did not attract many followers or provide much financial support. The Meyers also joined a small independent charismatic church in St. Louis called the Life Christian Center. She further honed her teaching skills by conducting a women's Bible class for her new church. By her own account, the class quickly grew from a few participants to an average weekly attendance of four hundred women. By 1979 she had taken a full-time position as an associate pastor with the church. In 1980, after conflicts with the senior pastor, Meyer decided to turn her weekly "Life in the Word" Bible studies into a full-time ministry. Dave, a soft-spoken, behind-the-scenes leader, later confessed that he was apprehensive about her taking a public ministerial role, but he believed that she was an effective teacher and decided to support her work wholeheartedly.[26]

For thirteen years Meyer's ministry did not reach much beyond the Midwest, where she held small monthly crusades in St. Louis and the surrounding area. "After one appearance before less than two dozen unenthusiastic listeners," *Charisma* reported, "Joyce asked if they had sold any tapes. 'No,' Dave replied, 'but somebody did return one.'"[27] She bought airtime on eight radio stations and achieved some notoriety in the Chicago and Kansas City markets, which led to meetings in those areas. But her enthusiasm outran her ability to manage a large ministry. "Early in my ministry, I had a big vision but no experience or training," she wrote. "I wanted to take out ads and hire an agency to promote my ministry. I could always sense deep inside that God didn't want me to do this."[28] Nor did her husband, who counseled Joyce to be cautious and establish a solid foundation for her ministry. They denied the assertion that Dave was the weak, subservient man behind the hard-charging, outspoken woman. According to their oldest son, David, "Mom makes jokes all the time about how she can't get a requisition through without Dad's permission. . . . He calls most of the shots. He's definitely a strong leader."[29] She listened carefully to his advice and allowed him to make most of the business decisions for her ministry. Gradually, her radio show grew to 150 stations.

By the mid-1980s, according to *Charisma*, she had moved out of her basement office and into a rented facility and hired twenty-five employees, and Dave had quit his job as a mechanical engineer to serve as administrative director. The ministry was officially established as a nonprofit corporation in 1986, and Meyer began publishing books in 1988. Her mainstay was her expanding radio program and small conferences until 1993, when Dave decided that she should focus on an international television ministry. She preached at Carlton Pearson's Azusa Revival in 1993, and her staff later cobbled together a television program that consisted of video clips from her live conferences, which initially aired on Chicago's WGN network and the Black Entertainment Network. The popular charismatic publisher Harrison House began publishing her books in 1994, and in 1998 she appeared on the cover of *Charisma* as "America's Most Popular Woman Minister."[30]

At the turn of the century, according to published reports, Meyer's radio program was heard on more than 260 stations in the United States and over 70 stations internationally, including countries in Europe, Asia, and the Americas. The *Life in the Word* television show, which changed its name in 2004 to *Enjoying Everyday Life*, was reportedly seen in 145 countries, on more than 250 local stations in the United States, and on several cable and satellite networks. She estimated that over 2 billion people were exposed to her telecast each day. The ministry claimed that its *Life in the Word* magazine, which also changed its name to *Enjoying Everyday Life* in 2004, went to at least 200,000 households; it duplicated almost 4 million teaching tapes each year; and it sold about 6 million copies of Meyer's books. Most of her fifty titles were published by Harrison House until 2002 when Meyer moved to Warner Faith publishers, a religious imprint of the mainstream media giant AOL Time Warner Books. In a statement released to *Charisma* by Warner Books, Meyer noted that the publisher's "vast distribution will complement the growth of my international radio and television ministry."[31] Those media outlets were vital to creating a large support base at home and abroad, which allowed her to market her message to a rapidly expanding audience. She correctly gauged the desires of the marketplace and positioned herself to capitalize on those opportunities. Getting on television and moving into secular media outlets gave her the ability to capture part of the self-help market that had become so prominent at the turn of the century.

Meyer was criticized for living a lavish lifestyle and for teaching the prosperity message that supposedly justified it. In November 2003 the *St. Louis Post-Dispatch* ran a series of articles that highlighted not only her difficult past, which led to her emphasis on emotional healing, but also the prosperity gospel that she and other ministers espoused. "Joyce Meyer Ministries," the newspaper reported, "is, without question, a well-oiled moneymaking machine."[32] Citing ministry reports, independent watchdog groups, and public tax records, the newspaper initially reported that her ministry bought and maintained her $2 million home; the homes of her children, which totaled another $2 million; a $10 million corporate jet; her husband's $107,000 Mercedes sedan; a $20 million, 158,000-square-foot office complex; and "nearly $5.7 million worth of furniture, artwork, glassware, and the latest equipment and machinery."[33] Furthermore, beginning in 2001, Meyer was engaged in a pitched battle with the Jefferson County, Missouri, tax assessor, who threatened to revoke her ministry's tax-exempt status.[34]

In 2003, MinistryWatch, an organization that monitors large Christian ministries, asked the Internal Revenue Service to investigate Meyer's ministry for possible tax code violations. An attorney for the ministry denied reports that the IRS contacted the ministry about its tax-exempt status and asserted that the ministry fully complied with IRS rules and regulations. *Christianity Today* reported that, amid criticism of "her $95 million-a-year television ministry, Meyer has announced plans to take a reduced salary in 2004 and personally use more of the income derived from her outside books sales." Joyce Meyer Ministries also increased its financial transparency by making annual financial reports for the years 2003 through 2005 available online and by making available an independent auditor's report of the ministry's finances. MinistryWatch upgraded its assessment of the ministry, applauding Meyer "for increasing the transparency of her organization," but maintained that "its audited financial statements" were still "not sufficient for donors to make the most informed decisions." Furthermore, she refuted the accuracy of the newspaper reports, which led the editors of the *St. Louis Post-Dispatch* to issue an apology for errors in its reporting of her finances. The editors acknowledged that two of the articles in the series "did not meet our standards for fairness and accuracy" and promised to take "corrective action to address the professional failures that led to these errors." In true Word of Faith fashion, Meyer defended her integrity and her lifestyle, insisting that her success was God-given—the result of unwavering faith and a dogged determination to promote her ministry and spread the gospel.[35]

Despite mounting opposition at the beginning of the twenty-first century, Meyer dominated the airwaves and her books and tapes were displayed prominently—not just in small Christian bookstores but in major secular outlets as well. The stability and business sense that her husband brought to her life and ministry was crucial to her success; Dave filled the supportive and administrative roles that spouses of male evangelists had filled for years. He positioned her to take advantage of the media outlets that allowed her to market her wares to the largest possible audience, thereby enhancing her role as a religious entrepreneur. Her ability to identify with the struggles other women faced, her commonsense approach to everyday problems, and her promise that those who sowed abundantly into her ministry would reap abundantly in their own lives made her popular to evangelicals around the world.

Other Women Ministers

One of Marilyn Hickey's contemporaries, Vicki Jamison-Peterson, had a moderately successful ministry in the 1970s and early 1980s, but its growth languished by the mid-1980s. Jamison-Peterson was one of the first prominent Word of Faith female evangelists, and her career demonstrated the influence Hagin's Word of Faith message had on women ministers, but it also exemplified the difficulties that many evangelists faced. Raised a Pentecostal, Jamison-Peterson had a conversion experience and reportedly spoke in tongues as a child, but she was never completely satisfied with her Christian life. She characterized it as "dull and boring"; she even lost her desire to live until—as she often claimed—she was miraculously healed from what doctors thought was cancer. She sought the counsel of an "old prophetess" who in 1966 introduced her to the teachings of Kenneth Hagin. "Within three months I was in one of his meetings," she recalled. "He came to speak at the Voice of Healing ministry (now known as Christ for the Nations) . . . taught on his theme Scripture verse, Mark 11:23, and suddenly there was a spiritual explosion inside me."[36] That experience led her to share his positive-attitude message with her family and friends, and it instilled in her the joy that was lacking in her life.

Jamison-Peterson attended the Lindsay's Bible institute in Dallas before joining Hagin in 1971 as a singer at his crusades.[37] She and her husband, Wes, traveled with Hagin for a year and a half before she was hospitalized with internal bleeding in 1972. The doctors were unable to stop her from hemorrhaging and had lost hope for her survival. Unwilling to give up, Jamison-Peterson employed the positive-confession techniques she learned from Hagin and, according to her personal testimony, within thirty minutes the bleeding had stopped. "From time to time the symptoms of the affliction try to come back upon me, trying to tell me I'm going to die," she later confessed. "But every time I stand upon the Word of God. . . . I declare, 'I am healed by God's power.' And the symptoms have always disappeared."[38] Such testimonies were vital for the success of Pentecostal and charismatic evangelists. All of the early healing evangelists—both men and women— told their life-changing stories hundreds, if not thousands, of times over the course of their careers. But this was especially important for women, because, as folklorist Elaine J. Lawless points out in her discussion of "oneness" Pentecostals, oral testimony was the primary method women used to pass down belief systems and religious rituals from generation to generation. Jamison-Peterson was one of a long line of Pentecostal and charismatic women who used this method to advance her ministry and transmit her beliefs. Her confidence in Hagin's Word of Faith message was prevalent in her own teaching and contributed to her modest success.[39]

In 1973 Jamison-Peterson began her own itinerant ministry, working out of her parents' home and securing the help of friends and family members to maintain her small but expanding organization. Her most successful venture was a daily television program for women called *It's a New Day,* which aired on CBN from 1974 through 1976. After watching her friends Kenneth and Gloria Copeland tape one of their early television series, she decided to make a pilot for her own show. When she discussed the project with Robertson, he told her that CBN had recently set aside thirty minutes of airtime for just such a program. She sang, preached, and interviewed leading charismatic women such as Gloria Copeland, Evelyn Roberts, and Kathryn Kuhlman.[40] The show resonated with evangelical women across the nation, and Robertson thought it was outstanding. One viewer's comments shed light on the intersection of the modern feminist movement with the emerging evangelical subculture and the role that these women evangelists played in bridging that gap: "We have 4 sons, ages 16, 14, 11, and 2; and that leaves me with very little time alone and quiet. However, when my husband leaves at 1:30 after lunch, I hurry to get the dishes done so I can prop my feet up and soak up all I can receive from 'It's A New Day.' It is so wonderful to see what God is doing for and through women. Who needs to join a 'Lib' group—Jesus always liberates!!"[41] Even though many conservative women eschewed feminism, they had become receptive to the message of liberation—a message that evangelicals wanted to keep within the confines of their conservative theology. Women such as Jamison-Peterson allowed conservative women to enjoy some of the benefits of changing cultural mores without having to completely abandon their traditional views.

But Jamison-Peterson wanted more than just a women's ministry—she sought "a broader ministry of seminars, teaching, and guest appearances on other TV ministries."[42] In March 1975 she appeared on TBN, where she developed a monthly miracle and healing program called *Vicki*. Later that year she started making regular guest appearances on Jim Bakker's PTL Network, conducting healing services for the studio and television audiences. From then on she put most of her energy into developing a full-blown healing ministry and producing special healing programs for a national television audience. The visibility she gained from these television appearances allowed her ministry to grow at an impressive rate.[43]

In 1977 she held several successful healing revivals in the Northeast, drawing large crowds and getting a warm response from the people and the local press. In 1978 she started a daily radio broadcast that was intended to further her work in New England.[44] Her favorite medium, though, was television. In 1982 she launched a program designed to promote divine healing and the charismatic revival in the Northeast. Shortly after the death of her twenty-five-year-old nephew, who had been mentored by Kenneth Hagin and had served as her crusade director, she decided to uproot and move from Dallas to Tulsa. "A week after Greg's death, the Lord spoke to me in a dramatic and unmistakable way," she later declared. "Sell your home and your office building. Move your ministry to Tulsa and begin a one-hour daily television program to go into New England." Two hours later she held an impromptu meeting with the ministry's board of directors, and they agreed to relocate the ministry to Oklahoma.[45] On September 13, 1982, "in a cramped and poorly equipped TV studio in Tulsa," Jamison-Peterson's healing ministry went back on the air with Oral Roberts's son Richard as her first guest. The show was well received and helped bolster her support in the Midwest and New England. Guests included Richard and Lindsay Roberts, Kenneth Hagin, T. L. and Daisy Osborn, Billye Brim, Nigerian evangelist Benson Idahosa, and actress Donna Douglas, who played Ellie Mae on *The Beverly Hillbillies*. Despite her initial success, Jamison-Peterson fell on hard times.[46] In the summer of 1983 the nonprofit television station in Worcester, Massachusetts, that carried her show into six New England states became a commercial station and removed all Christian programming, leading to a severe decline in donations to her ministry. Unable to return to a solid financial standing, she had to stop production of her television show, discontinue her magazine, and "cut away everything we could financially to continue our ministry."[47]

Although the details are unclear, other personal tragedies occurred in her life in the early 1980s that contributed to her loss of support. In 1984 she returned to public life with a new husband and a fresh focus for her ministry. For the remainder of the millennium Jamison-Peterson continued to hold small crusades in the United States and expand her international ministry, proclaiming Hagin's Word of Faith message and promoting her books, teaching tapes, and music albums. She made regular appearances on *Something Good Tonight: The Hour of Healing* with Richard and Lindsay Roberts and was a trustee of the International Charismatic Bible Ministries, an organization founded in 1986 by Oral Roberts, Marilyn Hickey, and other prominent charismatic ministers.[48] She was one of the first prominent female evangelists in the Word of Faith movement, she contributed to the expansion of the charismatic revival, and she served as a cultural mediator between modern feminism and conservative evangelicalism. Had she not experienced some major setbacks early in her career, she might have achieved the same level of popularity at the end of the century that Marilyn Hickey and Joyce Meyer enjoyed.

Other, lesser-known figures include independent ministers such as Anne Gimenez, Paula White, Billye Brim, Kate McVeigh, and Juanita Bynum. Most of these women achieved only modest success in the late twentieth century, but they represent an established set of female evangelists who benefited from the pioneering work of earlier women.

South Texas native Anne Gimenez was another pioneer among women ministers. She converted to Pentecostalism in 1949 at a tent meeting where T. L. and Daisy Osborn were preaching with Gordon and Freda Lindsay. She worked for an accounting firm for eight years before becoming a full-time itinerant evangelist, and she married John Gimenez in 1967. The couple co-founded Rock Church in Norfolk, Virginia, in 1968; initially catering to the "hippie" crowd, the church experienced impressive growth throughout the 1970s and 1980s. By 1986 they boasted a regular attendance of four thousand, an elementary school and high school, a bevy of outreach and service organizations, and a satellite campus for Oral Roberts University. Ten years later they claimed to have two hundred churches in their Rock Ministerial Fellowship. They began airing their Sunday-morning services on CBN in 1978, and in 1986 they launched their own twenty-four-hour Rock Christian Network. The network was never able to meet its financial obligations, however, and dissolved in 1988. In 1984 she ran unsuccessfully for a city council seat, but the couple remained active in their community.[49]

Gimenez championed women's rights and taught that even though wives were to submit to their husbands, they could still hold positions of leadership in the church. She encouraged women to develop a spirit of humility, work within the male-dominated social structure of the charismatic movement, and become successful without being too assertive. "A woman does not have to argue for or insist upon her place of leadership in God's kingdom," she stated in 1986. "Humbling, not demanding, is always the first step in the process of becoming a leader."[50] In the early 1980s she founded Women in Leadership, an organization designed to counter modern feminism but still promote female leadership in the church. She held a series of national and international conferences and wrote a book, *The Emerging Christian Woman*, which addressed gender issues in the church. In 1999 she was named senior pastor of the five-thousand-member Rock Church, making her one of the few women in America to pastor a megachurch.[51] Gimenez's role in promoting female leadership within the context of conservative religion did much to advance sexual equality in the charismatic movement.

Paula White, who co-founded and co-pastored a fifteen-thousand-member megachurch in Tampa, became hugely popular among Pentecostals and charismatics—especially among African Americans—at the turn of the century. One observer noted to *Ebony* magazine regarding White: "You know you're on to something new and significant when the most popular woman preacher on the Black Entertainment Network is a White woman." According to ministry reports, her "story is one of tragedy and triumph, poverty and prosperity. . . . A self-proclaimed 'messed up Mississippi girl'" from Tupelo, her father committed suicide when she was five years old. She was the victim of physical and sexual abuse as a child, and she suffered from depression and "a serious eating disorder." In an interview with the *Washington Post*, White noted that her mother married a "military man" when she was nine years old and that the family moved often before settling in the Washington, D.C., area, where she graduated from high school in 1984.[52]

In the 1980s, Pentecostal evangelist and pastor T. L. Lowery mentored White as a young adult, and during the 1990s she developed a close working relationship with Joyce Meyer and T. D. Jakes, becoming a featured speaker at several of their annual events. Her emphasis on emotional healing and financial prosperity, which reflected that of Meyer and Jakes, brought her a great deal of success as both a pastor and evangelist. She and her husband,

Randy, established the South Tampa Christian Center in 1991 and changed the name to Without Walls International Church in 1997. She began Paula White Ministries in 2001 and launched a weekly television program, *Paula White Today*, on BET. In 2005 her program could be seen on BET, TBN, DayStar, Word Network, Middle East TV, Far East TV, and several local stations throughout the United States. At the turn of the century she was poised to become one of the most popular women evangelists in the charismatic movement.[53] But notoriety also brought criticism.

In 2002 the *Tampa Tribune* ran a lengthy article highlighting the Whites' displays of wealth after they bought an eight-thousand-square-foot, five-bedroom, $2.1 million English manor home in a tony neighborhood overlooking Tampa Bay. The article also noted that Paula drove a Mercedes sedan and Randy drove a Cadillac Escalade, which was emblazoned with the scripture verse Psalm 37:4: "Delight yourself in the Lord and he will give you the desires of your heart." The Whites were never embarrassed by these displays, and shortly after they bought their new house Randy preached a ninety-minute sermon titled "Poverty or Prosperity" in which he extolled the virtues of the prosperity gospel. He included a PowerPoint presentation that chronicled every home the couple had owned, showing the progression from living in a small apartment early in their ministry to their mansion on the bay. In 2001 "they claimed a combined income of $600,000." Randy reportedly received from their church an annual salary of $179,000, Paula brought in $120,000, and the church gave them an $80,000 housing allowance. Michael Chitwood, the president of a financial services company that specialized in helping churches and ministries with their finances, told the *Tribune* that "[f]or the size of their church and its revenues [about $10 million annually], they're grossly underpaid." The rest of their income, they claimed, came from outside business ventures, book royalties, and speakers' fees.[54]

One business opportunity that the Whites participated in was promoting a fatty acid pill called Omega XL. This was part of an emerging trend of ministers becoming paid endorsers of health-related products. Texas evangelists James and Betty Robison and *The 700 Club* host Pat Robertson had already gained reputations as spokespeople for a vitamin company and a weight-loss shake, respectively. The Whites were featured in a thirty-minute infomercial after the CEO of Omega XL heard that Randy himself had benefited from the product. The Whites contributed some money to initially fund the infomercial, and they negotiated a deal with the company to receive a percentage of the product's sales profits. Although there

is historical precedent for similar activities, televangelists serving as pitch-
men for such products highlights evangelicals' growing commercial interest
in health-related issues. The CEO for TriVita, Inc., which produced the vi-
tamins that the Robisons endorsed, told the *Tampa Tribune* that "one of
the hottest topics in Christian television is health. . . . Every time we talk
about it the phones light up." Florida physician and Oral Roberts University graduate Don Colbert had become a best-selling author, speaker,
and self-proclaimed "Physician to God's Generals," appearing with many of
the top independent charismatic evangelists in the nation. According to his
website, Colbert "bases his plan for healing on God's Word, nutrition, exercise and common sense." An emphasis on healthy living and divine healing
was certainly not new in American religious history, but the nexus between
the consumer culture and contemporary notions about health was note-
worthy in modern evangelicalism.[55]

Billye Brim, a former Baptist and early leader in the Word of Faith
movement, attended some of Hagin's Tulsa revival meetings in 1967, when
she accepted the charismata. Her conversion led to a close association with
Hagin and with Kenneth and Gloria Copeland. From 1971 until 1980 she
edited Hagin's sermons into books and articles for *The Word of Faith*. Like
Marilyn Hickey, she believed that events in the Middle East had great eschatological significance, and she made it her mission to persuade American
evangelicals to support a modern Israeli state. Brim reported that, while
standing at her kitchen sink peeling potatoes for supper one day, she received a revelation from God that she was to begin a ministry that would
focus on the role modern Jews would play in biblical prophecy.[56] In 1980
she resigned from Kenneth Hagin Ministries to become a full-time evangelist. After her husband died in 1986 she became an authority among charismatics on end-times prophecy, holding small conferences and meetings
throughout the country.[57]

In 1995 Brim expanded her ministry's focus when she announced plans to
build a prayer center in the Ozark Mountains near Branson, Missouri. According to ministry reports, in just over a year she located 102 acres of un-
developed land on Bull Shoals Lake, raised enough money to pay for it, and
started building cabins and an administrative facility.[58] Although she did
not have the media exposure that other charismatic evangelists had, she had
gained some notoriety by the turn of the century. She had strong support
from established charismatic leaders such as the Hagins and Copelands, co-
hosting the *Believer's Voice of Victory* television show with Gloria Copeland,

contributing articles to the *Believer's Voice of Victory* magazine, and speaking at large conferences all over the world. Her own seminars, which generally focused on end-times prophecy, remained relatively small and were held in hotels and conference centers. All four of her children and at least one grandchild worked with her ministry. Brim's growing influence suggested a greater level of stability and acceptance, and the institutions she established and the involvement of family members allowed for the perpetuation of her ministry. At the dawn of the new millennium she continued to be an influential figure in the Word of Faith movement, and she embodied the traits of the modern charismatic woman—dutiful wife and mother as well as successful businessperson and evangelist.[59]

Kate McVeigh and Juanita Bynum were two more emerging stars on the horizon. McVeigh was part of the second generation of female charismatic evangelists who, like some of her predecessors, exemplified the power that positive thinking had on the charismatic revival, and she became a living testimony to the influence of Hagin's Word of Faith message. Her personal testimony focused on her childhood learning disabilities and low self-esteem: she attended special education classes from fifth through eleventh grade, was terrified to give oral presentations in school, was shunned or ridiculed by her basketball teammates, and was voted "least likely to succeed" by her high school classmates. With the encouragement of her mother, McVeigh was converted in 1983 at one of Hagin's revival meetings when Hagin came to her hometown of Detroit.[60]

After reading Hagin's book *The Believer's Authority,* McVeigh immersed herself in his teachings, reading his literature, listening to his sermon tapes, and repeating aloud statements that encouraged a positive attitude. When she returned for her junior year of high school, she noted, her attitude was profoundly different and her teachers, coaches, and classmates noticed a change in her behavior. No longer the shy, timid, insecure girl they once knew, she was bold, outgoing, and not easily intimidated. She claimed that her grades improved to the point that she was taken out of special education classes; her confidence increased on the basketball court; and she began witnessing about her newfound faith to her fellow students. Promoting the "life-changing power" of Hagin's message, *The Word of Faith* reported that "Kate's last year of high school was marked by excellent grades, record-breaking achievements on the basketball court . . . and an abundance of friends who liked and respected her." Upon graduating from high school in 1985, McVeigh enrolled in Rhema Bible Training Center (RBTC), where she learned the art of being a traveling evangelist from Kenneth Hagin Jr. This training proved useful as she started her own itinerant ministry in 1987.[61]

Despite her overwhelming fear of speaking in public, McVeigh applied Hagin's principles of positive thinking and claimed that they helped her overcome this obstacle in her life. "Sometimes the only way to break free from intimidation," she counseled in her book *Conquering Intimidation,* "is to just do it—to purpose in your heart that whether or not your knees are knocking, you're going to do it anyway because you believe that you are free! Now I speak in front of people nearly every week of my life, and it doesn't bother me at all." By century's end, her ministry reported, she was holding between 250 and 300 meetings a year, had published several books and pamphlets, was promoting her teaching tapes, and had started a radio broadcast that was heard on more than fifty stations nationwide. Her close association with prominent ministers such as Hagin, Detroit minister Keith Butler, and Joyce Meyer helped her promote her books, tapes, and crusades.[62] Although her work remained small, McVeigh's growing popularity and acceptance into the cadre of charismatic evangelists demonstrated how far women ministers had come in a traditionally male-dominated field. She never pastored a church or established lasting institutions, but she was able to create a moderately successful itinerant ministry and make her mark on the Word of Faith movement.

A former flight attendant and self-proclaimed prophetess, Juanita Bynum attended Chicago's St. Luke Church of God in Christ as a child. She made her debut as a recording artist on T. D. Jakes's *Woman, Thou Art Loosed!* compact disc, which was released in 1996, and in 1998 she published *No More Sheets Devotional,* where she recounted "what it is like to be a slave to sexual bondage and promiscuity." Her ministry, like Joyce Meyer's and Paula White's, focused on emotional healing and the prosperity message, but with a special emphasis on encouraging black women to take more prominent roles in ministry. Sociologist Shayne Lee sheds some light on how Bynum gained notoriety. After Bynum preached at one of Jakes's conferences in 1998, Jakes "made a fortune by selling many videos and tapes of her performance." A dispute over royalties erupted between Bynum and Jakes, and, citing anonymous sources familiar with the situation, Lee maintains that "Jakes responded by using his power and influence to have her blacklisted from preaching in many venues." This apparently had an immediate negative effect on her budding career. The two evangelists reconciled in 2003 when Bynum publicly apologized to Jakes at his "Woman, Thou

Art Loosed" conference. Her career quickly rebounded, and, Lee surmised in 2005, "Bynum is back on track as one of the highest-paid traveling evangelists in the country."[63]

Ministers' Wives

As conservative Christians became more accepting of female ministers, the wives of some prominent preachers and evangelists began stepping into the spotlight. Oral Roberts's daughter-in-law, Lindsay, immediately filled the role of the supportive wife when she married Richard in 1980 as he was beginning his own healing ministry. She traveled with him, participated in his healing services, and became an integral part of Oral and Richard Roberts Ministries. Unlike Richard's first wife, Patti, she did not try to establish her own ministry, independent of her husband and father-in-law. She willingly and dutifully supported their work any way she could. Over time, she accepted increasingly public roles within their ministry, and at the turn of the century she was hosting her own television show, publishing her own quarterly journal, and serving as executive vice-president of Oral Roberts Evangelistic Association (OREA).

Lindsay graduated from Rollins College in Winter Park, Florida, before entering law school at Oral Roberts University in the fall of 1979. She later claimed "that God had called me to go to law school, and that it would play a key role in my life. . . . At that time, very few women were entering the legal profession, but I had heard from God."[64] She met Richard during her first semester of law school as he was reeling from a very public divorce from Patti. In a matter of weeks they started making plans to marry in a small private ceremony in January 1980, and she decided to drop out of law school. Her primary responsibility, she believed, was to support her husband's budding career as an evangelist. In 1981 Richard crowed about his new bride's devotion: "I'm very grateful for my wife Lindsay, who stands by me in the ministry and supports me. . . . It is so important to me to know that I have someone standing by me as a true helpmate."[65] Her initial duties mainly included assisting with his healing services, answering ministry correspondence, and some light fund-raising.[66] Although her early involvement in fund-raising was not as extensive as that of other ministers' wives, Lindsay helped raise money for the struggling City of Faith Medical Center that Oral Roberts was building in Tulsa. The financial situation had become desperate, and she and the other members of the Roberts family and ministry were doing all they could to keep the project alive.[67]

Within two years of their marriage, Lindsay had begun accepting visible roles in Richard's ministry. She fully understood that, even then, this was unusual in charismatic and Pentecostal circles, and she claimed to be more than a little ambivalent about stepping into these new roles:

> In the early 1980's after Richard and I were married, the Full Gospel church world began to see more and more ministers' wives step out in ministry. Women were beginning to speak, teach and even preach in the churches. Some were even stepping out in great faith to minister to the needs of people. I knew that God had placed a lot inside me; but how, when and where it would ever come out—I just didn't know. I didn't really know whether women were supposed to preach, or take any active part in public services. And I still doubted whether I would be accepted in an active ministry role, and I didn't really want to jump into it.[68]

But in 1982 she announced that she had a special "anointing" in her right hand, which she claimed gave her the miraculous gift of healing. After one crusade meeting, Richard reported that "she touched me and the anointing came through her hand and hit me like a bolt of electricity. If I had been ill, I know I would have been healed instantly."[69] Lindsay later confessed that all she really wanted to be was "a good spectator, but I kept feeling the urge to participate" publicly in Richard's healing ministry.[70]

As with many other charismatics and Pentecostals, Lindsay's personal testimony was an important part of her ministry. Her father died of leukemia when she was a child, and her mother struggled to raise her three children alone. When Lindsay was eighteen years old her doctors told her that she would never be able to have children, and later—after two miscarriages—a large cyst was discovered on one of her ovaries. Despite these circumstances, she gave birth to their first child, Richard Oral Roberts, on January 17, 1984. The birth of a potential successor to the Roberts ministry thrilled both Oral and Richard, but their hopes were dashed when the infant developed breathing problems and died shortly thereafter. Although she eventually gave birth to three daughters, their son's death continued to affect her life and ministry. Doctors later found a small tumor in her breast, for which she claimed a miraculous healing, and she subsequently began highlighting breast cancer awareness on her *Make Your Day Count* television show. In 2002, *Miracles Now* magazine featured Cathy Keating, the wife of Oklahoma governor Frank Keating, promoting National Breast Cancer Awareness Month.[71] Roberts was as effective as any great charismatic evangelist in using her personal testimony to bolster the faith of her co-religionists and to convince others that modern-day miracles were possible.

A bright and talented woman, Lindsay maintained a hectic schedule of being a housewife, mother, author, editor, conference speaker, and administrator. Her first book, *Thirty-six Hours with an Angel,* was published in 1990, and by 2004 she had written or contributed to seventeen other books. She wrote a few short promotional articles for the ministry magazine *Abundant Life* as early as 1984, and ran her first full-length article six years later. By 1998 she was writing feature articles for *Abundant Life*'s successor, *Miracles Now,* and served as editor for that journal as well as a devotional magazine, *Daily Blessing,* that Oral Roberts began publishing in 1959.[72] In 2001 she launched her own quarterly journal for women, titled *Make Your Day Count.* Acknowledging the difficulties that modern women faced, this magazine was designed to meet the spiritual needs of women "on the go." In the inaugural issue, Lindsay wrote: "Women especially are bombarded by stress because they have so many responsibilities and hectic schedules. I understand what it's like to run from sunup to sundown, attempting to get everything done. . . . But because of the expectations placed on us, the stress we encounter, and the pressures that are unavoidable, we need to stay built up spiritually as well as physically and emotionally."[73] In 1987 she began hosting annual women's conferences, which drew large crowds and provided exposure for the growing number of female evangelists in the charismatic movement.[74] Her women's ministry was enhanced in 1996 when she started her own daily television program, *Make Your Day Count with Lindsay and Cheryl.*[75] According to a ministry publication, this was initially "a local outreach to the women of Tulsa, but because of its phenomenal success and popularity, it has expanded into a nationally syndicated program." Lindsay and her sister-in-law Cheryl Salem featured guests and information that they believed appealed to women and included "segments on cooking, health, and nutrition." She also co-hosted with her husband *Something Good Tonight: The Hour of Healing.*[76] In addition to her women's ministry, Lindsay continued to be involved in the administrative affairs of OREA. In 2004 Richard announced that she had been promoted to executive vice-president for OREA and would oversee the daily operations of the ministry.[77]

Despite her assertions to the contrary, Lindsay had a real knack for these public roles, readily identified with her audience, and, like other female ministers, served as a cultural mediator for an important segment of the charismatic movement. Astutely recognizing that many conservative Christian women were trying to live up to the "superwoman" ideal, she focused much of her ministry at the turn of the century on meeting the needs of these women. Although she never tried to establish her own career and always worked within the confines of her husband's ministry, she was a leader in a new generation of preachers' wives who asserted themselves publicly and gained reputations based on their own abilities.[78]

Although Kenneth Hagin Jr.'s wife, Lynette, never had the visibility that Lindsay had in her husband's ministry, Lynette was always an important part of Kenneth Hagin Ministries and gradually accepted a more public role. Early in their marriage she focused much of her attention on raising her children until she became director of RBTC in May 1982. But even then she served mainly behind the scenes in an administrative capacity, and she seemed most interested in ministering to women in a more traditional sense. She claimed to have first considered starting a women's ministry in 1977, but it was not until the late 1990s that she began to assert herself in more public roles. One of the first articles she wrote for *The Word of Faith* appeared in 1998, and in 2001 she sponsored a women's conference at Rhema Bible Church, which included, among others, herself, her daughter, Denise Hagin Burns, and her daughter-in-law, Melissa Robertson Hagin, as featured speakers. The following year she began contributing a monthly column, "Seed Thoughts," to their magazine, and in 2004 she started writing feature articles. According to ministry reports, she continued to direct RBTC and assist with the administration of Kenneth Hagin Ministries and Rhema Bible Church. She also co-hosted the *Rhema Praise* television program with her husband and conducted "All Faiths' Crusades" with him throughout the country.[79]

Conclusion

The women discussed in this chapter ushered in a new generation of charismatic leaders who reflected the changing attitudes of many evangelicals as they moved into mainstream American society and became more accepting of secular culture. They encouraged a receptive audience of conservative Christian women to take public leadership roles in their churches. They used the same message and ministry-building techniques that their male counterparts used, and by recounting their own personal hardships they identified with a broad segment of the American population. Most had the support of their spouses and other family members, and all had the ability to develop thriving ministries, either as independents or as part of their husbands' programs. Although few women gained the popular acclaim that many men enjoyed, they were still able to create a solid niche for themselves and have an important influence on the charismatic movement. They opened doors that, to a large extent, had previously been closed to women, and they forced many conservative Christians to rethink their views about gender roles in the church and society.

These women also struggled to reconcile their traditional views about women's roles in society with the new cultural milieu. Personal testimonies reveal their ambivalence about trading in their reputations for being meek, quiet, submissive women of God for the assertive, vocal, and public roles of modern evangelists and religious entrepreneurs. They were entering a "man's world" while trying to maintain their femininity and the support of conservative evangelical women. But even that support base was beginning to change. Although many older evangelicals retained traditional attitudes about women's roles, younger women internalized the pervasive messages of the feminist movement and its emphasis on sexual equality. They assumed that men and women were created equal and that women had the same right as men to pursue happiness. These younger women, especially, were ready and willing to accept the message of sexual equality even if it was packaged in traditional rhetoric about submissiveness. The women in this study made submissiveness an important part of their message, but they placed it in the context of submission to God and mutual submission between men and women. They also wove into their teaching the principles of Hagin's Word of Faith message, according to which women did not have to give up anything in order to achieve sexual equality. They could have it all—a career, wealth, health, and a happy family life—if they would simply have faith, "sow a seed" into their favorite ministry, and pattern their lives after the lives of these successful female evangelists.

1. Gloria Copeland at a healing revival (Courtesy Gloria Copeland and Kenneth Copeland Ministries).

2. T. L. Osborn, Kenneth E. Hagin, and Oral Roberts (Courtesy Rev. Kenneth E. Hagin, Kenneth Hagin Ministries, Inc.).

3. Kenneth E. Hagin (Courtesy Rev. Kenneth E. Hagin, Kenneth Hagin Ministries, Inc.).

4. Marilyn Hickey (Courtesy Marilyn Hickey Ministries).

5. Bishop T. D. Jakes of Dallas, Texas, delivers his sermon to a near-capacity crowd of mostly women, Thursday, July 29, 1999, at the Georgia Dome in Atlanta, as he begins his 1999 "Woman, Thou Art Loosed" conference (Courtesy Associated Press. Photographer: Bill Cranford).

6. Bishop T. D. Jakes preaches at the dedication of the new Potter's House sanctuary in Dallas, Sunday, October 22, 2000 (Courtesy Associated Press. Photographer: Bill Janscha).

7. Freda Lindsay sits for an interview with a Dallas television station (Courtesy Freda Lindsay and Christ for the Nations, Inc.).

8. Freda Lindsay (*center*) receives the Christian Woman of the Year Award in 1983 (Courtesy Freda Lindsay and Christ for the Nations, Inc.).

9. Freda and Gordon Lindsay (*at podium*) at a fund-raising event (Courtesy Freda Lindsay and Christ for the Nations, Inc.).

10. Joyce Meyer (Courtesy Joyce Meyer Ministries and Dario Acosta).

11. Frederick K. C. Price teaching at the Crenshaw Christian Center (Courtesy Crenshaw Christian Center, Inc. of Los Angeles County).

4

The New Black Charismatics

Frederick K. C. Price has been heralded by *Charisma* as one of the leading proponents of the prosperity message among African Americans. He emphasized faith, positive attitudes, and positive actions when teaching black Americans how to claim their earthly reward for being faithful Christians. In contrast to Martin Luther King Jr.'s image of the suffering servant, Price believed that black Christians should not have to suffer; instead, they could receive their physical and financial blessings in the here and now. King told his antagonists, "We will soon wear you down by our capacity to suffer, and in winning our freedom we will so appeal to your heart and conscience that we will win you in the process."[1] Price, on the other hand, rejected the notion that the faithful had to suffer: "Many people have the idea that somebody who lives by faith is supposed to be 'poor-mouthing' it; the bottoms of their shoes are out; the seat of their pants out; and their old car is clinking along on two cylinders and four bald tires; they have no place to live, and no food to eat. They think to live by faith means that you have to be some kind of *weird-o*. No sir! . . . When you are living by faith—the faith of God—you will be on top, and if you are not on top, or moving towards the top, then you are not living by faith."[2] Price believed that when preachers taught the pure, unadulterated word of God, faith would grow in the hearts of the hearers, and miracles, divine healing, and prosperity would be manifested in their lives.[3] I argue in this chapter that the black evangelists examined here were the natural heirs to the independent charismatic movement and the beneficiaries of the civil rights movement. They capitalized on the social and economic advances made by African Americans, and they used Kenneth Hagin's prosperity message to advance their ministries and

become successful and wealthy religious entrepreneurs in the late twentieth century.

The struggle for African American equality reached new heights in the
mid-1950s when blacks—and some whites—began to successfully challenge racial discrimination. Martin Luther King Jr. and other leaders galva-
nized black churches and advanced the civil rights movement, which gave
many African Americans the opportunity to receive a better education, get
better jobs, and achieve a higher standard of living. By the 1970s blacks were
becoming more integrated into mainstream American society, and in the
1980s and 1990s, although complete equity with whites certainly had not
been achieved, they were much more upwardly mobile than they had been
a half century earlier. In 1978, *Charisma* highlighted the impressive growth
of Pentecostalism among African Americans and ruminated on the role
black charismatics could play in bridging the racial divide within Pentecostal and charismatic circles.[4] In the late 1980s and early 1990s, *Charisma* ran
several articles and editorials promoting racial reconciliation. At one point
its publisher, Stephen Strang, even considered starting a new magazine devoted solely to the role of African Americans in the Pentecostal and charismatic movements.[5]

As Pentecostals and charismatics moved into the mainstream of middle-
class America, so too did African Americans. Although there is some debate about the origins and composition of the black middle class, most
scholars agree that this segment of American society expanded greatly in
the postwar era. According to sociologist Mary Patillo-McCoy:

> The unprecedented economic growth and prosperity after World
> War II, along with the social and political pressures of the civil rights
> movement, greatly expanded the black middle class in the 1950s and
> 1960s. The black class structure began to resemble the white class
> structure, with greater occupational diversity.... The period from
> 1945 to the early 1970s was extraordinary in terms of opening oppor-
> tunities for African Americans. Predominantly white educational in-
> stitutions were admitting black students in large numbers, businesses
> were recruiting at black colleges, and unions yielded to the pressure of
> their formerly excluded black coworkers.[6]

Stephan and Abigail Thernstrom report that between the late 1940s and
the early 1990s the number of black lawyers increased eighteen-fold; there

were nineteen times more black editors and reporters and thirty-three times more black engineers. They also note that in 1949 there were no black mayors of large U.S. cities and only two black members of Congress. In contrast, by the mid-1990s most major cities had had black chief executives, and more than forty African Americans had held seats in the House of Representatives.[7] The number of black middle-class citizens increased even more dramatically in the wake of the civil rights movement. "In 1960, only 385,586 black men and women in the entire country were professionals or semi-professionals, business owners, managers, or officials," Patillo-McCoy records. "By 1980, that number had grown to well over one million (1,317,080). Similar increases took place in the category of sales and clerical workers, which increased from 391,927 blacks in 1960 to well over two million such workers in 1980. By 1995, nearly seven million African Americans were employed in middle-class occupations."[8]

Despite these advances, African Americans continued to lag behind middle-class whites in terms of social mobility and relative position within that social class. Most blacks were considered lower middle class at century's end and tended to hold a larger number of "medium-level" occupations, such as clerks, salespeople, and well-paid factory workers. Most of the "higher-level" occupations, such as managerial positions, continued to be held by whites.[9] Middle-class blacks, particularly in urban areas, often lived in racially segregated neighborhoods, and they seldom strayed far from the poor inner cities they were trying to escape. As African Americans began to make more money and move out of the ghettos into predominantly white suburbs, they found that upwardly mobile whites soon moved to newer neighborhoods farther away from blacks. Black suburbs then developed along the fringes of the inner cities, making it difficult for the new black middle class to get too far away from their poor roots. Education levels among African Americans increased from 1960 onward, but they were always behind those of their white counterparts.[10]

Some scholars argue that an economic downturn and the rejection of affirmative action policies by politicians from the mid-1970s through the 1990s contributed to the slower progress that African Americans made toward economic and social equity.[11] By the end of the twentieth century, many blacks, having tasted the fruits of middle-class prosperity, knew that that lifestyle was within reach but were often unable to fully realize the American dream. They saw a few African Americans work their way into the upper echelons of business and politics and believed that they or their children could one day benefit from those advances.[12] Successful television evangelists such as Fred Price, T. D. Jakes, and Creflo Dollar were also considered proof positive that African Americans could work their way out of poverty, and they offered seemingly viable solutions through their prosperity theology, outreach programs, and economic development plans that upwardly mobile blacks could use.

Besides applying Hagin's principles of positive confession, many televangelists also encouraged African Americans to start small businesses, invest in the stock market, and gain more business savvy. Sociologist E. Franklin Frazier identified an entrepreneurial spirit among the black middle class in the 1920s, and many black neoconservatives emphasized a similar ethic in the 1980s and 1990s.[13] One survey comparing middle-class whites and blacks "found that 71 percent of affluent whites have a mutual-fund or brokerage account compared to 56 percent of blacks. About half as many blacks as whites, 24 percent compared to 46 percent, grew up in a household in which stocks were traded, and more blacks listed traditional bank accounts, insurance companies, and real estate as the key places where their assets are kept or invested, while a larger percentage of whites listed brokerages."[14] (Although conservative investment strategies seemed unwise in the 1990s, this diversity was beneficial during the economic slump of the early twenty-first century.) Furthermore, many black charismatic leaders held an ideological position similar to that of Robert L. Woodson, who founded the National Center for Neighborhood Enterprise. Contrary to the view of many traditional civil rights leaders, Woodson contends that the eradication of racism should not be a precondition to black advancement in American society; that blacks have become too dependent on government-funded welfare programs that perpetuate poverty;[15] and that leaders must encourage "the growing movement among blacks to, once again, rely on themselves for an improved life."[16] Black leaders, he continues, should develop new educational strategies that teach African Americans how to "tap resources within the black community" so they can own and operate their own businesses.[17]

By the mid-1980s many black churches, especially mainline denominations, had begun community development programs to encourage business ownership. Journalist Bill Alexander notes how "church programs have traditionally coped with community needs" such as "[f]amily counseling, blood pressure clinics, day care centers, senior citizen activities, and family community events." But many congregations in the post–civil rights era recognized the need for more economic development programs that addressed the root of many African American problems.[18] The independent charismatic churches and other full-gospel congregations also recognized the need for such advocacy. Fred Price offered practical advice for staying out of debt, but he primarily emphasized the supernatural aspects of God's plan for Christians to be wealthy. "The world's economic system is not designed for you to get ahead," he asserted in 1984. "It is designed to keep your nose to the grindstone. . . . You will never be financially independent of the circumstances through your job alone. Yes, we must work. . . . But God has a plan. The Father has a plan whereby you can become financially and materially independent of the circumstances. That plan is initiated through tithes and offerings."[19] Creflo Dollar's Project Change was designed to evangelize and reinvigorate his church's local community by providing social, educational, and employment services to local residents. Although he, too, focused on the "miraculous" ways God made Christians rich, many of his benevolent and economic programs had a notable effect on his community.[20]

T. D. Jakes proposed one of the most comprehensive community development programs of any modern independent evangelist. In 1998 he broke ground on "a 230-acre rehabilitation and education community in South Dallas" that was to include "a senior citizens home, a youth center, a mall, and grocery store," garnering the attention of then-governor George W. Bush and presidential hopeful Al Gore. Jakes's Potter's House church claimed to provide "two thousand homeless people with clothes, coats, and shoes for the winter" and to offer help to prisoners, prostitutes, AIDS victims, and substance abusers.[21] Probably his strongest endorsement for the entrepreneurial spirit among African Americans, however, came through his own example. Although he acknowledged the charismatic emphasis of "having faith" to attain wealth, he considered it only one part of the equation. In a 2001 interview with *Ebony*, Jakes asserted that faith and hard work were important components of economic empowerment. "It's very important that we don't just leave it on a church level of praying God will bless you or preaching God will bless you . . . because the reality is [that] most of my income comes from my for-profit ventures." He continued: "If I retired from preaching, I make enough from writing to take care of personal needs." Jakes sought to instill the Protestant ethic of hard work and thriftiness into his followers and community by creating new business opportunities and encouraging locals to spend their money closer to home. "In South Dallas, where I minister, something like a billion dollars flows out of our community for goods and services," he lamented. "We need to rectify this and develop businesses here."[22]

Of course, without the institutional structure these ministries provided, one wonders if their for-profit ventures would have been quite so successful. The confluence of business and ministry was so seamless that it was difficult to determine where one ended and the other began. All of these evangelists encouraged their followers to give to their ministries—be they evangelism, outreach, or community development—so the gospel could be proclaimed, the needy could find relief, and individual and corporate wealth could be attained. But in each case, the evangelists themselves reaped the financial rewards of those tithes and offerings.

This prosperity message has long appealed to people struggling to work their way out of poverty, regardless of their race. From their beginnings, the Pentecostal and charismatic movements were known for racial experimentation. Healing evangelists throughout the twentieth century challenged racial taboos by holding integrated services, and they often made a concerted effort to attract African Americans to their meetings. Poor blacks and whites were drawn to the message of healing and prosperity preached by most charismatic ministers, and as early as the mid-1950s integrated audiences appeared. In the 1950s and 1960s African Americans began to take visible roles in some healing ministries. Generally they were musicians, and they had a profound influence on the music and worship of the healing revivals and charismatic movement. Some even began their own evangelistic careers. White revivalists such as Kenneth Hagin, Oral Roberts, and Kenneth Copeland trained some of these young men in the 1970s and 1980s, while others came out of black Pentecostal church backgrounds.[23]

Frederick K. C. Price

One of the most important black charismatic evangelists in the late twentieth century was Frederick K. C. Price. The first African American preacher to become popular in the new generation of charismatic leaders, Price spawned several other successful ministries. Like Marilyn Hickey, he began his work in the mid-1970s and rose to prominence during the 1980s. Price embraced Hagin's Word of Faith doctrine as the centerpiece of his ministry, but he also addressed social issues such as race, poverty, and community development among African Americans.

Born in 1932 in Santa Monica, California, Price had little exposure to organized religion as a child and, according to ministry reports, was not converted to Christianity until after he married Betty Ruth Scott in 1953.[24] Shortly thereafter he felt called to ministry and served as an assistant pastor in a Baptist church from 1955 to 1957, but for nearly twenty years he struggled "to find a place where I could serve without problems."[25] Price wandered from denomination to denomination during the 1950s and 1960s, pastoring several congregations. In 1965 he went to West Washington Community Church, a Christian and Missionary Alliance congregation in southern California. While pastoring this church, he was influenced by Kathryn Kuhlman's books on miracles and came to believe that something was missing in his life and ministry.[26] Concerned about his spiritual development, dissatisfied with the meager growth of his church, and unhappy about the lack of joy and conviction he saw in his congregation and the rest of the religious world, he longed for a more dynamic religious experience. In his personal testimony he noted: "I was not witnessing these 'greater works' in my own ministry or in the ministry of others that I knew with two exceptions— Kathryn Kuhlman and Oral Roberts." In February 1970, Price claimed, he received the Holy Spirit, spoke in tongues, and began his charismatic ministry.[27]

Shortly thereafter Price read Kenneth Hagin's *The Authority of the Believer*, a book that he believed taught him how to put this supernatural power into action in his own life. He recalled that he had always "been a complainer, a cry baby who was always sick," and debt had forced him to work a second job during his early ministry to make ends meet. He worked at a variety of blue-collar jobs but was never able to make much financial progress. Hagin's teachings convinced him that faith in God and a positive attitude would ultimately lead to material gain and divine health. After putting Hagin's principles into action, Price claimed, his situation began to change and he started paying off the massive debt he had accumulated.[28] His humble beginnings, no-nonsense teaching style, and willingness to "stay connected" to his downtrodden followers were all part of his popular appeal. "People can see I have some smarts, but at the same time I'm just an average guy," he remarked to one interviewer. "I'll split verbs and I'll use anything that'll get the truth across. I think people like that."[29] His personal appeal and Word of Faith teaching attracted people to his small church.

In 1973 Price severed ties with the Christian and Missionary Alliance and started the independent Crenshaw Christian Center in Inglewood, California. Free from denominational restrictions, he reported that his church experienced phenomenal growth in the 1970s and 1980s. By 1977 the church had outgrown its fourteen-hundred-seat auditorium and began holding three services. When he tried to buy twenty-three acres from the Inglewood school board to construct a new facility, the city passed a zoning law limiting the church to building on only three acres. In 1981 he bought

Pepperdine University's thirty-two-acre campus in downtown Los Angeles for $14 million, and in September 1984 he began holding services there.[30]

In his book *Race, Religion and Racism*, Price was very critical of the way Pepperdine handled the transaction, claiming that the university took advantage of him and his church when they sold their campus to his ministry. "When my wife and I first got married," he wrote, "we as black people could not rent an apartment in the area where our church is situated. . . . Then, when Whites finally decided that too many Blacks were applying to get in, they left, and they left the whole neighborhood, including the property where the church is located, like a dump." According to Price, Pepperdine was supposed to have paid for improvements on their sewer system, but, he claimed, they did not make those improvements and Crenshaw Christian Center had to pay the city of Los Angeles $200,000 to connect to the sewer system after buying the property. "That is cold-blooded," he railed. "The previous owners knew that no white people were going to buy the property, that it would be bought either by Hispanics or Blacks, and their attitude was, 'Let them pay through the nose!' Two hundred thousand dollars just to hook up to the sewer system—all of which should have been paid by the people who occupied the property when the improvements along the Vermont Corridor were originally made." According to *Charisma*, he broke ground on his ten-thousand-seat FaithDome in 1986 and moved his sixteen-thousand-member church into the $9 million facility in the fall of 1989. Attendance continued to grow slowly throughout the 1990s; by the end of the century his church boasted twenty thousand members.[31]

David Hazard has attributed much of Price's national popularity to his television program, begun in April 1978 on the relatively new Trinity Broadcasting Network. A month later Price switched to a local Los Angeles station in order to reach a larger audience; he quickly expanded to four other major markets, including Washington, D.C., Chicago, Detroit, and New York City. He used his television and radio shows to reach black Americans with the Word of Faith message, which he believed would teach them how to get out of debt and improve their lives. "I have a very heartfelt desire for black America to receive the real word of God," he said in 1988. "They've had religion. There's no shortage of religion. They've had emotion. No shortage of emotion. They've had music. No shortage of music. But the word of God—the power-filled word that people can take and apply to their lives and change their circumstances—they don't know that."[32] He was one of the few televangelists who spent almost his entire sixty-minute program teaching. He boasted that he did not waste time pleading for money and entertaining people with choir music. Price believed that if people were taught what the Bible said about finances, divine health, and other practical aspects of daily life, they would be inspired to change their lifestyles. "Teaching is informative," he told a reporter in 1987. "It gives people something to use. It is more tangible than preaching though you can have a degree of both in any message depending on the individual." Many media experts doubted that Price's format would be successful, but eight years after he started the *Ever Increasing Faith* program it proved to be quite popular with many Americans. According to public opinion polls cited in *Religious Broadcasting,* a third of the people who tuned in to religious programs on Sunday mornings watched Price's show. More than half of the African American households in New York and Washington, D.C., that watched religious programming on Sundays tuned him in. By 1987 the show was seen on almost a hundred broadcast and cable outlets around the country; at the turn of the century Price claimed to have a television audience of 33 million people, and the program was seen in fifteen of the twenty largest U.S. markets.[33]

As Price's television ministry grew, so too did the demand for his literature and audiotapes—in the late 1980s Price claimed that more than two hundred thousand people were on his mailing list. At the end of the century he claimed to have written fifty books that had sold over 2 million copies since 1976. Price's ministry, like that of other independent ministers, depended financially on supporters who watched his program and sent regular donations. In an effort to cultivate that relationship with his television audience, Price began conducting crusades in the United States in 1982. By 1986 he was holding crusades in major cities, with a reported attendance of more than forty-two thousand at one meeting. Aside from the personal contact with his audience that crusades afforded, Price explained that they "encourage the television audience to continue to support the Ever Increasing Faith program. It costs megabucks to be on television. Commercial television is financed by sponsors who pitch their products intermittently during the show," but Christian television was sponsored solely by viewers' freewill offerings. Because he did not focus on fund-raising on his television program, cultivating these relationships was especially important to the success of his ministry. He often boasted that he would rather go off the air than plead for money to fund the program.[34]

Price used Hagin's Word of Faith teaching to encourage positive attitudes and self-help among blacks and to catapult himself to the forefront of a new generation of charismatic leaders. He was, in the words of *Charisma* reporter Paul Thigpin, the most prominent "forerunner of this recent black charismatic wave" that emerged in the last quarter of the twentieth century.[35] His confidence, hard work, determination, and intuition quickly brought him to the forefront of this movement. Oddly enough, it was whites, not blacks, who first accepted him. Hagin promoted Price's ministry in the early years, speaking at his church and making him a featured speaker at the popular Campmeetings held in Tulsa. According to Hazard, this exposure gave Price a platform from which to reach blacks around the country with the Word of Faith message.[36]

Price sought to help African Americans by teaching faith in God, the power of positive thinking, and practical ways to improve one's life. He won the Horatio Alger Award in 1998, which was a testament to his emphasis on self-help and positive thinking. This award was given by the Horatio Alger Association of Distinguished Americans, which, according to their website, sought to "recognize the achievements and accomplishments of . . . extraordinary Americans who have risen from humble beginnings to achieve personal and professional success."[37] In 1988 Price noted: "If they'll listen to me, they'll find out how to do something for themselves. They won't need me, or anyone else. They'll learn how to pray for themselves, apply God's word for themselves. They can become independent of their circumstances."[38] His emphasis on positive thinking and self-actualization further demonstrates the influence of popular culture on evangelicalism and the charismatic movement. These ideas, which had been advanced by Norman Vincent Peale and other Protestant leaders in the 1950s, had filtered into the evangelical subculture and were being used by African American charismatic evangelists to build their ministries and empower their followers.

Price also believed that whites should take responsibility for their role in oppressing blacks, and in the early 1990s a single incident unleashed his fury on what he considered the biggest problem in modern Christianity. In 1992, at the Rhema Bible Church in Tulsa, Kenneth Hagin Jr. preached a sermon about interracial dating and marriage in which he argued that if parents did not want their children dating members of other races, they should teach those values at an early age. "I can't tell your kids who to go with and who not to go date," Hagin reportedly stated. "Not my responsibility." He continued: "If you don't want your kids dating somebody, then you control it. But you control it a long time before they ever get to be dating age." He maintained that Christian parents could choose to allow their children to practice interracial dating, but he assured them that they were not racist if they chose otherwise.[39] When a group of black ministers informed Price of Hagin's sermon, Price confronted his friend and asked him to recant his views publicly. Hagin apologized to Price privately and publicly, but Price was not satisfied with a simple apology; he wanted Hagin to renounce those views and take a public stance against racism.[40] Convinced that this issue needed to be addressed, Price preached a yearlong series of televised sermons titled "Race, Religion and Racism," which became a three-volume book condemning racism in the church.[41]

In this series of sermons, Price argued that Hagin's views reflected the racist attitudes held by many whites and that the church needed to speak out against the latent racism ingrained in American society—especially in the South. "This minister," Price retorted, "is instructing his congregation to teach their children before the children reach dating age. Many white people, especially southern Whites, have trained their children this way. Racism is not in the genes, it starts in the home."[42] Stressing that he did not think all white people were racist, he acknowledged that some blacks had developed a "reactive racism" toward whites. This reactive racism, Price proclaimed, helped blacks "keep their sanity in the face of the racist actions and attitudes black people are confronted with on a daily basis," but their racism, while understandable to Price, was not justified.[43] For him the issue was not interracial dating and marriage but rather the underlying assumption that blacks were inferior to whites, who tried to justify the position that the two races should not intermingle.[44]

Price wanted to use this incident as a catalyst to launch a movement for change in the church and American society. "I am not angry with any individual person," he insisted, "but I am angry about a situation that until now, apparently, nobody has fully addressed." He characterized his anger as a "holy, righteous indignation" that arose not because his longtime friend hurt his feelings but because the church and the nation still had not effectively dealt with the problem of racism.[45] "I am dealing with a symptom here, not the man," Price contended. "But he represents something. When you are a leader you stand in the pulpit and minister to people, people are going to believe that what you say is from God. That is how racism in America became the mess it is today, because of so-called leaders and ministers talking in this way. Nobody has challenged them. That day is over."[46] Price asserted that slavery was practiced in America for almost three centuries because the church refused to take a stand against it. He further argued that after Emancipation the church continued its "ostrich syndrome, hiding its head in the sand" and refusing to correct the ills that persisted in American society.[47] His assault on these attitudes and practices made Price a controversial figure, but he continued to influence the development of the charismatic movement at century's end.[48]

In accordance with his long-standing policy not to respond publicly to criticism, Hagin said little about the controversy. According to *Charisma*, however, he did respond to Rhema supporters privately, assuring them that he tried to apologize to Price personally for the offense and to his church for any hard feelings his statements may have caused. He pointed out that there were interracial couples in his church who remained loyal to him, that he performed wedding ceremonies for mature couples regardless of race, that key members of his pastoral staff were black, and that many prominent Word of Faith ministers were black. "If people would just take a look at the fruit of this ministry and would talk to people who know me . . . they would understand that I am definitely not a racist, nor am I a bigot in any way," he wrote in a letter to his supporters. "If I could take the words back, I would . . . but I can't. I can only apologize for having said them and pray that the hurt and confusion will be healed."[49] Before and after the controversy, the Hagins consistently featured black speakers at their popular Campmeeting revivals held every year in Tulsa, including prominent evangelists Leroy Thompson and Keith Butler.

Hagin continued to react to Price by issuing a veiled call for peace and unity among charismatics in general and within the Word of Faith camp in particular. Although neither Price nor the controversial incident was ever mentioned, three articles appeared in *The Word of Faith* in 1998 and 2001 suggesting that Hagin desperately wanted to put the situation behind him. In one article Hagin maintained that Christians could effectively spread the gospel only when they had unity of purpose and did not publicly criticize the mistakes of others: "When conflicts arise, you can either take the low road or the high road. You can take the low road and wallow in the mire, allowing bad feelings or offenses to pull you down. Or you can take the high road and rise up, living above the situation."[50] He continued: "You can choose to dwell on the hurtful things that others have done or said. . . . Or you can hide God's words inside your heart until they become a part of your mind as well. And when somebody does you wrong, out comes love and forgiveness."[51] Although this incident created a breach between these pillars of the Word of Faith camp, it did not seem to hurt either ministry's influence on the charismatic movement.

Price always felt called to minister to blacks, but this incident heightened his sense of responsibility to represent African Americans and combat racism in American society. He was one of the most prominent black charismatic preachers to minister to blacks from the ghetto—not from white suburbia—and he had one of the largest churches and television ministries in America. In *Race, Religion and Racism* he stated: "I believe that the Lord has raised me up for a time like this: to be, as it were, a catalyst to find the solution to what I consider to be America's biggest challenge."[52] The 1990s were an opportune time for Price to address this issue, since many whites—and several religious groups—recognized their role in the perpetuation of racism in American society.[53] By the beginning of the new millennium, Price had combined his Word of Faith teaching on divine health and prosperity with an emphasis on breaking the bonds of racism.

Many of the new black independent ministers followed Price's lead in promoting social and political activism, engaging in community outreach, and providing leadership training and life skills to African Americans, especially young men. Several came from Baptist or Church of God in Christ backgrounds and worked to forge ties with some mainline Protestant and black Pentecostal denominations, but the Word of Faith movement had the most visible impact on these new leaders.

T. D. Jakes

Thomas Dexter Jakes, one of the most popular African American evangelists in the 1990s, began his independent ministry in 1982 but did not gain national prominence until the early 1990s. By the turn of the century he was one of the most recognizable religious figures in the United States. Many of his contemporaries likened his fame and influence to that of Billy Graham, who crossed denominational, political, and socioeconomic divides. Although Jakes's audiences were primarily black and his message of economic empowerment was directed toward African Americans, his ability to relate to different racial and ethnic groups contributed to his success. His greatest appeal was his message of emotional healing, which he directed first to women and later to men. His emphasis on emotional healing, racial equality, prosperity, and spiritual renewal was popular with Pentecostals, charismatics, and mainline evangelicals. But Jakes also had his detractors, who criticized his lavish lifestyle and the prosperity theology that justified it. They argued that he, like other televangelists, had compromised the gospel message of salvation and liberation by embracing the materialistic and hedonistic culture of modern America.[54]

T. D. Jakes was born on June 9, 1957, in South Charleston, West Virginia, to Ernest and Odith Jakes, a businessman and schoolteacher, respectively. Despite his parents' divorce and his father's struggle with kidney disease, Jakes maintained that he was raised in a loving and relatively stable home where he learned the value of hard work and developed an entrepreneurial spirit that was essential to his success. To earn money as a child he reportedly delivered newspapers, sold Avon products, and peddled vegetables from his mother's garden. His father had a successful janitorial service in the Charleston area, but he developed kidney disease when Jakes was only ten years old. According to ministry reports, Jakes spent six years caring for his sick father.[55] This experience, he explained to *Ebony* in 2001, contributed to his commitment to emotional healing in his ministry: "I think it's because I was in such pain myself that I can relate to people who have been through trauma. . . . I was forced to be responsible and deal with issues that relate to life and death."[56] It took many years of hardship and toil for those lessons to manifest themselves in a prominent national ministry.

Jakes was raised a Baptist, but as a teenager he turned to Pentecostalism at a storefront Apostolic church. He soon began preaching part-time at small churches in the Charleston area while pursuing a degree in psychology at West Virginia State University. A bivocational minister, he and ten others founded the Greater Emanuel Temple of Faith in Montgomery, West Virginia, in 1980. Laid off from his job at Union Carbide in 1982, he supplemented his meager income as a part-time minister by digging ditches and holding revival meetings for small churches in the area. His wife, Serita, recalled how when the unemployment money ran out "he was digging ditches with his brother to lay gas lines and preaching revivals to subsidize their income. I worked as a DJ at a Christian radio station at night, but little did I realize that it was deflating his masculine instinct to want to take care of his family." Jakes persevered through these hard times and began building what became a prominent international ministry. From 1982 through 1985 he conducted a local radio ministry called "The Master's Plan"; in 1983 eighty people attended his first "Back to the Bible" conference. He continued to work in relative obscurity for the remainder of the decade, but his preaching earned him some notoriety in the region.[57]

In 1990, Jakes moved his hundred-member church from the impoverished mining town of Montgomery to Charleston. The church grew quickly, and by 1996 it had more than a thousand members. Jakes admitted that his congregation's growth stemmed partly from a general spiritual revival among black churches, but he asserted that its interracial flavor was rooted in his ability to minister to people who were hurting—emotionally, financially, spiritually, and physically. "I don't believe you can have a Pentecostal experience and have any type of exclusion," he told *Charisma* in 1994. "What really happened is our church closed its eyes and opened its doors and allowed anybody to come in." In addition to addressing the problems of unemployment and poverty that accompanied the slump in the West Virginia coal industry, he began social programs for prisoners, former convicts, the homeless, AIDS victims, and those with drug and alcohol addictions. As one church official commented to *Charisma:* "The ministry is to hurting people, and hurting people know no color." Jakes preached a message of hope for the hurting, but he claimed not to embrace what he called a "microwave concept of faith. . . . You need to understand that some things that God promises to His people will *not* be zapped into your life," he implored. "You have to persevere even while you are waiting on the promise." His encouraging message and dynamic preaching style transcended racial, socioeconomic, denominational, and, most importantly, gender barriers. In 1992 he started a ladies' Sunday school class titled "Woman, Thou Art Loosed!" that mushroomed into a thriving—and lucrative—cottage industry. His message of emotional healing for women put Jakes on the road to international fame and financial success.[58]

A year later he published his first book, *Woman, Thou Art Loosed!* It addressed issues such as divorce, molestation, depression, and discrimination—issues he thought the church had neglected for far too long. He believed Christians were focusing on the "sweet by and by while we're living in the nasty here and now."[59] His message to women was that no matter how old their emotional scars were, they still needed to be healed.[60] This ministry to women began, ironically, with his wife. "I was the first 'Woman, Thou Art Loosed!' conference," Serita told *Christianity Today.* Early in their marriage she came home exhausted and depressed: "I was overwhelmed with all of the roles that I was having to take on at one time," she said. "I asked my husband to step outside our relationship and minister to me." That conversation allowed him to explore the emotional and physical baggage that many women carried with them from childhood to adulthood.[61] In his book he pleaded with churches and pastors to minister to these hurting women. "The church must open its doors and allow people who have a past to enter in," he maintained. "We must divorce our embarrassment about wounded people" and help these women who were sexually, emotionally, and physically abused.[62]

Woman, Thou Art Loosed! also represented a major financial risk for Jakes. He initially published the book himself, and printing the first five thousand copies almost completely drained their savings account. The book sold out within two weeks. By the spring of 1994 it was in its fourth printing and had sold almost seventy-five thousand copies. By century's end more than 2 million copies were in print, and it had spawned a series of national conferences, devotional guides, a play, a Grammy-nominated gospel album, and a movie, propelling Jakes to national prominence almost overnight.[63] In 1997, twenty-two thousand women attended his annual "Woman, Thou Art Loosed!" conference in Tampa. Two years later he set an attendance record at the Georgia Dome in Atlanta of eighty-four thousand participants, breaking Billy Graham's 1994 record of seventy-eight thousand.[64] Jakes got a huge boost when he signed a seven-figure book deal with Putnam Publishing Group, a division of the world's second-largest publisher, Penguin Putnam. His influence was compared to that of Martin Luther King Jr. and Billy Graham as his books were marketed successfully to both religious and secular audiences. By 2001 he had published at least twenty books—ten of which were Christian best-sellers—and his public relations firm noted that he was Penguin Putnam's third-best-selling author (behind Tom Clancy and Patricia Cornwall).[65] Shayne Lee notes, however, that Jakes used ghostwriters for many of his books, a common practice among independent evangelists. Leonard Lovett, a well-known Pentecostal theologian and author, served as one of Jakes's ghostwriters: "I ghostwrote the third book, *Water in the Wilderness*. It took me about a week sitting up in my apartment there to really write the thing and another guy took it, went over my stuff, and we passed it on to the head of Pneuma [publishing company], and Jakes consented. That's how we ended up doing two or three of his other books." Jakes later required his ghostwriters and assistants to sign a waiver preventing them from discussing the work they did for him.[66] Book sales and conferences, however, were not the only measures of Jakes's success.

In the 1990s Jakes launched a weekly television show and a nationally syndicated radio program and moved his ministry to Dallas. In 1993 he began his weekly television broadcast, *Get Ready with T. D. Jakes,* on TBN and BET. He received his big break on TBN after the network's founder, Paul Crouch, heard Jakes speak at Carlton Pearson's Azusa Revival and offered him airtime on the prominent religious network. Jakes's visibility increased dramatically.[67] In 1994, according to ministry reports, he established T. D. Jakes Ministries, a nonprofit organization, to produce his conferences and television ministry. The following year he began a short-lived nationally syndicated radio program called *Get Ready*. In 1996 Jakes made one of the most important moves of his career by relocating his ministry to Dallas.[68]

Jakes had indicated in 1994 that he was not interested in moving to a major metropolitan area. He told *Charisma* that a megachurch in Washington, D.C., had offered him a pastorate in 1991, but he chose to stay close to his modest roots in West Virginia. In 1995 the local media began to scrutinize Jakes's ministry more closely. In April the *Charleston Gazette* ran a front-page story about Jakes's success and the opulent lifestyle his newfound wealth afforded him. In July he and Serita bought a seven-bedroom mansion replete with tennis courts, an indoor swimming pool, and a bowling alley for $630,000. They also bought a four-bedroom, three-bathroom house on the adjacent property for $240,000. Readers deluged the newspaper with letters criticizing the attention it gave to Jakes's lifestyle and prosperity message. One letter to the editor in May 1995 defended Jakes: "I wish all these people calling in would leave the Bishop T. D. Jakes alone. He's a good man. He's helped me. If you send him enough money, he can save your soul also." Another reader, R. A. Clise, suggested that Jakes was being singled out because he was a successful black preacher: "What is the hoopla over Bishop Jakes? Is it now a 'big deal' that his success is evident to the public because he is a minister, because he is black, or both?" Not all of the responses to the *Gazette*'s article favored Jakes, however. An unidentified reader wrote on April 14, 1995: "With all the controversy over Bishop Jakes, I think someone should look at his past practices with Jakes Contracting Services. As a former employee, I find this man not to be an upstanding member of the community and wonder how in the world people can be swayed in such a way." *Gazette* reporter Lawrence Messina criticized Jakes and his brother Ernest for trying to evict a family from their home after they bought their property, which had been seized and sold by the Internal Revenue Service to collect money for back taxes. The family had inherited the property and the existing tax debt, and they claimed to be unable to pay off the debt. Ernest argued that they were within their legal right to evict the current residents: "We're not out of line. It's just normal business, just business. We buy and sell real estate all the time. It's not anybody taking advantage of anybody." After more than a year of such attacks, Jakes decided to move his ministry to Dallas.[69]

In 1996 Jakes bought healing evangelist W. V. Grant's Eagle's Nest Family Church in the Oak Cliff area of South Dallas for $3.2 million. The property, according to published reports, had been assessed at $30 million, but Grant was unable to make the mortgage payments. That summer Jakes moved fifty families associated with the ministry to the twenty-eight-acre facility, which was dubbed the Potter's House.[70] The first Sunday he opened for membership, a reported fifteen hundred people joined his new church. Within a year, he claimed, ten thousand members were meeting in the five-thousand-seat facility. "I came here fully expecting to go through the long road of building from the grass roots," he told *Ebony*.[71] The rapid growth surprised him, as did the challenges of ministering to an impoverished inner-city clientele. A few local pastors resented his overnight success, thinking they would lose members to the newcomer, but according to *Charisma*, most of Jakes's colleagues welcomed him to the community and supported his work in Oak Cliff. There was also some speculation about Jakes mixing his faith with politics, but he never seemed interested in entering the political arena as a candidate.[72]

At century's end Jakes had one of the nation's fastest-growing megachurches. By 1998 the Potter's House church claimed two hundred employees and sixteen thousand members. Four years later it claimed nearly thirty thousand members and had built a multimillion-dollar facility capable of seating eight thousand.[73] According to the ministry's website, the main sanctuary was larger than two football fields and used state-of-the-art technology. Two hundred pew seats at the front of the auditorium were equipped with power and data terminals so the audience could download the speaker's computer presentations. It claimed to be one of the first churches in the country to install a large-venue touring concert sound system. Jakes also installed the latest digital audio and video production equipment in the facility and made extensive use of the internet to promote his ministry and proclaim his message. "I think as we go into the 21st century, you have to incorporate every vehicle of modern technology to become an expression of healing and restoration for people in need," he remarked in 2001.[74] His dynamic personality, use of modern technology, and compassionate message all contributed to Jakes's success.

As his nonprofit and for-profit programs sought to boost a struggling local economy, Jakes also wanted the Potter's House to become an effective social institution in the Dallas area. Although he continued to promote racial and ethnic diversity, his Texas ministry appealed mainly to African Americans. In 2003 he claimed his congregation was 77 percent black, 13 percent white, and 7 percent Hispanic, with the remaining 3 percent coming from seventeen different nationalities. He preferred not to use the term "black church," but he recognized the unique characteristics that made black congregations distinctive. "The church has always been a central place of meeting and focal point for our culture," he noted. "Even how we see our ministers tends to be a little bit different because many of the great heroes of the African American community have come out of the church."[75]

Jakes planned not only to be a role model to other African Americans but also to make the Potter's House "a full-service, user-friendly church that is very similar to a mall in concept in that it's one-stop shopping. You can go there and find counseling, motivation, inspiration, [and] entertainment. You can go there and find everything." His message of economic empowerment appealed to blacks in South Dallas. Through his entrepreneurial efforts he hoped to teach people how to build their own institutions and stop the flow of money leaving Oak Cliff for goods and services elsewhere. Through his nonprofit and for-profit ventures he sought to teach people— especially African Americans—that faith in God must be coupled with hard work, ingenuity, and an entrepreneurial spirit.[76] One of his associates contended, "We are firm believers that those who have the wealth aren't going to give it up. We have to develop our own wealth."[77] In 1998 Jakes launched his City of Refuge, a two-hundred-acre rehabilitation and education center in South Dallas. He planned to add a youth center, senior citizens home, mall, and grocery store while continuing to offer traditional social programs such as literacy tutoring, youth mentoring, domestic-violence counseling, and AIDS outreach.[78]

One successful outreach program the Potter's House offered was a mentoring program run by Serita Jakes. Lamenting the decline of femininity in modern culture, she started a debutante program that encouraged traditional womanliness, social grace, chastity, spirituality, and emotional development in teenage girls. "I noticed that the femininity my parents instilled in me was beginning to go into baggy jeans and T-shirts," she explained to *Charisma*'s Valerie G. Lowe. "It seems like a laceless generation."[79] Serita also directed the human resources department at the Potter's House, and through her speaking engagements she taught wives how to support their husbands' ministries.[80]

Shortly after establishing himself as a prominent national religious figure, Jakes took his message of emotional healing to men—especially black men. His first "ManPower" conference was held in Detroit in 1993 and reportedly attracted two thousand men. The following year attendance more than tripled, and by 1995, *Charisma* reported, he was attracting as many as twenty thousand men to these conferences.[81] In 2002 Jakes claimed that "ManPower" had 250 paid staff and 550 volunteers who worked to make the conference a success for the twenty-three thousand attendees.[82] At these conferences Jakes promoted black male empowerment and encouraged men to develop godly character. He considered the conferences "a religious locker room chat time for the boys."[83] Jakes wanted the world "to understand that not all our men are strung out on crack, wife-beaters or child-molesters. Women," he said, "get ready to be loved, cared for and treated fairly. There's a new breed of men coming up."[84] By 2005 he had combined all of his major crusades—"Woman, Thou Art Loosed!" "ManPower," "Mega Youth Experience," and "Megakidz"—into one huge event he called "Megafest," which was held in Atlanta's Georgia Dome, World Congress Center, Phillips Arena, and International Plaza.[85]

Jakes offered hope for the hurting and downtrodden, and he made it clear that "Christianity is not the white man's religion." He maintained that black men could overcome their problems of poverty, crime, and discrimination by being God-centered, hardworking citizens. His message of economic empowerment resonated with African Americans as he encouraged them to develop an entrepreneurial spirit.[86] "I think we're facing more economic issues than we've ever faced before," he told the *Dallas Morning News.* "We're no longer fighting over where we ride on the bus. We want to own the bus, and that solves the seating problem. . . . You just buy the bus and you sit anywhere you want to."[87] But he also criticized whites for not doing enough to help minorities realize the American dream of financial independence. Much of his criticism centered on an unfair justice system that, he believed, kept black men in an endless cycle of crime and poverty. He tried to correct this situation by starting a national prison ministry.[88]

In 2000, *Time* magazine recognized Jakes as "one of America's most influential new religious leaders." Many observers called him a black Billy Graham for the new millennium.[89] Vinson Synan told journalist David Van Biema that Graham and Jakes were the only evangelists who could fill the Georgia Dome, but he noted that Jakes did it without the benefit of fifty years of fame.[90] Jakes downplayed the comparisons to Graham and Martin Luther King Jr.: "I don't think God is in the business of duplicating people," he told CNN. "I think he makes one designer original, and then he breaks every mold. My goal is not to be Dr. Graham or Dr. King or anyone else. My goal is to be the best T. D. Jakes I can possibly be."[91] His charismatic personality, engaging preaching style, and empowering message gave him a broad appeal. While reaching out to African Americans and addressing their needs, he emphasized racial and ethnic harmony. He overcame poverty and became a successful minister, author, television personality, and cultural icon who befriended famous athletes and lived an unapologetically lavish lifestyle. He believed he deserved the physical comforts he earned, and through his ministry he tried to teach others how to pull themselves out of poverty and despair through faith in God and hard work.

Jakes also represents the quintessential religious entrepreneur. Biographer Shayne Lee contends that "Jakes generates many followers and critics because he personifies American ideals and postmodern features that resonate with a diversity of psychosocial needs and cultural tastes." He "saturates the [religious] marketplace with an incessant flow of images and products" that appealed to a large segment of the American population who were searching for a therapeutic, self-help message that mainline churches were not offering. Jakes's emphasis on emotional healing and the prosperity message resonated with a generation of postmodern Christians who sought immediate answers for the emotional and financial problems they faced. His critics argued that he compromised the true message of the gospel by "matching Christianity with the existential cravings of contemporary Americans," but Jakes instinctively understood what people wanted from religion, and he successfully marketed his spiritual wares to a receptive audience.[92]

Creflo Dollar

Creflo Dollar also preached a self-help gospel and encouraged an entrepreneurial spirit among his followers. He was firmly rooted in the Word of Faith theology, and although he never claimed to target a particular audience, his prosperity message resonated with upwardly mobile African Americans. Born and raised a Methodist in the Atlanta suburb of College Park, according to ministry reports, Dollar was converted to Pentecostalism as a teenager. He dreamed of pursuing a career as a professional athlete, but those dreams were dashed when he sustained a career-ending injury at West Georgia College in the early 1980s. Discouraged and disappointed, he began to give serious consideration to one day becoming a minister.[93]

Dollar later reported that he and his roommate, Ken Terry, began a weekly Bible study called World Changers Bible Study. They started in their dorm room with just a few people, but by the time Dollar graduated about three hundred students were attending the study each week.[94] After college he reportedly served as a high school history teacher in the Fulton County, Georgia, school system and as an educational therapist for the Brawner Psychiatric Institute of Atlanta.[95] He never received formal ministerial training: "I never went to seminary," he boasted. "I learned everything I know through *knee-ology*. That's where you get on your knees and let God teach you." He was proud of the fact that he learned his lessons through the hard-knocks "school of life" and that his work ethic and ability to withstand criticism allowed him to succeed where many people failed.[96]

Like many other evangelists, Dollar remembered the difficulties of the early years—allegedly living on government-surplus food and being, in his words, "neck-deep in debt."[97] He called them the "silent years": "Those are the years where your character is developed. That's when . . . you're the only person who shows up for Bible Study, and you preach to empty chairs." He had a dream for his ministry, but he lacked the tools to realize that dream until he immersed himself in the teachings of Kenneth Hagin, Kenneth Copeland, and Oral Roberts. He learned from these men how to organize his ministry and broaden his appeal.[98] His close associates knew him as a tireless worker: "Not many people know this," admitted one of his longtime employees, Cynthia T. Walker, "but in the earlier years Pastor Dollar literally did everything himself. He played the piano, led praise and worship, did the announcements and preached all in one service."[99] His commitment to the ministry, his willingness to overcome adversity, and his charismatic personality eventually led to professional success and financial gain.

According to ministry reports, Dollar held the first service of World Changers Church International (WCCI) in an elementary school cafeteria on February 7, 1986, with eight people in attendance. He hoped the congregation would grow to five hundred within a couple of weeks, but it took almost three years to reach that goal and move into a permanent facility. It grew quickly thereafter, expanding to four Sunday services by 1990. In early 1991 Dollar found himself at a spiritual and professional crossroads, not knowing what direction he should take his ministry next. He believed his church should not only minister to his south Atlanta community but touch the rest of the world as well. He broke ground on a $17 million World Dome in the fall of 1991, gradually paying for it as he acquired the cash.[100] It was not an easy project, as neighborhood groups and the county government often opposed the church's expansion. He discovered that as he became more successful, the criticism of his ministry and resistance to his church's growth increased. The church's neighbors claimed that traffic congestion, parking problems, and flooding accompanied the expansion.[101]

Dollar finally moved into the eighty-five-hundred-seat structure on December 24, 1995. He had by then gained some notoriety in the charismatic world, and his church and ministry grew at a phenomenal rate. Giants in the charismatic revival, such as Roberts, Copeland, and Price, noted Dollar's influence and heaped praise on the up-and-coming evangelist. In 2001

Roberts remarked, "Creflo and Taffi Dollar are just now reaching their stride . . . in bringing God's renewal to the Body of Christ and this unsaved generation." Copeland recognized Dollar's role in spreading the charismatic movement to African Americans. He claimed that shortly after Martin Luther King Jr. was assassinated God told him: "I am going to raise up a black man who will bring more souls into the Kingdom of God than any before him, both black and white and all other groups alike." Several black evangelists carried out that "prophecy," and Dollar was an important figure among them.[102] Dollar considered Copeland his spiritual father and acknowledged the Texas evangelist's influence on his ministry.[103] "Without a doubt, Kenneth Copeland's teachings on the Anointing and how it 're-moves burdens and destroys yokes,' has made a profound impact on my life and ministry in every way imaginable."[104]

One of Dollar's most important local outreach programs was Project Change International. Founded in 1996, Project Change developed a phone counseling team, a food-distribution center, anti-drug campaigns, and mentoring programs for low-income families, and it promoted local economic development. According to its first director, Tommie Garner, "Project Change is a ministry God called forth to bring change to Atlanta, the nation, and the world. . . . The way to restore communities is to restore families. The way to restore families is one individual at a time." By 1999 it boasted more than sixty programs that promoted innovation, creativity, and an entrepreneurial spirit.[105] But this local outreach was only one part of the equation. Dollar used Creflo Dollar Ministries (CDM), established in 1990, to promote his global vision for evangelizing the world and building his own empire.

CDM was the outreach arm of Dollar's ministry that scheduled his conventions and meetings, supervised his partners program, and sold his books, tapes, and other promotional products. It was also responsible for his overseas ministry. Dollar held his first international crusade in London in 1990; CDM opened its first international office in 1996 in the United Kingdom; by 2001 it reported having offices in Australia, South Africa, and Canada, which were small operations that maintained close contact with the home office in Atlanta. Dollar held his first U.S. crusade in 1990 as well, but the early meetings were small. As his popularity grew, he bought a small Cessna airplane to expedite his travel; within just a few years, according to CDM, he purchased a Gulfstream Lear Jet. By the turn of the century his conventions were reportedly drawing crowds of three thousand to fifteen thousand, depending on the region and venue.[106]

Like most other evangelists, Dollar used radio and television to promote his ministry. He began a local radio broadcast in 1986 on two Atlanta stations, but his television show, *Changing Your World*, was most successful.[107] He started a local program in 1990, and within ten years he claimed to be on more than 150 television stations in the United States, 8 cable and satellite networks, and 36 international stations. The television program cost a reported $2–3 million a month to produce, which was funded by regular partner donations.[108]

Dollar also had several for-profit business ventures that contributed to his success. One of these was the record label Arrow Records, which his wife, Taffi, began in 1998. Taffi earned a degree in Mental Health and Human Services from Georgia State University and met her future husband at a Bible study on the campus of West Georgia College. CDM staff noted that she was initially very shy and reserved, often shunning the attention cast on her family. Like other spouses of famous evangelists, she preferred to remain behind the scenes as an administrator, supporter, and mother. Aside from being president and CEO of Arrow Records, she was also executive director of World Changers Ministries, supervisor of WCCI's Women's Fellowship, co-pastor of their church, and, in the late 1990s, a speaker at conferences and on their broadcasts.[109] She took a public role in the ministry, which typified the changing nature of the evangelist's wife at the turn of the century. Many wives became equal partners in their husbands' ministries and often became celebrities in their own right. But this celebrity status came at a price to the Dollar family.

In 1999 and 2000 Creflo Dollar was involved in two separate scandals that garnered considerable public attention. One involved the divorce of boxing great Evander Holyfield, who was a member of Dollar's church; another involved money given to officers of the South Fulton Police Department by WCCI. In August 1999 a Fayette County judge ruled that Dollar must be deposed in the divorce case of Holyfield and his estranged wife, Dr. Janice Holyfield. Dr. Holyfield's attorney, John Mayoue, estimated that his client's estranged husband had given $7 million to Dollar and his ministry during the couple's marriage. He believed that nearly $4 million had been donated during the sixty days prior to Holyfield's filing for divorce from his wife on March 26, 1999, with $3 million of that total being given five days before the filing. The judge ordered Dollar to provide financial information to Mayoue regarding Holyfield's donations to help the attorney assess how much of the boxer's earnings Dr. Holyfield should receive. Dollar refused to divulge the information, citing issues involving separation of church and state, pastor-parishioner confidentiality, and his religious objections to divorce. The judge found Dollar in contempt and ordered his arrest when he failed to attend a scheduled deposition in December. Dollar's attorney filed an appeal with the Georgia Supreme Court, which was dismissed on a technicality, and another warrant was issued for Dollar's arrest. In March 2000 the Holyfields agreed to settle their divorce out of court, thereby releasing Dollar from the judge's order. This incident produced unwanted publicity for Dollar at the same time another controversy was swirling about him.[110]

In November 1999 Dollar gave one hundred police officers a thousand dollars each at an appreciation breakfast held at his church. He claimed the money was given as a gesture of appreciation for the officers' service to the community, but critics charged that the gifts were improper and might be viewed as creating a "conflict of interest." The Fulton County ethics commission agreed when it ruled that the gifts broke the county's code of ethics and ordered the officers to return the money. Some of Dollar's detractors claimed that the gifts were given in response to traffic citations Dollar had received a month earlier, which contained fines totaling $150. Dollar questioned the wisdom of handing out thousand-dollar gifts for a $150 fine, but he publicly apologized for the action, acknowledging that it might be misconstrued by some people. Aside from these incidents, most of the controversies surrounding Dollar involved criticism of his prosperity theology.[111]

Dollar's message appealed to many evangelicals because it fit nicely into their upwardly mobile worldview. Much of Dollar's success lay in his ability to apply Hagin's Word of Faith message to the issues that seemed most important to his audience. As African Americans continued moving into the middle classes in the 1980s and 1990s, Dollar focused on prosperity, family values, and developing an entrepreneurial spirit that promised personal success. At the beginning of the new millennium he was poised to become one of the most influential leaders in the charismatic movement in general and the Word of Faith camp in particular.

Conclusion

None of the ministers discussed in this chapter relied solely on itinerant evangelism for their support; instead, they established churches and parachurch institutions that provided the stability necessary for perpetuating their ministries. Many clearly embraced the theological and political conservatism of modern white evangelicalism, but they all promoted, in one way or another, social justice and racial equality. These men created for themselves religious empires and encouraged self-reliance among young, up-wardly mobile black professionals as well as among the emotionally scarred, debt-ridden members of society who sought comfort in their promise of hope for the hurting. These shrewd businessmen placed the interests of their religious empires first and were undeterred by the theologians, jour-nalists, and others who criticized their eagerness to sacrifice the traditional gospel message of meekness and humility for the message of personal ful-fillment and self-actualization.

In 1990 *Charisma* heralded the rise of the "New Black Charismatics," and throughout the decade it touted the accomplishments of independent evangelists, Church of God in Christ leaders, and neo-Pentecostals. *Charisma* journalist Paul Thigpen identified six common characteristics of the new breed of charismatic leaders and churches. First, they preached some variation of Hagin's Word of Faith message. Second, their churches or min-istries were established after 1980 and experienced rapid growth, usher-ing in the age of the modern megachurch. Third, most adherents of these churches were young adults in their twenties and thirties. Fourth, their con-gregations were predominantly black but tended to have a multicultural or multiracial emphasis. Fifth, husbands and wives generally functioned as co-pastors, each having considerable official responsibility for maintaining their congregations. And sixth, the new leaders were relatively young men and women whose teaching focused on practical issues and whose wor-ship styles drew "from contemporary musical sources."[112] These qualities not only characterized Price, Jakes, and Dollar but also described a host of black pastors and evangelists who made their mark on the independent charismatic movement.

5

Politics and Prosperity

In 2002, Atlanta pastor and evangelist Eddie Long told an audience of twenty-three thousand black men that their generation had to become more aggressive than previous generations in fighting racism in America. "Your masculinity was robbed from you because you were locked up and tamed" by society, he charged. "We're still doing the same things our daddies did and trying to get success out of it. . . . Now is the time to break the curse of racism" and take control of the businesses, political institutions, and social institutions that had long been dominated by whites.[1] This message of empowerment resonated with his upwardly mobile, mostly black audience. They not only wanted a caring, compassionate pastor who offered hope for a better life in the hereafter; they also wanted a pastor who would give them the practical skills and encouragement necessary to succeed in life. In that respect, Eddie Long fit the mold of the new black charismatic minister.

In addition to Fred Price, T. D. Jakes, and Creflo Dollar, lesser-known black ministers established themselves as religious entrepreneurs who sought to satisfy the social and economic needs of African Americans. Nearly all of these men pastored large churches, conducted evangelistic crusades, sponsored radio and television programs, and produced promotional literature. They taught Hagin's Word of Faith theology, encouraged African Americans to start their own businesses, and generally engaged in some sort of social or civic activism. Nearly all of them were politically and socially conservative, which represented a slight change in the political climate among African Americans. Although most black voters remained faithful to the Democratic Party, many were not comfortable with that party's position on certain social issues, such as homosexuality and abortion. This allowed some of these evangelists to woo some black voters to the political right.

The 1970s and 1980s marked a general decline of black mainline churches and the growth of charismatic and neo-Pentecostal churches. Anthony Pinn observes how the emergence of radical black groups in the 1960s, the splintering of the civil rights movement's leadership, and the rise of the black middle class contributed to a growing sense that, for many African Americans, the church had become irrelevant. As they achieved an unprecedented level of freedom and economic success in the 1950s and 1960s, many became less interested in promoting black advancement for all and more interested in self-promotion. Cornel West noted that "the message was clear: beneath the rhetoric of Black Power, and black control and black self-determination was a budding, 'New,' black, middle class hungry for power and starving for status."[2]

By the late 1980s and early 1990s, many middle-class blacks had experienced the spiritual emptiness of financial success, the continued difficulties of latent racism, and "a cultural uncertainty" of what it meant to be black. They longed for the stability and sense of community that religious institutions provided. One "restored" Christian commented on the trauma that many middle-class blacks had faced: "We've had bad marriages, we've had bad careers, and, personally it was a relational thing for me. I thought for a long time I was master of my universe, but then you find you need something real. Something authentic through the church, through your own personal relationship with God."[3] Independent charismatic ministries were not only in a position to fulfill the physical needs of poor blacks but also offered the emotional healing and social connections that many people wanted.[4] As middle-class African Americans returned to church, they were able to provide much of the financial support that allowed these large ministries to reach out to poor blacks. Just as their mainline counterparts had done years earlier, this new generation of black Christians sought to address the social and economic concerns of African Americans.

Keith Butler

Detroit native Keith Butler was one of Kenneth Hagin's most loyal and successful protégés. He emphasized the prosperity message, promoted black entrepreneurialism, established lasting institutions, and was reportedly one of the first black Republicans to participate in Detroit politics. *Charisma* magazine and ministry publications reported that Butler was raised a Baptist but converted to Pentecostalism as a teenager and attended Anderson Memorial Church of God in Christ in downtown Detroit. In May 1978 he and his wife, Deborah, graduated from Hagin's Rhema Bible Training

Center (RBTC) and returned home to establish the Word of Faith International Christian Center (WOFICC). Butler recalled that only a handful of people attended the first Sunday service in January 1979; over the next twenty years, however, he built a thriving ministry, replete with satellite churches, a Christian school, television and radio programs, Bible training centers, outreach ministries, and a twenty-thousand-member congregation. In its first fifteen years, WOFICC met in eight different locations, quickly outgrowing each one. In 1995 it reportedly had over ten thousand members, and Butler was looking for property to accommodate his expanding empire. In the summer of 1996 he claimed to have paid just over $9 million for a 110-acre facility that had been a Duns Scotus friary in the Detroit suburb of Southfield. The existing structures nicely accommodated his ministry programs, and in 1997 he began building a five-thousand-seat sanctuary for his church.[5]

Butler's first daily radio program, *The Word of Faith,* aired on a local Christian station in 1979; his first weekly television broadcast was shown locally two years later. Butler expanded his broadcast ministry—and his influence—in 1994 when he started the *Living Word* television and radio programs. Within a year, his ministry magazine noted, *Living Word* was seen in Michigan, Georgia, Pennsylvania, Mississippi, Jamaica, and England. Although Butler did not dominate the airwaves like Price, Jakes, and Dollar, by century's end his program was seen on several local stations, three domestic networks, and two international networks.[6] His increased national exposure also allowed him to establish satellite churches in Pennsylvania, Georgia, Mississippi, Florida, Arizona, and Michigan. By 2002 his ministry boasted fourteen Word of Faith International Christian Centers in the United States and one in the U.S. Virgin Islands.[7]

Butler was also active in foreign missions. In 1995 he helped Marilyn Hickey conduct an evangelistic crusade in Pakistan. They held a ministry training school for twelve hundred pastors and Christian workers during the day and claimed to have had crowds of up to twenty thousand for the evangelistic meetings at night. By 1997 he supervised or financially supported more than fifteen churches in Pakistan, sixty in Africa, and several in the Caribbean.[8]

Butler followed a growth pattern similar to that of his mentor, Kenneth Hagin. Although he was never a traveling evangelist, Butler established lasting institutions that ensured his influence on the charismatic movement. His Word of Faith Bible Training Center and Layperson's Bible School provided doctrinal and practical instruction for ministers and Christian workers. Unlike Hagin's RBTC, these were not accredited institutions and did not offer formal degrees.[9] In 1993 he began holding the Living Word Convention and Ministers' Conference, which featured established and up-and-coming charismatic preachers such as Marilyn Hickey, Buddy Harrison, Jerry Savelle, Creflo Dollar, and R. W. Schambach.[10] Two years later he formed the Word of Faith International Ministerial Association, which sought to provide fellowship, inspiration, instruction, wisdom, and advice to its members. The ministry's magazine reported that the association began with nearly a hundred members but grew to more than six hundred by 1997.[11] In 1996 he started the Christian Business Association, later called the Kingdom Business Association, to help business owners and aspiring entrepreneurs develop their business skills.[12] The entrepreneurial spirit that dominated the leadership of the charismatic movement manifested itself in organizations like this in nearly every modern ministry.

At the turn of the century Butler's ministry was becoming denominational in nature, and as his institutions grew and solidified, his stature increased within the charismatic movement. His influence in Detroit flourished in the late 1980s and early 1990s as well. Butler believed that conservative Christian moral principles should be an integral part of public policy, and he worked hard to instill those principles in the public sphere. As leader of the Detroit Coalition for Academic Excellence he fought to keep family planning services, such as contraceptive distribution and abortion referrals, out of Detroit's school-based health clinics in 1987. His success on this issue allowed his coalition to continue its fight to influence the policies of Detroit's public school system. He promoted education as a means for social mobility and criticized public educators for "making it difficult for minorities, underclass and middle-class America to get to college and pay for it. . . . The best way out of poverty," he insists, "is still a great education."[13]

Butler took his civic activism a step further when he ran for public office, and in 1989 he became the first black Republican elected to the Detroit City Council since before World War II. *Charisma* reporter Steve Beard noted in 1992: "While most Americans are familiar with the liberal views espoused by black personalities like Jesse Jackson, . . . the recent Supreme Court confirmation of Clarence Thomas brought to the forefront many new faces and ideas within the black community. . . . Side by side with pastors from around the nation, Butler rallied popular black support for Thomas to thwart the efforts of the civil rights establishment." Criticizing the dependency and lack of incentive that he believed was fostered by the modern American welfare system, Butler called for a return "to self-help and the Judeo-Christian work ethic" among African Americans. "I hope to make the world a better place through my work as a pastor and as a public servant," he said. "I want to minister the gospel of Jesus Christ and win the lost. But I also want to work within the political process to ensure that Judeo-Christian values are installed in the public policy and public life of this nation." He believed that black charismatic churches could be agents of social change in American society, replacing the influence of more liberal mainline churches: "These charismatic churches believe that the old attitudes, as well as most of the liberal social agenda, have destroyed our community. We can no longer just stand by and let it happen. We have to get out and do something about it."[14]

In 2005, when the forty-nine-year-old Butler announced his candidacy for the U.S. Senate, he echoed to *Charisma* the same rhetoric that political and social conservatives across the nation were espousing. "I had to take a very hard look at these United States, which was founded on the principles of religious freedom," Butler said. "But now liberal judges are rendering extinct any form of religious expression." Some political pundits placed his candidacy in the context of a political revolution. Butler was one of four black candidates for either senator or governor in 2006, who, if they won their respective races, could "break the Democrats' near monopoly on black voters, remaking the American political landscape." Most pundits rejected the idea that those elections were as important as Butler believed them to be, since black Republican candidates historically did not translate into black Republican votes. But those pundits also noted that simply "fielding so many competitive [black] candidates represents a Republican revolution." The Republican Party was making better efforts to include black candidates, and those candidates appealed to the social conservatism of African Americans, wooing some voters to the GOP. Butler's conservative agenda resonated with parishioners and voters alike, and he exemplified the kind of conservative social action promoted by other black charismatics.[15]

Butler's wife and their three children all supported his social and political activism and participated in his ministry. Their two oldest children, Keith II and Michelle, graduated from RBTC and returned to serve as ministers on the WOFICC staff. Deborah Butler, an ordained minister, provided managerial and administrative support, directed their women's ministry, was a gifted public speaker, and regularly contributed articles to the ministry's magazines.[16] Like her husband, she spoke out on social issues and encouraged women to be bold in their Christian witness and not be inhibited by traditional social mores about female meekness. "Being a women [*sic*] does not subordinate your status as a believer, a follower of Jesus Christ, or as a person," she contended in June 1987. A decade later she argued that women should use their freedom in Christ to assert themselves in society: "Now ladies, you know in order to dominate, we have to stand in the preeminent position Christ has given us." Echoing Daisy Osborn and other ministers, she promoted sexual equality and empowerment among conservative evangelical women.[17]

Keith Butler's legacy lay mainly in his role as a leader in the Word of Faith movement and as a politician. He advanced the prosperity message, and his continued support of the Hagins through the controversies of the 1990s endeared him to many of the "faith camp" faithful. He also established churches and created institutions that perpetuated his ministry and made him an important figure in the evangelical world. His social activism and political conservatism resonated with many in the burgeoning black middle class. Although African Americans generally remained loyal to the Democratic Party, Butler's success as a Republican politician indicated a sea change in the political sensibilities of black voters and in the willingness of whites to vote for a black candidate.

Carlton Pearson

Tulsa evangelist and pastor Carlton Pearson was mentored by Oral Roberts in the early 1970s and had close ties to Hagin and the Word of Faith movement. Autobiographical accounts note that Pearson was born in San Diego in 1953 and raised in the Church of God in Christ, where he was first mentored by COGIC bishop J. A. Blake. The first in his family to attend college, he entered Oral Roberts University in the fall of 1971 and was immediately tapped by Roberts to join the ORU World Action Singers. This opportunity not only paid for his college but allowed Pearson to learn a great deal from this renowned healing evangelist. Pearson and Roberts's son Richard became a successful singing duo in the early 1970s and traveled together extensively, promoting the charismatic revival.[18] *Charisma* reported that Pearson started the Souls A' Fire choir at ORU, which he hoped would be a racially mixed group with an African American flavor. "But ORU didn't want that," he told the charismatic publication in 1999. "They told me, 'We want a black choir singing black songs. We want you to march in and do your black thing.' . . . They wanted to let everybody know they had black students at the school."[19] This was important to Roberts's ministry because it highlighted the interracial nature of the charismatic movement and helped promote a progressive image at the fledgling school. It also helped to encourage black Pentecostals and charismatics to attend ORU. Many of the predominantly white Pentecostal denominations had colleges that catered to their churches, but the historically black denominations—like COGIC—did not have liberal arts schools where they could send their children. Roberts wanted to show the world that his ministry and university were colorblind, and Carlton Pearson was instrumental in promoting that image. Pearson graduated from ORU in 1975 and went to work for the Oral Roberts Evangelistic Association, touring with Richard, appearing on Oral's television show, and working with the ministry's correspondence program. In 1977 he decided to pursue a career as an independent evangelist, establishing Higher Dimensions Ministries.[20]

Charisma reported that Pearson's ministry team struggled at first: six months after its formation all but one of the team's members quit. But Pearson persisted, and between 1977 and 1981 he traveled widely, even leading the first racially integrated ministry to tour apartheid-ridden South Africa. In the early 1980s he recognized that the future of the charismatic revival lay not in the work of "superstar evangelists" but in the stability that churches and parachurch institutions provided. On August 31, 1981, he and his white college roommate, Gary McIntosh, started Higher Dimensions Evangelistic Center, a racially mixed church in the Tulsa suburb of Jenks.[21] Pearson recalled that the first storefront meeting had seventy-five people in attendance but that they were soon tearing out walls to accommodate the more than five hundred congregants who streamed into this interracial church. Dogged by lack of funds and qualified personnel, Pearson continued to work as a traveling evangelist while McIntosh carried on the work of sustaining a local church. The congregation continued to grow, and by the mid-1980s it was a popular place for ORU students and many Tulsa residents.[22]

Pearson's emphasis on racial and spiritual unity was also evident in the annual Azusa conference that he began in 1988. It was named for the Azusa Street revival in Los Angeles, which featured interracial services and helped spread Pentecostalism throughout the world. Pearson wanted to capture the spirit of unity and equality that he believed characterized the early Pentecostal movement. He maintained that later charismatic renewal occurred more slowly among black Christians because they were too busy trying to liberate themselves from white oppression and create a place for themselves in American society. In 1987 he told *Bridge Builder* magazine: "Blacks have been trying to establish themselves—getting a decent home, a car, money in the bank, education, building a church"—and they simply did not have the time or energy to focus on spiritual unity and renewal.[23] Pearson said he started the Azusa conference to "give blacks a point of identification with the broader charismatic movement" and to expose them to the resources that whites had long enjoyed.[24] That conference eventually formed the basis for the Azusa Fellowship, a network Pearson oversaw that claimed more than six hundred churches and pastors.[25]

The Azusa conference also helped promote charismatic evangelists such as T. D. Jakes and Joyce Meyer who were starting to gain national prominence in the early 1990s. Shayne Lee, in his biography of T. D. Jakes, analyzes Pearson's influence on the charismatic movement through the Azusa Revival and Azusa Fellowship. Lee contends that "Pearson's high visibility and contacts" with important charismatic and Pentecostal power brokers such as Oral Roberts, Paul Crouch, and *Charisma* founder and publisher Stephen Strang allowed him to serve as a bridge between established white charismatic leaders and emerging black charismatic and neo-Pentecostal leaders.[26] The training Pearson received from white leaders such as Oral Roberts allowed him to cross racial boundaries easily and promote cooperation within the charismatic community. But his ministry experienced considerable controversy. At the turn of the twenty-first century he was criticized for teaching a doctrine that many considered heretical.

Pearson promoted a Christian message that was, in essence, tolerant of non-Christian belief systems. His "Gospel of Inclusion" maintained that Jesus's death reconciled all humans to God and that everyone would be saved except "those who, in their heart, intentionally and consciously reject the grace of God."[27] In 1999 this teaching split the Higher Dimensions Evangelistic Center and isolated Pearson from many of his co-religionists. In 2005 he claimed that he had lost 90 percent of his five-thousand-member church and that it was in foreclosure. He resigned from ORU's board of regents, and Oral and Richard Roberts, along with board president Marilyn Hickey and other evangelical leaders, distanced themselves from him. "They've cut me off completely," he told the *Atlanta Journal-Constitution* in a 2005 interview. "People I've gotten out of jail have abandoned me. People who I've written $1,000 checks to keep their ministry going have dropped me." He even claimed that none of his former preaching friends called him when he was diagnosed with prostate cancer. T. D. Jakes flatly rejected the Gospel of Inclusion and told *Charisma* that he considered Pearson's views heretical: "While I do consider Carlton Pearson to be a friend, I believe his theology is wrong, false, misleading and an incorrect interpretation of the Bible."[28]

This controversy may also have hurt Pearson's chances of being elected mayor of Tulsa. Pearson speculated that he lost the Republican primary in February 2002 because many Tulsans "weren't sure that they should risk putting somebody like me in office."[29] His annual Azusa conference, which, according to *Charisma*, typically averaged between seventy-five hundred and ten thousand attendees each night, never got above forty-five hundred in 2002. He admitted that his teaching hurt his church and reputation, but he was unapologetic for his emphasis on tolerance and believed that his ministry would eventually rebound. This recovery never materialized. Pearson was marginalized by other charismatics, and he never regained the influence he once had as a bridge between the white charismatic power brokers and emerging black leaders within the movement.[30] He continued to pastor his church, oversee the Azusa Interdenominational Fellowship of Christian Churches and Ministries, and promote tolerance, unity, and diversity through his music and evangelistic crusades, but he was never again a major figure among evangelical or charismatic leaders. His significance lies in the fact that he was an early example of the influence that men like Oral Roberts had on important black leaders in the modern charismatic movement. He began his career as a singer and broadened his ministry to promote racial and theological unity. Becoming an extraordinary power broker in his own right, he brought together the old guard of white charismatic leaders and the female and African American evangelists who were emerging stars in the charismatic movement.

Eddie Long

Eddie Long, pastor of New Birth Missionary Baptist Church in Atlanta, followed a path similar to that of T. D. Jakes. The son of a Baptist minister and businessman, Long was born and raised in Charlotte, North Carolina, at the height of the civil rights movement. Published reports assert that he developed a strong sense of social justice and an entrepreneurial spirit, which made him a controversial figure among African Americans and allowed him to build one of the largest megachurches in Atlanta. He was a self-described "nerd" whose high school guidance counselor allegedly told him he was too dumb to go to college. Long received a bachelor's degree in business administration from North Carolina Central University in 1976 and soon joined the Ford Motor Company as a sales representative. Despite his initial success, Ford reportedly fired him for claiming personal expenses on his business account; in 1979 he found himself unemployed in Richmond, Virginia. Making an obvious connection to a parable recorded in the Bible, Long recalled that he worked for a short time making pig feed before joining the Honeywell corporation, where he remained until 1987. That year he was asked to pastor the three-hundred-member New Birth Missionary Baptist Church.[31]

Charisma reported that the congregation quickly grew to two thousand members as Long reached out to young black men and women in his community. "Long's candor has been a recipe for success," the evangelical publication crowed in 1999. "He isn't afraid to talk about the days when he was almost homeless, when his marriage failed, when some Christian leaders told him God would never use a divorced man in ministry."[32] By 1994 New Birth boasted eleven thousand members and was considered the fastest-growing church in the South, reportedly gaining three hundred new members each month.[33] Published reports note that the church moved from a 500-seat chapel to a $3.7 million, 3,700-seat sanctuary in 1991. Long received a $3 million business loan to purchase 170 acres near Atlanta's Hartsfield International Airport, which, within a year, sold for a reported $14 million. Long retired all the church's debt and bought 240 acres in Conyers, a suburb east of Atlanta. At the turn of the century he had completed a 10,500-seat, $45 million complex for the church and, according to the *Atlanta Journal-Constitution*, had settled into an exclusive residential neighborhood where the median price for homes was $325,000. Long claimed to have a staff of nearly one hundred, an annual budget of $20 million, and a church membership of twenty-five thousand. Early on he had little media exposure, relying on his members to tell their friends about his congregation. Long's success, much like that of his contemporaries Creflo Dollar and T. D. Jakes, lay partly in his desire to reach out to the surrounding community. He offered ministries for teenagers, young men, single women, the homeless, prisoners, and drug addicts.[34]

Although Long's outreach programs were directed toward poor or at-risk African Americans, his church membership was composed largely of young black professionals. They admired Long for his message of love and acceptance, his entrepreneurial spirit and success, and his emphasis on the charismatic experience within black Baptist churches. "We need to be able to explain what [the charismatic experience] is about," he told *Charisma* journalist Marcia Ford in 1994. "Once people have been enlightened, they often find that it's like a breath of fresh air." In an effort to encourage Baptist leaders to promote "gifts of the spirit" in their churches, he helped establish the Full Gospel Baptist Church Fellowship.[35]

Long's supporters also appreciated his strong sense of social justice, which did not fit the traditional mold of liberal black preachers and did not always sit well with black political leaders. Long claimed to be neither Democrat nor Republican, but his political and theological sensibilities were clearly conservative. In 1999 the president of Atlanta's Concerned Black Clergy, a civil rights organization, compared him to a black Jerry Falwell because of his refusal to support most marches and demonstrations for racial equality.[36] Long, on the other hand, believed his mission as a black minister was to create a new paradigm for Christian social justice and to reform American society according to biblical standards, which meant, in part, creating a God-centered public education system. His church provided financial support to local schools, and he was invited to speak at Southwest DeKalb High School after one student fatally shot another student in 1997. After preaching a sermon to the student body, which included an altar call and was described by one observer as an all-out religious revival, the Georgia American Civil Liberties Union complained that his speech violated the separation of church and state.[37] Long unapologetically argued that education was "the key to correcting the national moral decline" and called for a return to the Christian principles upon which, he believed, American education was founded, even recommending that the Ten Commandments be displayed in public schools across the country.[38]

Long also sparked controversy in 2004 when he organized and led a protest march in downtown Atlanta that advocated education reform, healthcare reform, economic reform, and a controversial constitutional amendment opposing gay marriage. He was accompanied by Dr. Martin Luther King Jr.'s youngest daughter, Bernice King, who was an elder at Long's church and who, according to the *Atlanta Journal-Constitution,* opposed her mother, Coretta Scott King, on the issue of same-sex marriage. Although Long claimed not to speak for Dr. King on the issue of gay marriage, he began his march near King's gravesite, clearly linking his own cause with the civil rights movement. Civil rights activist and congressman John Lewis charged that Long and King were misrepresenting the slain civil rights leader's message of love and acceptance. "If Dr. King were here today, he wouldn't participate in this march," Lewis intoned. "During the civil rights movement, we were trying to take discrimination out of the Constitution." Critics also claimed that Long and other conservative African American religious leaders were trying to get federal funding for their faith-based initiatives. "If you look at the black pastors who've come out with the faith-based money," charged Timothy McDonald, head of the African-American Ministers' Leadership Conference, "they're the same ones who have come out with campaigns on the gay marriage issue." Furthermore, Long's critics contended that Long was being used by white political conservatives to tap into black megachurches for potential voters. Nevertheless, Long held fast to his conservative views. His approach to correcting social ills was often more in line with the views of white conservatives—and those of Keith Butler—than with those of traditional black liberals.[39]

Long defied stereotypes, and his rhetoric was at times militant. He argued that his generation of black men had to become more aggressive in fighting racism in America, and his message of empowerment resonated with his upwardly mobile African American audience. They wanted a caring, compassionate pastor who provided badly needed social services and hope for the future, and a mentor who would give them the practical skills and encouragement necessary to succeed in a postmodern, post–civil rights world. In that respect, Eddie Long fit the mold of the new black charismatic minister. His effort to combine an emphasis on racial equality and social justice with modern conservative rhetoric resonated with many young black Americans. Long also faced considerable opposition for his support of a constitutional amendment banning gay marriage and for his anti-gay stance. His critics charged him with blurring the lines between church and state, suggesting that he favored a theocracy in which conservative evangelical religious principles would be codified into civil law. And he was criticized for promoting the prosperity gospel so popular among many charismatics and evangelicals.

The Prosperity Message

Despite the calls for racial equality and social justice, Hagin's prosperity message remained the centerpiece of many of these ministries. The pioneers of the charismatic movement—particularly Katherine Kuhlman, Oral Roberts, and Kenneth Hagin—fostered an openness and ecumenism almost unprecedented in the holiness/Pentecostal tradition. They not only reached out to the disinherited but also welcomed into their fold people from a wide array of socioeconomic and theological positions. The prosperity message that later came to dominate the movement was used by rich and poor alike to justify one's social standing or to provide the promise for a better life in the future.

This teaching was abused by some ministers and denounced by a host of critics, both from within the charismatic movement and from without. In the 1970s, according to David Harrell, the New York City–based African American pastor and evangelist Frederick J. Eikerenkoetter II ("Reverend Ike") was one of the first to threaten the integrity of the charismatic movement with his "unabashed love of money and other material things."[40] Reverend Ike gained a substantial following through his church, television and radio programs, and *Action!* magazine. He offered his disciples tips for how to make more money and keep it, taught that the lack of money—not the love of money—was the root of all evil, and routinely dropped people from his mailing list if they fell behind on their contributions to his ministry. Although most late-twentieth-century evangelists did not publicly credit Reverend Ike for inspiring them to adopt the prosperity message, some privately admitted that he had a significant impact on the spread of the controversial teaching.[41]

The prosperity message received limited attention outside charismatic and Pentecostal circles until the late 1980s when some high-profile televangelists, such as Jim Bakker and Jimmy Swaggart, were engulfed in scandal. Their lavish lifestyles and questionable conduct became the focus of media scrutiny, and for many Americans they became the face of modern evangelicalism. Mainstream evangelicals struggled to distance themselves from these "false prophets" and their message promoting conspicuous consumption and instant gratification. In 1990 theologian Michael Horton compiled a theological critique of the prosperity message. "The world sees televangelists as the spokesmen for the evangelical movement," he noted. "It does not distinguish between those who preach the gospel 'once for all given to the saints' and those who preach a fraudulent gospel. So when the world examines televangelism . . . and concludes that televangelism is materialistic, exploitative, [and] power-hungry . . . it condemns the whole evangelical movement . . . not just fraudulent televangelists."[42] Horton and his co-religionists sought to dispel the notion that these charismatic televangelists represented the entire evangelical subculture.

Critic Art Lindsley charged proponents of the prosperity message with advancing "quick, easy solutions to complex problems. They tend to reduce the Christian life to knowing the right technique or formula, or following the prescribed steps to achieve prosperity. Thus, the Christian life is reduced to methods of success rather than to the gradual, life-long, and painful task of forming character."[43] Furthermore, they accused these ministers of placing too much emphasis on personal experiences and not enough on biblical certainty or the widely accepted standards for biblical interpretation. The result, they claimed, was a market-oriented message where ministers based their success on the size of their audiences and the income generated through their ministries. The evangelical media critic Quentin Schultze stated: "Televangelists easily slip into a marketing mentality that adjusts the message to the hopes and dreams of the audience. This would not be a problem except for the selfish desires of the viewers. What *are* the hopes and dreams of unbelievers? Health, wealth, and happiness? So give it to them! TV leads to market-driven gospels, not to the historic gospel of salvation from sin."[44]

While many evangelicals sought to discredit the prosperity gospel, others carried it further into the evangelical mainstream. Sociologist Milmon Harrison notes that the success of Bruce Wilkinson's *The Prayer of Jabez* (Multnomah Publishers, 2000) among mainline evangelicals "shows how the worldview so characteristic of the Word of Faith Movement has come to resonate among contemporary Christians even outside the movement." Wilkinson contends that, by praying the one-sentence prayer of an obscure Old Testament figure who asked God for material gain, modern Christians can receive similar financial blessings. Critics, Harrison contends, view this as evidence "of the commercialization and self-centered materialism of contemporary evangelical Christianity."[45]

In the 1990s, Word of Faith preacher Leroy Thompson carried the prosperity message to new heights. Ministry reports noted that he began as a small-town Baptist preacher from Darrow, Louisiana, and was exposed to the teachings of Fred Price and Kenneth Hagin in the early 1980s. In 1984 he changed the name of his 104-year-old Mt. Zion Baptist Church to the Word of Life Christian Center and began promoting the "gifts of the spirit." Over the next fifteen years his church reportedly grew from seventy-five members to more than seventeen hundred, and he became a popular speaker within the Word of Faith movement. Price mentored him from 1983 through 1986 and introduced him to Hagin. Thompson first spoke at Hagin's Campmeeting in 1993 and was a featured speaker at the popular summer event the following year.[46] At the turn of the century he kept a full speaking schedule and had developed close working relationships with other successful ministers, such as Carlton Pearson, Creflo Dollar, and Kenneth Copeland.[47]

Although many Word of Faith ministers tried to have well-rounded ministries emphasizing prosperity, healing, social justice, and healthy family relationships, Thompson made the prosperity message the cornerstone of his ministry. He criticized the notion that sickness and poverty were marks of holiness. "We have begun to understand that God wants our bodies well—healed and whole," Thompson stated in one of his most popular books, *Money, Thou Art Loosed!* "But I think we have taken hold of the healing message better than we've taken hold of the prosperity aspect of our redemption. Yet healing and prosperity are part of the same package, so to speak."[48] He enthusiastically defended the right of preachers to be wealthy and live comfortably. When Christians make generous financial contributions to pastors and evangelists, they would receive financial blessings in return. "When you put God first, He will honor and bless you. In other words, when your church is blessed and your pastor has plenty of money in his pocket (without your being critical or concerned about it), then you are in a position for God to give you your increase. Folks need to release the mentality that the preacher is supposed to be broke. . . . [T]he higher your pastor goes in finances, the higher you can go too."[49] He unabashedly promoted a health-and-wealth gospel whereby Christians could justify maintaining a lavish lifestyle as long as they supported their preachers and used their money to promote evangelism.[50]

Neo-Pentecostalism

The popularity of the charismatic movement also led to the growth of neo-Pentecostalism among mainline African American denominations. In large part, this phenomenon developed in tandem with the rise of independent black evangelists from the 1970s through the 1990s. In the late 1960s and early 1970s, John R. Bryant, considered the father of the neo-Pentecostal movement among blacks, combined his belief in the charismata with the popular emphasis on black pride at his African Methodist Episcopal (AME) Church. Holding a master's degree from Boston University and, at the time, pursuing a doctorate at Harvard, the pastor "began teaching his young, intellectual congregation that Pentecostalism was a reintegration of their cultural roots, and that the Holy Spirit could liberate and empower them." Before long, Bryant's church reportedly grew from several hundred to several thousand members, and, witnessing his success, other denominational churches began to adopt Pentecostal beliefs and worship styles.[51]

In 1981, John A. Cherry and his wife, Diana, started the Full Gospel AME Zion Church in Temple Hills, Maryland, with twenty-four members. Fifteen years later they reportedly had seventeen thousand members and sixty ministries and were adding two hundred people to their rolls each month. By the turn of the century the burgeoning neo-Pentecostal movement had affected several black Baptist and Methodist denominations, including the National Baptist Convention USA, the AME Church, and the AME Zion Church. Scholars quickly recognized the movement's impact on black churches. Sociologist Lawrence H. Mamiya and religion expert Robert M. Franklin highlighted neo-Pentecostalism's dual emphasis on social activism and spiritual development as reasons for its broad appeal to the black middle class. Mamiya even predicted that by 2050 "half of all black Christians will have embraced some form of Pentecostalism."[52]

Conclusion

The renewed emphasis on spirituality, social responsibility, and expressive worship styles among mainline African American Christians helped to bolster the charismatic and neo-Pentecostal movements among blacks. Independent evangelists had fertile fields for cultivating their brand of Christianity and continuing their move toward the center of evangelical Protestantism in the twenty-first century. Their message resonated with a new generation of African Americans who could not readily identify with traditional black churches and their leaders. The men and women who flocked to these ministers and churches wanted to take a different path in achieving equality and finding fulfillment in their spiritual lives. The new breed of black charismatic ministers understood this and were able to articulate a message that young upwardly mobile black Americans found palatable. These developments among African Americans were part of a broader trend in the expansion of the charismatic movement, which had become an important force in American society at the turn of the twenty-first century.

These ministers also played key roles in spreading the prosperity gospel to mainline evangelicals. Theologians and sociologists have been critical of the consumer-oriented, materialistic flavor of American Christianity, and the evangelists examined here have been some of the primary proponents of that doctrine. Their huge megachurches, far-reaching television ministries, and popular books and conferences served to spread that message to millions of Americans of all racial, ethnic, and socioeconomic backgrounds. The acceptance of these ideas is a testament to the evangelists' ability to successfully market their wares to a receptive audience.

Conclusion

In 1977 Oral Roberts predicted that the "next great outpouring of the Holy Spirit, and the mighty healing power of God, is to be upon black people."[1] He was not the only person to make that prediction, nor was he the only evangelist who worked to bring it to fruition. But while Roberts, Kenneth Hagin, Asa Allen, and other white evangelists might have provided the spark for the charismatic revival among African Americans, they were not responsible for fanning that flame into a raging fire. Fred Price, T. D. Jakes, Creflo Dollar, and other black ministers were the key figures in the modern charismatic movement at the end of the twentieth century. On the heals of the civil rights movement, they discovered that many African Americans were receptive to their message and able to support their ministries. Likewise, Aimee Semple McPherson, Kathryn Kuhlman, Daisy Osborn, and other women laid the foundation for a generation of female evangelists to establish ministries that equaled—and sometimes surpassed—those of their male counterparts. Those evangelists capitalized on the new opportunities the feminist movement had made available to women. "They are real bitches," Daisy Osborn concluded about modern feminists in 1991. "And they've been out there bitchin'! . . . But then *we* can come in and take the benefit."[2] A new breed of religious entrepreneurs emerged in the late twentieth century who took the messages of racial and sexual equality, economic empowerment, and self-actualization to audiences that were ready to receive and internalize them. The civil rights and feminist movements, a generally healthy U.S. economy combined with greater opportunities for upward mobility, and a cultural emphasis on self-help and positive thinking laid the groundwork for a generation of conservative Christians to seek and accept the ideas that these independent charismatic evangelists proclaimed. Likewise, these evangelists astutely recognized the cultural transformations taking place in American society and shaped their message and ministries to appeal to this new generation of seekers.

Cultural alienation was part of the Pentecostal experience from its inception. Pentecostals and charismatics nearly always considered themselves different from the rest of the world, and that feeling of separation shaped their worldview. "No twentieth century pentecostal totally escaped a feeling of rejection," notes David Harrell in *All Things Are Possible,* and the more radical healing evangelists' "sense of rejection and persecution seemed clearly linked with the insecurity of their early lives."[3] As charismatics moved into the mainstream of American society, those feelings of rejection waned but never disappeared. Nearly all the evangelists in this study emphasized the hardships they endured and their ability to overcome those difficulties. Many experienced poverty or abuse, came from broken homes, or had some physical or learning disability. Their rags-to-riches stories, which highlighted their ability to overcome seemingly insurmountable odds, appealed to their sometimes downtrodden but nearly always upwardly mobile audiences. Many African Americans were not too far removed from the ghettos in which they were raised, and they continued to confront latent racism and the bitterness it evoked. Women of all social, economic, racial, and ethnic backgrounds came to terms with abusive fathers or husbands and with feelings of inadequacy and rejection. Charismatic evangelists offered their audiences hope for economic empowerment, emotional healing, and physical and spiritual renewal. They also encouraged racial and sexual equality among conservative evangelicals and provided role models for women and African Americans to follow.

Daisy Osborn, Freda Lindsay, and Gloria Copeland bridged the gap between the female evangelical pioneers and the independent evangelists who emerged in the late twentieth century. They carved out spaces for themselves within their husbands' ministries and proved successful in subtly challenging the sexual mores of their day. While championing the egalitarian companionate model of the modern marriage, they also exemplified the "superwoman" ideal by maintaining their households, attending to the administrative needs of their husbands' ministries, and gradually accepting more public roles within those ministries. Marilyn Hickey, Joyce Meyer, Lindsay Roberts, and others further advanced the notion of sexual freedom among charismatics by establishing their own evangelistic associations or taking even larger roles in their husbands' ministries. They used Roberts's ministry-building techniques and Hagin's prosperity message to advance their own careers, just as their male counterparts did.

The ambivalence these women expressed about moving into public ministry both reflected and reinforced the views of their conservative constituencies. Although many evangelical women—especially younger ones—had been influenced by and sympathized with modern notions of sexual equality being advanced in secular society, they remained uncertain about how much those ideas should be promoted in their churches. They knew that the patriarchal leadership in many of those churches, denominations, and parachurch organizations would be resistant to any change in the status quo. Keenly aware of the need to challenge that status quo without alienating the women they hoped to reach, the independent evangelists examined here marketed their liberal ideas through conservative rhetoric and emphasized the traditional doctrine of female submission to male authority.

The "new black charismatics" not only promoted racial equality in the post–civil rights era but also advanced a growing entrepreneurial spirit among African Americans. Black charismatic evangelists were among the most recognizable figures in modern evangelicalism, even rivaling the popularity of Christian icons such as Billy Graham and Martin Luther King Jr. For many conservative black Christians, these ministers served alongside sports figures such as Michael Jordan and Tiger Woods as role models for future black leaders. By exemplifying and promoting an entrepreneurial spirit that many upwardly mobile African Americans were adopting in the late twentieth century, they encouraged economic development in black communities. Their espousal of politically, socially, and theologically conservative views placed them within the mainstream of American evangelicalism and drew the ire of traditional black leaders.

The emphases on emotional healing and financial prosperity proved to be the most distinctive features of the modern charismatic movement. Joyce Meyer and T. D. Jakes struck a delicate nerve with evangelical women when they burst onto the national scene in 1993 with their teaching about emotional healing. Through hundreds of books, magazine articles, videotapes, and audiotapes available on the subject, Meyer and Jakes skillfully crafted their message and method to reach a vast audience of women who were searching for respite from their emotional wounds. Although they acknowledged—and sometimes encouraged—ecstatic experiences at their meetings, emphasizing the charismata was never a central part of their teaching. This allowed them to appeal to a broader, non-charismatic audience and helped them to become important figures in the larger evangelical subculture.[4]

In 1975 David Harrell noted the growing importance of the prosperity message, which "almost supplanted the earlier emphasis on healing" and "often came across like crass materialism."[5] But black ministers quickly recognized that this message resonated with upwardly mobile, middle-class African Americans. In his study of the Word of Faith movement among African Americans, sociologist Milmon F. Harrison highlights the long tradition of black churches catering to "the material, social, political, and spiritual needs of their followers."[6] Black ministers such as Father Divine and "Sweet Daddy" Grace established urban ministries that attracted poor and dispossessed African Americans with the promise of a better life in the here and now, not just in the "sweet by-and-by." Furthermore, Harrison argues that Reverend Ike and Johnnie Colemon, a black female minister who founded the Universal Foundation for Better Living, were responsible for introducing African Americans to the New Thought metaphysical principles that undergirded the modern Word of Faith movement.[7] Although black churches and ministers have always promoted economic development among African Americans, the social conditions of post–civil rights America gave new impetus to the idea that black Americans could achieve the same level of financial success and stability that white Americans could. Modern charismatic evangelists latched on to that idea and successfully promoted it among African Americans.

This book has identified some of the important figures in the most recent phase of charismatic revival in the United States and has shown how and why these ministers became so significant. They were able to take theologically, socially, and politically liberal ideas from social movements such as the civil rights and feminist movements and repackage them so they appealed to a conservative audience. Each of these evangelists catered to a niche market, but they did not become so narrowly focused that they lost their broad appeal among evangelicals in general and charismatics in particular. Their emphasis on emotional healing and prosperity resonated with a generation of Americans who suffered from abuse and depression and who, after years of being economically disadvantaged, felt that they, too, deserved to enjoy the American dream. This new phase in the charismatic revival proved to be the beginning of a new day for many Americans, and they intended to take full advantage of the opportunities laid before them.

Notes

Introduction

1. Peter W. Williams, *America's Religions: From Their Origins to the Twenty-first Century* (1990; Urbana: University of Illinois Press, 2002), 343.

2. Robert Mapes Anderson, *Vision of the Disinherited: The Making of American Pentecostalism* (New York: Oxford University Press, 1979).

3. Anthony F. C. Wallace, *Religion: An Anthropological View* (New York: Random House, 1966).

4. Roger Finke and Rodney Stark, *The Churching of America, 1776–1990* (New Brunswick, N.J.: Rutgers University Press, 1992). For brief critiques of *The Churching of America*, see the following book reviews: Laurence R. Iannaccone, *Contemporary Sociology* 22 (September 1993): 653–54; George M. Marsden, *Church History* 62 (September 1993): 449–51; Edwin S. Gaustad, *Journal of Religion* 73 (October 1993): 640–42; Wade Clark Roof, *Social Forces* 72 (December 1993): 597–98; Kent Redding, *American Journal of Sociology* 99 (January 1994): 1130–32; Jon Butler, *American Historical Review* 99 (February 1994): 288–89; Joel A. Carpenter, *Journal of American History* 80 (March 1994): 1448–49.

5. R. G. Robins, *A. J. Tomlinson: Plainfolk Modernist* (New York: Oxford University Press, 2004), 21–24. Robins bases his work on the models advanced by Thomas Bender, *Community and Social Change in America* (New Brunswick, N.J.: Rutgers University Press, 1978); R. Stephen Warner, "Work in Progress toward a New Paradigm for the Sociological Study of Religion in the United States," *American Journal of Sociology* 98 (March 1993): 1044–93; and Rodney Stark and Laurence R. Iannaccone, "A Supply-Side Reinterpretation of the 'Secularization' of Europe," *Journal for the Scientific Study of Religion* 33 (September 1994): 230–52.

6. Shayne Lee, *T. D. Jakes: America's New Preacher* (New York: New York University Press, 2005), 182.

7. George Marsden, ed., *Evangelicalism and Modern America* (Grand Rapids, Mich.: Eerdmans, 1984), vii–xvi; Randall Balmer, *Mine Eyes Have Seen the Glory: A Journey into*

the Evangelical Subculture in America, expanded ed. (New York: Oxford University Press, 1993), xiii–xvi.

8. Marsden, *Evangelicalism and Modern America,* vii–xvi; Balmer, *Mine Eyes Have Seen the Glory,* xiii–xvi; William Martin, *With God on Our Side: The Rise of the Religious Right in America,* rev. ed. (New York: Broadway Books, 2005), 10–23.

9. Matthew A. Sutton, "'Between the Refrigerator and the Wildfire': Aimee Semple McPherson, Pentecostalism, and the Fundamentalist-Modernist Controversy," *Church History* 72 (March 2003): 160–63.

10. Ibid., 162–63.

11. Balmer, *Mine Eyes Have Seen the Glory,* 133.

12. Quoted in W. Martin, *With God on Our Side,* 212.

13. Ibid., 210–14.

14. David Edwin Harrell Jr., *Pat Robertson: A Personal, Religious, and Political Portrait* (San Francisco: Harper and Row, 1987), 114.

15. Ibid., 117.

16. Ibid., 124–25.

17. Ibid., 131. Although charismatics and other evangelicals began to cooperate more in the 1970s and 1980s, that cooperation did not always translate into a unified political bloc. Using polling data from Pat Robertson's failed bid to win the Republican nomination in the 1988 presidential election, William Martin contends that Robertson had a strong base of support among Pentecostals and charismatics but had little support among other Republicans and evangelicals. Most evangelicals—especially Southern Baptists—were not comfortable with his charismatic theology, his belief in glossolalia and divine healing, and his "penchant for interpreting international developments in the light of biblical prophecy." But Martin also asserts that Robertson's defeat did not mean the demise of the Religious Right. Many observers believed that his candidacy would only push conservative evangelicals further into the political mainstream, and they would become an important political and social force in American society. *With God on Our Side,* 295–98.

18. David Edwin Harrell Jr., *White Sects and Black Men in the Recent South* (Nashville: Vanderbilt University Press, 1971), 92.

19. Ibid., 131.

20. See Leonard I. Sweet, ed., *Communication and Change in American Religious History* (Grand Rapids, Mich.: Eerdmans, 1993), for a collection of essays addressing this topic.

21. Denise Hawkins, "Shoutin' It from the Housetops," *Charisma,* June 1995, 22–29.

22. Anthony B. Pinn, *The Black Church in the Post–Civil Rights Era* (Maryknoll, N.Y.: Orbis Books, 2002), 135.

23. Ibid., 137–38.

24. Harvie M. Conn, *The American City and the Evangelical Church: A Historical Overview* (Grand Rapids, Mich.: Baker Books, 1994), 191.

25. Richard Kyle, *The Religious Fringe: A History of Alternative Religions in America* (Downers Grove, Ill.: InterVarsity Press, 1993), 328.

26. Scott Thumma, "Exploring the Megachurch Phenomena: Their Characteristics and Cultural Context," http://hirr.hartsem.edu/bookshelf/thumma_article2.html (accessed June 3, 2003).

27. Ibid. See also E. S. Caldwell, "Trend toward Mega Churches," *Charisma*, August 1985, 31, 35–36, 38.

28. Adrienne S. Gaines, "Revive Us, Precious Lord," *Charisma*, May 2003, 37–44.

Chapter 1

1. Vinson Synan, ed., *The Century of the Holy Spirit: One Hundred Years of Pentecostal and Charismatic Renewal, 1901–2001* (Nashville: Thomas Nelson, 2001), 1; Vinson Synan, *The Holiness-Pentecostal Tradition: Charismatic Movements in the Twentieth Century*, 2nd ed. (1971; Grand Rapids, Mich.: Eerdmans, 1997), 89–92; Williams, *America's Religions*, 277–80.

2. Williams, *America's Religions*, 269–74; Synan, *The Holiness-Pentecostal Tradition*; Synan, *The Century of the Holy Spirit*, 15–37; David Edwin Harrell Jr., *All Things Are Possible: The Healing and Charismatic Revivals in Modern America* (Bloomington: Indiana University Press, 1975), 11.

3. Anderson, *Vision of the Disinherited*, 289.

4. Ibid., 289–90; Harrell, *All Things Are Possible*, 10–13.

5. Quoted in Robert Owens, "The Azusa Street Revival: The Pentecostal Movement Begins in America," in Synan, *The Century of the Holy Spirit*, 58–59.

6. Synan, *The Century of the Holy Spirit*, 4–5. Randall J. Stephens offers an excellent analysis of the use of periodicals in spreading Pentecostalism in its early years in "'There Is Magic in Print': The Holiness-Pentecostal Press and the Origins of Southern Pentecostalism," *Journal of Southern Religion* 5 (December 2002), available at http://jsr.as.wvu.edu/2002/Stephens.htm (accessed May 5, 2002).

7. Owens, "The Azusa Street Revival," 39–68. *Charisma* publisher and founder Stephen Strang and editor J. Lee Grady wrote numerous editorials, especially in the 1990s, highlighting the racial and sexual equality they believed existed in Pentecostalism's early years.

8. Vinson Synan, "The Holiness Pentecostal Churches," in Synan, *The Century of the Holy Spirit*, 99–107; Harrell, *White Sects and Black Men*, 41–43.

9. Vinson Synan, "The 'Finished Work' Pentecostal Churches," in Synan, *The Century of the Holy Spirit*, 141.

10. Ibid., 141–46. For a complete discussion of the doctrinal and racial issues that separated Pentecostals in the early years, see Synan, *The Holiness-Pentecostal Tradition*.

11. Religious historian David Edwin Harrell Jr. provides brief sketches of some of the more important early leaders in *All Things Are Possible*, 12–21; Grant Wacker and

James R. Goff Jr. have edited a collection of essays that provides a more complete account of these men and women, *Portraits of a Generation: Early Pentecostal Leaders* (Fayetteville: University of Arkansas Press, 2002).

12. Susan C. Hyatt, "Spirit-Filled Women," in Synan, *The Century of the Holy Spirit,* 234.

13. Ibid., 234–43; Synan, *The Holiness-Pentecostal Tradition,* 190–91; Harrell, *All Things Are Possible,* 15–16; Wayne E. Warner, *The Woman Evangelist: The Life and Times of Charismatic Evangelist Maria B. Woodworth-Etter* (Metuchen, N.J.: Scarecrow Press, 1986).

14. Synan, *The Century of the Holy Spirit,* 9–10; Hyatt, "Spirit-Filled Women," 248–51; Grant Wacker, *Heaven Below: Early Pentecostals and American Culture* (Cambridge: Harvard University Press, 2001), 32–34; Richard G. Peterson, "Electric Sisters," in *The God Pumpers: Religion in the Electronic Age,* ed. Marshall Fishwick and Ray B. Browne (Bowling Green, Ohio: Bowling Green State University Popular Press, 1987), 118–21.

15. Synan, "The 'Finished Work' Pentecostal Churches," 131–34; Edith L. Blumhofer, *Aimee Semple McPherson* (Grand Rapids, Mich.: Eerdmans, 1993), 141–43; Synan, *The Holiness-Pentecostal Tradition,* 200–202; Daniel Mark Epstein, *Sister Aimee: The Life of Aimee Semple McPherson* (New York: Harcourt Brace Jovanovich, 1993), 135–54.

16. Wacker, *Heaven Below,* 144–48; Harrell, *All Things Are Possible,* 16; Blumhofer, *Aimee Semple McPherson,* 145–47; C. Douglas Weaver, *The Healer-Prophet: William Marrion Branham, a Study of the Prophetic in American Pentecostalism* (1987; reprint, Macon, Ga.: Mercer University Press, 2000), 43; Epstein, *Sister Aimee,* 95, 154–73.

17. Blumhofer, *Aimee Semple McPherson,* 212–13.

18. Ibid., 202. Pentecostals typically focused on the apostles' use of glossolalia in Acts 2 when creating their Christian community, but McPherson used the passage in Hebrews to appeal to a broader audience that may not have accepted the Pentecostal tradition of glossolalia emphasized in Acts 2.

19. Blumhofer, *Aimee Semple McPherson,* 203.

20. Ibid., 205–6; Wacker, *Heaven Below,* 251–56, 260–62. David Harrell discusses the importance of dispensational premillennialism in Oral Roberts's ministry as well. See *Oral Roberts: An American Life* (Bloomington: Indiana University Press, 1985), 447–48.

21. Blumhofer, *Aimee Semple McPherson,* 155–56; Harvey Cox, *Fire from Heaven: The Rise of Pentecostal Spirituality and the Reshaping of Religion in the Twenty-first Century* (Reading, Mass.: Addison-Wesley, 1995), 128–34; Stephen J. Pullum, *"Foul Demons, Come Out!": The Rhetoric of Twentieth-Century American Faith Healing* (Westport, Conn.: Praeger, 1999), 152–53; Elaine J. Lawless, *God's Peculiar People: Women's Voices and Folk Tradition in a Pentecostal Church* (Lexington: University Press of Kentucky, 1988). In *Heaven Below,* church historian Grant Wacker notes that "early pentecostals assumed that their personal faith stories bore normative implications for others. Consequently they devoted much of the time in their worship services—maybe a third of the total—to public testimonies about their spiritual journeys." He describes a typical three-step

sequence: first, adherents "explained the problems that drove converts to seek a life-transforming spiritual experience in the first place"; second, they described their conversion experience; and third, they "elaborated the benefits received" (58).

22. Blumhofer, *Aimee Semple McPherson*, 213.

23. Epstein, *Sister Aimee*, 184–201; Blumhofer, *Aimee Semple McPherson*, 181–200.

24. Epstein, *Sister Aimee*, 85.

25. Blumhofer, *Aimee Semple McPherson*, 274–302; Epstein, *Sister Aimee*, 286–314; Stanley M. Burgess, ed., *The New International Dictionary of Pentecostal and Charismatic Movements*, rev. ed. (Grand Rapids, Mich.: Zondervan, 2002), s.v. "McPherson, Aimee Semple"; Synan, *The Holiness-Pentecostal Tradition*, 200–202; Synan, "The 'Finished Work' Pentecostal Churches," 134–36.

26. Weaver, *The Healer-Prophet*, 13–14; Aimee Semple McPherson, *The Foursquare Gospel* (Los Angeles: Echo Park Evangelistic Association, 1946), 22–23; Blumhofer, *Aimee Semple McPherson*, 232–80, 363–64; Epstein, *Sister Aimee*, 247.

27. Burgess, *New International Dictionary*, s.v. "McPherson, Aimee Semple"; Blumhofer, *Aimee Semple McPherson*, 236–41; Synan, "The 'Finished Work' Pentecostal Churches," 134–36; Epstein, *Sister Aimee*, 215–41.

28. Blumhofer, *Aimee Semple McPherson*, 242–43.

29. Burgess, *New International Dictionary*, s.v. "McPherson, Aimee Semple"; Blumhofer, *Aimee Semple McPherson*, 253–57.

30. Blumhofer, *Aimee Semple McPherson*, 268.

31. Burgess, *New International Dictionary*, s.v. "McPherson, Aimee Semple"; Hyatt, "Spirit-Filled Women," 259; Epstein, *Sister Aimee*, 263–66.

32. Blumhofer, *Aimee Semple McPherson*, 269–70; Epstein, *Sister Aimee*, 276–77.

33. Burgess, *New International Dictionary*, s.v. "McPherson, Aimee Semple"; Blumhofer, *Aimee Semple McPherson*, 344–50; Epstein, *Sister Aimee*, 369–71, 375–76; Synan, "The 'Finished Work' Pentecostal Churches," 134–36.

34. Burgess, *New International Dictionary*, s.v. "McPherson, Aimee Semple"; Blumhofer, *Aimee Semple McPherson*, 371–73, 383–85; Burgess, *New International Dictionary*, s.v. "McPherson, Rolf Kennedy"; Weaver, *The Healer-Prophet*, 167; Synan, *The Holiness-Pentecostal Tradition*, 200–202; Wacker, *Heaven Below*, 6, 77; Synan, "The 'Finished Work' Pentecostal Churches," 136–38.

35. Blumhofer, *Aimee Semple McPherson*, 18–20.

36. For a broader discussion of how fundamentalists used modern culture and mass media to espouse their views during the interwar period, see Douglas Carl Abrams, *Selling the Old-Time Religion: American Fundamentalists and Mass Culture, 1920–1940* (Athens: University of Georgia Press, 2001).

37. Cox, *Fire from Heaven*, 123–38.

38. David Edwin Harrell Jr., "Divine Healing in Modern American Protestantism," in *Other Healers: Unorthodox Medicine in America*, ed. Norman Gevitz (Baltimore: Johns Hopkins University Press, 1988), 215–17.

39. Ibid., 217–27, quote on 219.

40. David Barrett, "The Worldwide Holy Spirit Renewal," in Synan, *The Century of the Holy Spirit,* 388.

41. Synan, *The Holiness-Pentecostal Tradition,* 253–54.

42. Ibid., quote on 223–24; Harrell, *All Things Are Possible,* 135–49, 225–33.

43. For scholarly overviews of the charismatic movement see Synan, *The Holiness-Pentecostal Tradition;* Synan, *The Century of the Holy Spirit;* and Harrell, *All Things Are Possible.* For a typology of evangelical and charismatic thought see Harrell, *Pat Robertson,* 107–55.

44. Harrell, *Pat Robertson,* 70.

45. Ibid., 50–82; Ben Armstrong, "Trend toward Televangelism," *Charisma,* August 1985, 48–49, 51–52, 54; Hal Erickson, *Religious Radio and Television in the United States, 1921–1991: The Programs and Personalities* (Jefferson, N.C.: McFarland, 1992), 156–58; J. Gordon Melton, Phillip Charles Lucas, and Jon R. Stone, eds., *Prime-Time Religion: An Encyclopedia of Religious Broadcasting* (Phoenix: Oryx Press, 1997), 57–59; George H. Hill, *Airwaves to the Soul: The Influence and Growth of Religious Broadcasting in America* (Saratoga, Calif.: R & E Publishers, 1983), 37–38.

46. Dennis Roberts, "Trinity Broadcasting Network: The Dream Almost Didn't Happen," *Charisma,* June 1983, 18–24; Melton, Lucas, and Stone, *Prime-Time Religion,* 73–76, 355–58; Erickson, *Religious Radio and Television,* 188–89; Armstrong, "Trend toward Televangelism," 48–49, 51–52, 54; "Interview with Paul and Jan Crouch," *Charisma,* June 1983, 24–25, 88, 90; Ken Walker, "Twenty People Who Touched Our Lives," *Charisma,* August 1995, 37–41; J. Lee Grady, "Wired to Reach the World," *Charisma,* June 1998, 43–44, 46–48, 50; J. Lee Grady, "Answering TBN's Critics," *Charisma,* June 1998, 46–47; J. Lee Grady, "Jan Will Be Jan," *Charisma,* June 1998, 48.

47. Armstrong, "Trend toward Televangelism," 48–49, 51–52, 54; Melton, Lucas, and Stone, *Prime-Time Religion,* 50–51; Valerie G. Lowe, "Ministry Leaders Plan to Launch Black Christian TV Network," *Charisma,* December 1996, 29–30.

48. Harrell, *All Things Are Possible,* 41–45, quotes on 43. I have used *All Things Are Possible* as a template for sketching the life and ministry of Oral Roberts, but a much more complete account is found in Harrell's biography *Oral Roberts.*

49. Harrell, *All Things Are Possible,* 41–45; Harrell, *Oral Roberts,* 485–90; Oral Roberts, *Expect a Miracle: My Life and Ministry* (Nashville: Thomas Nelson, 1995), 142–43, 149–51.

50. Kenneth Copeland and Gloria Copeland, *The First Thirty Years: A Journey of Faith* (Fort Worth: Kenneth Copeland Publications, 1997), 63.

51. Quote in Harrell, *All Things Are Possible,* 46; Harrell, "Divine Healing," 220–22.

52. Harrell, *All Things Are Possible,* 47.

53. Ibid., 49; O. Roberts, *Expect a Miracle,* 122–26.

54. Harrell, *All Things Are Possible,* 45–49; O. Roberts, *Expect a Miracle,* 151–52.

55. Copeland and Copeland, *The First Thirty Years,* 169–70.

56. O. Roberts, *Expect a Miracle,* 126–27, 378–82.

57. Quote in Harrell, *Oral Roberts,* 462; Harrell, *All Things Are Possible,* 158; Harrell, "Divine Healing," 226.

58. Harrell, *All Things Are Possible,* 50.

59. Ibid., 49–52.

60. Harrell, *Oral Roberts,* 448–51.

61. Harrell, *All Things Are Possible,* 150.

62. O. Roberts, *Expect a Miracle,* 368–75.

63. Quote in Harrell, *All Things Are Possible,* 154; O. Roberts, *Expect a Miracle,* 158–63. Interestingly, fellow Tulsan Kenneth E. Hagin established Rhema Bible Training Center in 1973, which became an important training ground for charismatic evangelists and pastors.

64. Harrell, *Oral Roberts,* 452–60.

65. Harrell, *All Things Are Possible,* 154–55.

66. "Blacks Still Not Wanted at Many Christian Colleges," *Journal of Blacks in Higher Education* 17 (Autumn 1997): 81.

67. Harrell, *Oral Roberts,* 487.

68. O. Roberts, *Expect a Miracle,* 231–32.

69. Valerie G. Lowe, "Carlton Pearson Aims at Racial Unity," *Charisma,* March 1999, 40; David Hazard, "A Narrow Way and a Lonely Place," *Bridge Builder,* May–June 1988, 5–8; Carlton Pearson, *I've Got a Feelin' Everything's Gonna Be All Right* (Tulsa: Harrison House, 1992), n.p. For a brief discussion of racial themes in Roberts's ministry see Harrell, *Oral Roberts,* 446–47; and O. Roberts, *Expect a Miracle,* 136–38, 221–32.

70. Harrell, *All Things Are Possible,* 156.

71. O. Roberts, *Expect a Miracle,* 368–75; Ralph Carmichael, http://www.spaceagepop.com/carmicha.htm (accessed April 16, 2003).

72. Harrell, *Oral Roberts,* 439–40; O. Roberts, *Expect a Miracle,* 368–75.

73. Harrell, *Oral Roberts,* 439–46.

74. Wayne Warner, *Kathryn Kuhlman: The Woman behind the Miracles* (Ann Arbor: Servant Publications, 1993), 203–5; Hyatt, "Spirit-Filled Women," 257.

75. Vinson Synan, "The Pentecostal Century: An Overview," in Synan, *The Century of the Holy Spirit,* 9–10; Hyatt, "Spirit-Filled Women," 248–51; Wacker, *Heaven Below,* 32–34; Peterson, "Electric Sisters," 118–21.

76. W. Warner, *Kathryn Kuhlman,* 49–58; Jamie Buckingham, *Daughter of Destiny: Kathryn Kuhlman . . . Her Story* (Plainfield, N.J.: Logos International, 1976), 42–45.

77. W. Warner, *Kathryn Kuhlman,* 61–66, 68–72; Buckingham, *Daughter of Destiny,* 58, 72; Burgess, *New International Dictionary,* s.v. "Kuhlman, Katherine."

78. W. Warner, *Kathryn Kuhlman,* 81–99; Buckingham, *Daughter of Destiny,* 75–84, 112–13.

79. W. Warner, *Kathryn Kuhlman,* 81–99, 101–4, 108–11, 124; Buckingham, *Daughter of Destiny,* 75–84, 112–13; Stephen Strang, "Heroine of Healing," *Charisma,* July–August 1977, 35; Rebekah Scott, "The Legacy of Kathryn Kuhlman," *Charisma,* August 1995, 33;

Burgess, *New International Dictionary,* s.v. "Kuhlman, Katherine"; Stephen Strang, "A Gift of Healing," *Charisma,* October–November 1975, 6–9.

80. W. Warner, *Kathryn Kuhlman,* 113–19; Buckingham, *Daughter of Destiny,* 85–106.

81. W. Warner, *Kathryn Kuhlman,* 124–29; Buckingham, *Daughter of Destiny,* 68, 98.

82. W. Warner, *Kathryn Kuhlman,* 131–34; Buckingham, *Daughter of Destiny,* 98–106; S. Strang, "A Gift of Healing," 6–9; Scott, "The Legacy of Kathryn Kuhlman," 33; Burgess, *New International Dictionary,* s.v. "Kuhlman, Katherine."

83. W. Warner, *Kathryn Kuhlman,* 134–35, 137–41, 154–59; Buckingham, *Daughter of Destiny,* 63, 116; Roberts Liardon, *Kathryn Kuhlman: A Spiritual Biography of God's Miracle Working Power* (Tulsa: Harrison House, 1990), 43–44, 65–66; Burgess, *New International Dictionary,* s.v. "Kuhlman, Katherine"; Synan, "The Pentecostal Century," 10; David Edwin Harrell Jr., "Healers and Televangelists after World War II," in Synan, *The Century of the Holy Spirit,* 327; Harrell, *All Things Are Possible,* 136. Warner and Buckingham elaborate on the theological basis of Kuhlman's belief in divine healing and argue that she believed and practiced this doctrine consistently throughout her entire career.

84. W. Warner, *Kathryn Kuhlman,* 20–21, 159–60; S. Strang, "A Gift of Healing," 6–9. Physician William A. Nolen later refuted her claims of divine healing but nevertheless thought she was sincere in her belief in miracles. See his *Healing: A Doctor in Search of a Miracle* (Greenwich, Conn.: Fawcett, 1974).

85. W. Warner, *Kathryn Kuhlman,* 207–9; Liardon, *Kathryn Kuhlman,* 100; Buckingham, *Daughter of Destiny,* 193–209; S. Strang, "A Gift of Healing," 6–9; Scott, "The Legacy of Kathryn Kuhlman," 33; Burgess, *New International Dictionary,* s.v. "Kuhlman, Katherine"; Vinson Synan, "Streams of Renewal at the End of the Century," in Synan, *The Century of the Holy Spirit,* 363.

86. W. Warner, *Kathryn Kuhlman,* 193, 228; Buckingham, *Daughter of Destiny,* 206–9; Helen Kooiman Hosier, *Kathryn Kuhlman: The Life She Led, the Legacy She Left* (Old Tappan, N.J.: Fleming H. Revell, 1976), 103–8, 146–51; S. Strang, "A Gift of Healing," 6–9; "Kuhlman Foundation Closed," *Charisma,* December 1982, 18; Scott, "The Legacy of Kathryn Kuhlman," 33; Burgess, *New International Dictionary,* s.v. "Kuhlman, Katherine"; S. Strang, "Heroine of Healing," 35. Strang interviewed Kuhlman just ten months before her death and asked who would succeed her when she died. She curtly responded that Jesus would return before then and refused to discuss the matter further. Strang believed that she knew she was in poor health and simply ignored the reality of her impending death.

87. In the midst of her health crisis in the spring of 1975, Kuhlman hired a controversial personal administrator, Tulsa car salesman Dana "Tink" Wilkerson. He alienated Kuhlman from most of her close associates and ultimately profited from a mysterious rewriting of her will shortly before her death. Her original will stipulated that most of her estate would go into the Kathryn Kuhlman Foundation trust fund, which would perpetuate her ministry and provide for the well-being of five longtime employees. The new will, dated December 17, 1975, which left much of her estate to Wilkerson, was not

discovered by her close friends until two weeks after her death. See W. Warner, *Kathryn Kuhlman,* 231–33, 237–41, 281; Buckingham, *Daughter of Destiny,* 1–5, 277–92.

88. Harrell, *All Things Are Possible,* 66–75, 194–203; Pullum, *"Foul Demons, Come Out!"* 67–86.

89. Harrell, *All Things Are Possible,* 66–67; Pullum, *"Foul Demons, Come Out!"* 68–71; Melton, Lucas, and Stone, *Prime-Time Religion,* 1–4; Erickson, *Religious Radio and Television,* 21–23.

90. Harrell, *All Things Are Possible,* 67–75, quote on 68, 195–96; Pullum, *"Foul Demons, Come Out!"* 68–71; Melton, Lucas, and Stone, *Prime-Time Religion,* 1–4; Erickson, *Religious Radio and Television,* 21–23.

91. Pullum, *"Foul Demons, Come Out!"* 71–73, 84.

92. William Hedgepeth, "Brother A. A. Allen on the Gospel Trail: He Feels, He Heals, and He Turns You On with God," *Look,* October 7, 1969, 29.

93. Harrell, *All Things Are Possible,* quote on 99, 201–2.

94. A. A. Allen, "Are You in Bondage?" *Miracle Magazine,* September 1958, 28.

95. A. A. Allen, "How God Feels about Segregation," *Miracle Magazine,* May 1963, 8–9. Allen typically did not draw much attention to the integrated nature of his ministry. Aside from a few comments to reporters, a handful of articles in *Miracle Magazine,* and a special "integration issue" of his magazine in September 1969, he wrote little about racism. The fact that his integrated revivals and baptismal services were so widely accepted suggests that racial equality was simply commonplace in his ministry.

96. Harrell, *All Things Are Possible,* 98–99, quote on 198, 201–2; "Men and Women Used by God: Gene Martin," http://www.iahm-europe.org/html/men_women/gene_martin/default.html (accessed April 26, 2003); David Davis, "The Dawn of a New Day in Gospel Music," *Miracle Magazine,* September 1969, 11, 15; "Gospel Team Doing Their Thing for God," *Miracle Magazine,* February 1970, 21.

97. "Holy Ghost–Filled Ministers Declare Revival Solves Serious Problems: Racial—Denominational—Personal," *Miracle Magazine,* July 1967, 9.

98. Ibid.

99. Harrell, *All Things Are Possible,* 74.

100. Ibid., 201.

101. A. A. Allen, "You Can Have the Power to Get Wealth!" *Miracle Magazine,* January 1963, 3.

102. Sherry Andrews, "Keeping the Faith," *Charisma,* October 1981, 24–30; Harrell, *All Things Are Possible,* 185–86.

103. "A Great Heritage of Faith—You're Still a Part of the Vision!" *Connections* 26 (Winter 2001): 2–3; Harrell, *All Things Are Possible,* 136, 185–86; Andrews, "Keeping the Faith"; Kenneth E. Hagin, "Looking to the Future," *The Word of Faith,* September 1986, 2–5.

104. "We're Preparing Laborers to Reap the Precious Fruit of the Earth," *The Word of Faith,* June 1986, 8–9; Hagin, "Looking to the Future," 2–5; comments by friends about Hagin's fifty years in ministry, *The Word of Faith,* October 1984, 15–17; Kenneth Hagin Jr.,

"Trend toward Faith Movement," *Charisma*, August 1985, 67–70; Andrews, "Keeping the Faith"; Harrell, *All Things Are Possible*, 186; "Campmeeting '98: Fan the Flame," *The Word of Faith*, October 1998, 13–16; "Campmeeting 2000: So Much More Than You've Seen Before," *The Word of Faith*, October 2000, 12–14, 16, 18; Burgess, *New International Dictionary*, s.v. "Hagin, Kenneth E."; Jeff Dunn, "Faith That Just Won't Stop," *Charisma*, August 2000, 70–71; "The Ministry behind the Ministry," *The Word of Faith*, September 1989, 9; Kenneth E. Hagin, interview by David Edwin Harrell Jr., May 24, 1973, Birmingham, Alabama, audiotape in author's possession.

105. Hagin, "Trend toward Faith Movement."

106. Kenneth E. Hagin and Kenneth Hagin Jr., interview by David Edwin Harrell Jr., December 12, 1983, audiotape in author's possession. Some of his harshest critics included Hank Hannegraff, *Christianity in Crisis* (Eugene, Ore.: Harvest House, 1997); David Hunt and T. A. McMahon, *The Seduction of Christianity* (Eugene, Ore.: Harvest House, 1985); D. R. McConnell, *A Different Gospel* (Peabody, Mass.: Hendrickson, 1988); John Ankerberg and John Weldon, *The Facts on the Faith Movement* (Eugene, Ore.: Harvest House, 1993); Michael Horton, ed., *The Agony of Deceit* (Chicago: Moody Press, 1990).

107. Quoted in Andrews, "Keeping the Faith," 27; Kenneth Hagin Jr., interview by David Edwin Harrell Jr., March 29, 2001, Tulsa, Oklahoma, audiotape in author's possession.

108. "Rhema Bible Training Center," *Charisma*, October 1981, 30–31.

109. Quoted in Andrews, "Keeping the Faith," 25.

110. Michael Horton, "The TV Gospel," in Horton, *The Agony of Deceit*, 123.

111. McConnell, *A Different Gospel*; Milmon F. Harrison, *Righteous Riches: The Word of Faith Movement in Contemporary African American Religion* (New York: Oxford University Press, 2005), 5–8.

112. Hagin, "Trend toward Faith Movement"; Derek E. Vreeland, "Restructuring Word of Faith Theology: A Defense, Analysis, and Refinement of the Theology of the Word of Faith Movement" (paper presented at the annual meeting of the Society for Pentecostal Studies, Tulsa, Oklahoma, March 2001). For a synopsis of positive confession theology see L. Lovett's entry in Burgess, *New International Dictionary*, s.v. "Positive Confession Theology."

113. Hagin, "Trend toward Faith Movement"; announcements of various events, *The Word of Faith*, February 1981, 15; "About Joel Osteen," http://www.joelosteen.com/site/PageServer?pagename=AboutJoel (accessed May 18, 2005); "*New York Times* Best Sellers List," http://www.nytimes.com/pages/books/bestseller/index.html (accessed May 18, 2005).

114. Paul Thigpen, "The New Black Charismatics," *Charisma*, November 1990, 58–67.

115. Hagin, "Trend toward Faith Movement."

116. Comments by friends about Kenneth E. Hagin's fifty years in ministry, *The Word of Faith*, October 1984, 16.

117. "'Best Campmeeting Ever' Focuses on the Supernatural," *The Word of Faith*, October 1982, 11.

118. For more on how Price's and Hagin's ministries affected Grier's life, see *The Word of Faith*, October 1981, 6.

119. Price spoke at Campmeetings and other Rhema functions, and Hagin and Harrison House continued to promote his books and tapes throughout the 1970s and 1980s. See "Behind the Scenes," *The Word of Faith*, September 1974, 5; *The Word of Faith*, December 1974, 7; *The Word of Faith*, March 1975, 8; *The Word of Faith*, October 1981, 6; "'Best Campmeeting Ever' Focuses on the Supernatural," 5–10; *The Word of Faith*, October 1985, 13–14.

120. Advertisement for Campmeeting 1993, *The Word of Faith*, April 1993, n.p.; "Rhema Bible Training Center Day," *The Word of Faith*, October 1979, 9; quote in "Winter Bible Seminar '97—A Taste of Heaven on Earth," *The Word of Faith*, May 1997, 12; Keith Butler's home page, http://www.wordoffaith-icc.org/home.htm (accessed April 20, 2001).

121. Summary of Thompson's message on faith at Campmeeting 1993, *The Word of Faith*, October 1993, 10–13; summary of Thompson's message at Campmeeting 1994, *The Word of Faith*, October 1994, 13–14; summaries of Butler's and Thompson's messages at Campmeeting 1996, *The Word of Faith*, October 1996, 12–13; *The Word of Faith*, October 1997, 19–20; "Campmeeting '98: Fan the Flame," *The Word of Faith*, October 1998, 13–16; Leroy Thompson's home page, http://www.eiwm.org (accessed March 12, 2001).

Chapter 2

1. T. L. and Daisy Osborn, interview by David Edwin Harrell Jr., September 6, 1991, Tulsa, Oklahoma, transcript in author's possession.

2. Historian Margaret Caffrey examines the changing dynamics of the contemporary American family that emerged around 1920. Many of these changes "focused on the rooting out of hierarchy and the attempt to make democracy a reality," emphasizing a greater degree of autonomy and individuality in family members. Conversely, there was also an attempt "to preserve the authoritarian and hierarchical family as an unchanging ideal." These two positions reflect the tension that many fundamentalist Christians felt in trying to hold on to the past while facing dramatic social changes over which they had little or no control. See "Women and Families" in *American Families: A Research Guide and Historical Handbook*, ed. Joseph M. Hawes and Elizabeth I. Nybakken (Westport, Conn.: Greenwood Press, 1991), 243. For a discussion of the "superwoman" concept see chapter 9 in Ruth Rosen's *The World Split Open: How the Modern Women's Movement Changed America* (New York: Viking Penguin, 2000).

3. Alan Brinkley, *The Unfinished Nation: A Concise History of the American People*, vol. 2, *From 1865*, 4th ed. (Boston: McGraw-Hill, 2004), 637–38, 659–60; Betty Friedan, *The Feminine Mystique* (New York: Norton, 1963); Eugenia Kaledin, *Mothers and More: American Women in the 1950s* (Boston: Twayne, 1984).

4. R. Marie Griffith, *God's Daughters: Evangelical Women and the Power of Submission* (Berkeley: University of California Press, 1997), 4, 14, 200.

5. Brenda E. Brasher, *Godly Women: Fundamentalism and Female Power* (New Brunswick, N.J.: Rutgers University Press, 1998), 1–7, 20, quotes on 3, 4, 20.

6. Julie Ingersoll, *Evangelical Christian Women: War Stories in the Gender Battles* (New York: New York University Press, 2003), 1–8.

7. Ibid., 29.

8. Ibid., 16.

9. Ibid., 1–2. Historian David G. Hackett provides an overview for studying the history of gender and American religion in "Gender and Religion in American Culture, 1870–1930," *Religion and American Culture* 5 (Summer 1995): 127–57.

10. Ingersoll, *Evangelical Christian Women*, 101.

11. Ibid.

12. Ibid., 106.

13. Ibid., 100–107.

14. Brasher, *Godly Women*, 170–75; Ingersoll, *Evangelical Christian Women*, 127–36. See also Margaret Lamberts Bendroth, *Fundamentalism and Gender, 1875 to the Present* (New Haven: Yale University Press, 1993).

15. Caffrey, "Women and Families," 223–57; Sheila M. Rothman, *Woman's Proper Place: A History of Changing Ideals and Practices, 1870 to the Present* (New York: Basic Books, 1978); Glenna Matthews, *"Just a Housewife": The Rise and Fall of Domesticity in America* (New York: Oxford University Press, 1987).

16. Harrell, *All Things Are Possible*, 169–72.

17. Osborn interview; T. L. and Daisy Osborn, *God's Unbeatable Husband and Wife Team*, 1982, sound cassette located at the Holy Spirit Research Center, Oral Roberts University, Tulsa, Oklahoma. For general comments about the Osborns' influence on the modern charismatic revival see Stephen Strang, "The Miraculous Quest of T. L. and Daisy Osborn," *Charisma*, January 1987, 16–18, 20–21.

18. Walker, "Twenty People Who Touched Our Lives."

19. Daisy Washburn Osborn, *The Woman Believer* (Tulsa: OSFO Books, 1990), 9, 66–67; Daisy Osborn, *New Life for Women* (Tulsa: OSFO Publishers, 1991), 9; S. Strang, "Miraculous Quest," 16–18, 20–21.

20. Osborn interview.

21. Ibid.; S. Strang, "Miraculous Quest," 16–18, 20–21; Osborn, *The Woman Believer*, 9, 68–70; Daisy Washburn Osborn, *Five Choices for Women Who Win* (Tulsa: OSFO Books, 1986), 204.

22. Osborn, *The Woman Believer*, 70–74, quotes on 71, 72.

23. Ibid., 74.

24. Ibid., 75–79; Osborn interview.

25. Osborn interview.

26. Ibid.

27. Ibid.; Daisy Osborn, *Women and Self Esteem* (Tulsa: OSFO International, 1991), 23–25.

28. Osborn interview.

29. Osborn, *New Life for Women,* back cover, 13.

30. Osborn interview.

31. Osborn, *New Life for Women,* 98.

32. Osborn, *Five Choices for Women Who Win,* 25–26, 43–46, 51, 75, 92, 100.

33. Osborn interview; Osborn, *Five Choices for Women Who Win,* 61.

34. Osborn interview.

35. Ibid.

36. Osborn, *The Woman Believer,* 12.

37. Daisy Washburn Osborn, *Woman without Limits* (Tulsa: OSFO International, 1990), 13.

38. Quotes in Osborn, *The Woman Believer,* 131, 133; see also Osborn, *New Life for Women,* 96–98.

39. Quotes in Harrell, *All Things Are Possible,* 53, 54.

40. Ibid., 165–68.

41. Mrs. Gordon Lindsay, *My Diary Secrets* (Dallas: Christ for the Nations, 1976), 9–18; Sherry Andrews and Rob Kerby, "Freda Lindsay: The Widow Who Accepted the Mantle," *Charisma,* January 1984, 22–23, 25–28.

42. Lindsay, *My Diary Secrets,* 9–18, quotes on 16, 18; Andrews and Kerby, "Freda Lindsay."

43. Lindsay, *My Diary Secrets,* 18–23, quote on 23; Andrews and Kerby, "Freda Lindsay."

44. Lindsay, *My Diary Secrets,* 39–40.

45. Ibid., 55–56.

46. Ibid., 49.

47. Ibid., 51–52.

48. Ibid., 24–30, 38–56; Andrews and Kerby, "Freda Lindsay."

49. Quote in Lindsay, *My Diary Secrets,* 60; Andrews and Kerby, "Freda Lindsay."

50. Lindsay, *My Diary Secrets,* 61.

51. Lindsay, *My Diary Secrets,* 104–5.

52. Ibid., 110.

53. For a complete account of Branham's and Gordon Lindsay's roles in the healing revival see Harrell, *All Things Are Possible,* 27–41, 53–58, 159–69; Weaver, *The Healer-Prophet;* and Andrews and Kerby, "Freda Lindsay."

54. Lindsay, *My Diary Secrets,* 145.

55. Ibid., 174–75.

56. Ibid., 149–50.

57. Ibid., 187–95.

58. Ibid., 171, 174; Andrews and Kerby, "Freda Lindsay."

59. Lindsay, *My Diary Secrets,* 178.

60. Ibid., 179–86; Andrews and Kerby, "Freda Lindsay."

61. Lindsay, *My Diary Secrets,* 277; Osborn interview.

62. Lindsay, *My Diary Secrets,* 204.

63. Ibid., 234–37, quotes on 235.

64. Andrews and Kerby, "Freda Lindsay," 28.

65. Lindsay, *My Diary Secrets*, 288.

66. Ibid., 343–47.

67. Andrews and Kerby, "Freda Lindsay."

68. Lindsay, *My Diary Secrets*, 336–38; Andrews and Kerby, "Freda Lindsay"; Osborn interview.

69. Lindsay, *My Diary Secrets*, 265–66.

70. Ibid., 335–42, 390.

71. Ibid., 338–39; Gary Haynes, "Christ for the Nations in Dallas Celebrates Fifty Years of Ministry," *Charisma*, June 1998, 26–27.

72. Brasher, *Godly Women*, 170–75.

73. Copeland and Copeland, *The First Thirty Years*, 19.

74. Ibid., 22–25, 30.

75. Ibid., 29–32, quote on 29.

76. Gloria Copeland, *God's Will for You* (Fort Worth: Kenneth Copeland Publications, 1973), [9–12].

77. Ibid., [11].

78. Gloria Copeland, "Receive Your Inheritance!" *Believer's Voice of Victory*, April 1996, 20–23; quote in G. Copeland, *God's Will for You*, [12].

79. G. Copeland, *God's Will for You*, [12].

80. Quote in ibid., [13]; Copeland and Copeland, *The First Thirty Years*, 32–35.

81. G. Copeland, *God's Will for You*, [12–14]; Copeland and Copeland, *The First Thirty Years*, 42.

82. Kenneth Copeland, "The Only Financial Backer You Need," *Believer's Voice of Victory*, October 2000, 4–7.

83. Gloria Copeland, *God's Will Is Prosperity* (1980; reprint, Fort Worth: Kenneth Copeland Publications, 1992), 21.

84. Stephen Strang, "Kenneth Copeland," *Charisma*, June 1979, 16–22, 24; "It's Harvest Time," *Believer's Voice of Victory*, July–August 1997, 16–29; G. Copeland, *God's Will for You*, [14–15].

85. G. Copeland, *God's Will for You*, [15–16].

86. Ibid.; "It's Harvest Time"; G. Copeland, *God's Will Is Prosperity*, 47; quote in Copeland and Copeland, *The First Thirty Years*, 67.

87. Copeland and Copeland, *The First Thirty Years*, 63.

88. Ibid., 79.

89. Photos suggest that she played a supportive role with limited visibility in the early years. *Believer's Voice of Victory*, May 1974, 1, and July 1974, n.p.

90. Gloria Copeland, "Super Sunday," *Believer's Voice of Victory*, May 1974, 1, 3.

91. "Jesus Country News," *Believer's Voice of Victory*, October 1974, 3.

92. Kenneth Copeland, "A Message to Our Readers," *Believer's Voice of Victory*, September 1976, 2.

93. See the following articles by Gloria Copeland in *Believer's Voice of Victory:* "The Word Is Spirit Food," August 1977, 2–3; "The Hundred Fold," October 1977, 1–4; "Choose the Good Part," February 1978, 3; "Love in the Home," May 1978, 5; "God's Covenant People," October 1978, 4; "Choose the Good Part," January 1979, 6; "The Hundred-fold Return," April 1979, 3–6; "A Personal Testimony," September 1979, 4–5. These early speaking engagements fell within the Pentecostal and charismatic tradition of allowing women to testify in public services and to minister to other women.

94. Kenneth Hagin also returned to his healing roots in 1979, feeling that he was not fulfilling his "call" as a healing evangelist and had not used his "gift" of healing effectively. He even opened his own daily healing school at Rhema Bible Training Center in October 1979. "Prayer and Healing School to Be Held Daily," *The Word of Faith*, October 1979, 3.

95. Copeland and Copeland, *The First Thirty Years*, 94.

96. See the following articles by Gloria Copeland in *Believer's Voice of Victory:* "Reaping a Harvest of Healing," November 1979, 5; "1981 Itinerary," January 1981, 6–7; "Special Video Tape Offer: 'Healing School,'" February 1981, 7; "Believer's Voice of Victory: Television Series," March 1983, 10; "Special Speaking Engagements: Gloria Copeland," April 1983, 10; "Fresno Victory Crusade Report," July 1983, 6–7.

97. "Gloria Copeland 1994 Christian Woman of the Year," *Believer's Voice of Victory*, July 1995, 6–7, quote on 6.

98. Copeland and Copeland, *The First Thirty Years*, 169–70.

99. "An Invitation . . . ," *Believer's Voice of Victory*, July 1978, 7.

100. Gloria Copeland, "Doing Our Part . . . Together," *Believer's Voice of Victory*, May 1983, 4–6.

101. "Grounds for Success," *Believer's Voice of Victory*, April 1985, 9; "Kenneth Copeland Ministries Headquarters Update," *Believer's Voice of Victory*, December 1985, 13; "Kenneth Copeland Ministries International Headquarters Update," *Believer's Voice of Victory*, May 1986, 5; "It's Harvest Time."

102. In 1990 the Copelands founded Eagle Mountain International Church, and in 1997 they built a thirteen-hundred-seat auditorium. In 1997 they estimated that their television program appeared on almost five hundred stations and reached about 300 million homes worldwide. In the 1990s they developed a movie production team and started an internet website to further their work. At century's end KCM reports claimed that the Copelands had written over sixty books, that their magazines were sent to almost seven hundred thousand households around the world, and that all of their teaching materials were translated into twenty-two languages. They even started an international prison ministry, which reached a reported sixty thousand new inmates a year and received more than thirty thousand pieces of mail from prisoners each month. In 2002 they estimated that their evangelistic efforts—working through KCM and other ministries—had garnered 56,568,607 born-again believers. "It's Harvest Time"; Copeland and Copeland, *The First Thirty Years*, [211]; "Fifty-six Million Souls . . . and Still Counting," *Believer's Voice of Victory*, July 2002, 4–5.

103. Anita Baker, "Tarrant Airstrip Where Two Died," *Fort Worth Star-Telegram*, September 18, 1997; Veronica Alaniz, "Officials Unsure Why Helicopter Was at Airfield," *Dallas Morning News*, September 19, 1997; Selwyn Crawford, "Sheriff Sheds Little Light on Copter Crash," *Dallas Morning News*, September 24, 1997; "Secular Limelight Catches Up with Televangelist Ministry," *Dallas Morning News*, October 14, 1997; Veronica Alaniz, "Questions Remain in '97 Copter Crash," *Dallas Morning News*, September 17, 1998; Jack Douglas Jr., "Error by Pilot Cited in Sheriff's Copter Crash," *Fort Worth Star-Telegram*, March 13, 1999.

104. Selwyn Crawford, "Higher Profile: Tragedies Place Evangelist Copeland's Worldwide Ministry in the Public Eye," *Dallas Morning News*, October 14, 1997.

105. Veronica Puente, "Biker Arrested in Girl's Death," *Fort Worth Star-Telegram*, September 29, 1997; "Copeland Ministries Assesses Safeguards after Girl Killed," *Fort Worth Star-Telegram*, September 30, 1997; Neil Strassman, "Cyclist Will Not Be Charged," *Fort Worth Star-Telegram*, October 31, 1997.

106. Neil Strassman and Jack Douglas Jr., "Officers Warned Copeland of Racing Dangers," *Fort Worth Star-Telegram*, November 16, 1997.

107. Neil Strassman, "Claim Alleges County Improprieties at Rally," *Fort Worth Star-Telegram*, March 27, 1998.

108. Neil Strassman, "Family Sues Copeland Ministries," *Fort Worth Star-Telegram*, June 27, 1998.

109. Neil Strassman, "'98 Copeland Motorcycle Rally Canceled," *Fort Worth Star-Telegram*, May 19, 1998.

110. Brett Hoffman, "Bikers Gather for Christian Rally," *Fort Worth Star-Telegram*, May 4, 2002; Lawrence Jenkins, "Bikers Rally Is Heaven on Wheels," *Fort Worth Star-Telegram*, May 11, 2002.

111. Thunder Over Texas Motorcycle Rally, http://www.thunderovertexas.com/ (accessed June 19, 2006).

112. Susan Kwilecki makes a similar observation in "Contemporary Pentecostal Clergywomen: Female Christian Leadership, Old Style," *Journal of Feminist Studies in Religion* 3 (Fall 1987): 57–75.

Chapter 3

1. "Richard Roberts: On the Air!" *Abundant Life*, October 1984, 13–17.

2. Lindsay Roberts, "Does God Want You to Be All That You Can Be?" *Abundant Life*, January–March 1988, 14–15.

3. Rosen, *The World Split Open*; Harrell, *All Things Are Possible*.

4. Marilyn Hickey Ministries, http://www.mhmin.org/ (accessed April 20, 2001); "Celebrating Twenty-five Years of Covering the Earth with His Word, 1976–2001," *Outpouring*, special edition, May 2001, 3–5; David M. Hazard, "Marilyn and Wally Hickey: They Make a Great Team," *Charisma*, October 1985, 26–27, 29–30, 32, 37; Melton, Lucas, and Stone, *Prime-Time Religion*, 138–40; Stanley M. Burgess and Gary B. McGee, eds.,

Dictionary of Pentecostal and Charismatic Movements (Grand Rapids, Mich.: Regency Reference Library, 1988), s.v. "Hickey, Marilyn"; Marilyn Hickey, "Two Shall Become One," *Charisma*, July 1994, 44, 46–48; Stephen Strang, "Marilyn Hickey: She Makes the Bible Come Alive," *Charisma,* February 1979, 15–17; Marilyn Hickey, *Break the Generation Curse* (Denver: Marilyn Hickey Ministries, 1988): 70–71; Marilyn Hickey, "It's Time to Break the Family Curse!" *Outpouring,* November 1988, 12–13.

5. Marilyn Hickey Ministries, http://www.mhmin.org/ (accessed April 20, 2001); S. Strang, "Marilyn Hickey," 15–17; Hazard, "Marilyn and Wally Hickey"; Burgess and McGee, *Dictionary of Pentecostal and Charismatic Movements,* s.v. "Hickey, Marilyn"; "Celebrating Twenty-five Years," 3–5; "Today with Marilyn: One Step Closer to Covering the Earth with God's Word," *Outpouring,* November 1986, 9–11.

6. S. Strang, "Marilyn Hickey," 15–17; Steven Lawson, "Miracles," *Charisma,* December 1985, 90; Steven Lawson, "Miracles Come to Prime-Time TV," *Charisma,* October 1986, 74; "Today with Marilyn," 9–11.

7. Marilyn Hickey, "Dear Friend," *Outpouring,* September 1987, 2.

8. "Vote Yes for Christian Television," *Outpouring,* September 1987, 8–9.

9. Marilyn Hickey, "Fulfilling the Dreams God Has Given You!" *Outpouring,* May 1988, 9–11; Marilyn Hickey, "Watchman in the Night!" *Outpouring,* July 1988, 5; Marilyn Hickey Ministries—Fact Sheet, sent to author May 2, 2002; "Television Ministry: Today with Marilyn and Sarah," *Outpouring,* special edition, May 2001, 2; Peterson, "Electric Sisters," 126–29.

10. Advertisement for Marilyn Hickey's National Word Women Convention held in Tulsa, April 25–28, 1984, *Charisma,* March 1984, 18; advertisement for Marilyn Hickey's International Word Women Convention in Denver, October 24–27, 1984, *Charisma,* August 1984, 70; Joy Strang, "Spiritual Growth Taught at Women's Conferences," *Charisma,* May 1985, 85; "Women's Revival," *Charisma,* July 1987, 62–63; "Women's Christian Army News," *Outpouring,* February 1987, 7; Melton, Lucas, and Stone, *Prime-Time Religion,* 138–40; Peterson, "Electric Sisters," 126–29.

11. Quotes in Marilyn Hickey, "What Comes First?" *Charisma,* January 1985, 11–12; Marilyn Hickey, "Trend toward Women in Ministry," *Charisma,* August 1985, 80–81, 83–86; "What Is a Decatrend?" *Charisma,* August 1985, 16–18.

12. "Egypt Origin of Satellite Conference," *Charisma,* April 1982, 12; "Christians See Improvement in Guatemala," *Charisma,* January 1983, 16; Stephen Strang, "Marilyn Hickey Ministers in Nigeria and Poland," *Charisma,* November 1984, 107.

13. "A Million Cups of Milk for Ethiopia," *Charisma,* January 1985, 114; untitled article, *Outpouring,* October 1986, 2; "Marilyn Hickey Helps Bring Relief for Calcutta's Children," *Outpouring,* November 1988, 14; "Covering Australia with the Word!" *Outpouring,* January 1989, 11.

14. "Television—Reaching Japan for Christ," *Outpouring,* April 1989, 3; Marilyn Hickey, "Missions Possible," *Outpouring,* June 1989, 12–13; "Hungarians Hear Hickey: Bible Encounter a Hit behind the Iron Curtain," *Charisma,* June 1989, 32; "Marilyn Hickey Hits Hot Spots," *Charisma,* July 1989, 30.

15. Letter from Bradley K. Jordan, *Outpouring*, October 1989, 15; "Chinese Seek 'First Love,'" *Charisma*, April 1991, 22; "A Journey Underground," *Charisma*, January 1997, 39–41.

16. Melton, Lucas, and Stone, *Prime-Time Religion*, 138–40; "Hickey Leads Crusade in Pakistan," *Charisma*, August 1995, 26; Greg Burt, "Thousands of Pakistanis Come to Christ during Marilyn Hickey Event," *Charisma*, October 1999, 37–38.

17. Marilyn Hickey Ministries—Fact Sheet; Hazard, "Marilyn and Wally Hickey"; "Celebrating Twenty-five Years," 3–5; Stephen Strang, "Preface," *Charisma*, January 1979, 8; "Transitions," *Charisma*, January 1989, 30; "Hickey Chosen as Woman of the Year," *Charisma*, September 1989, 38.

18. Marilyn Hickey Ministries—Fact Sheet; Burgess and McGee, *Dictionary of Pentecostal and Charismatic Movements*, s.v. "Hickey, Marilyn"; Walker, "Twenty People Who Touched Our Lives"; Hazard, "Marilyn and Wally Hickey."

19. Marilyn Hickey Ministries, http://www.mhmin.org/ (accessed April 20, 2001).

20. Marilyn Hickey Ministries, http://www.mhmin.org/ (accessed April 20, 2001, and June 19, 2006); Marilyn Hickey Ministries—Fact Sheet; "Celebrating Twenty-five Years," 3–5.

21. "Popular TV Preachers," STLtoday.com, November 18, 2003, http://www.stltoday.com/stltoday/news/special/joycemeyer.nsf/0/4E2FA20598C3EA2986256DE30018CF37?OpenDocument (accessed June 19, 2006).

22. For a discussion of post-feminism see Rosen, *The World Split Open*, 274–75; and Amy Erdman Farrell, *Yours in Sisterhood:* Ms. *Magazine and the Promise of Popular Feminism* (Chapel Hill: University of North Carolina Press, 1998), 180, 213 n. 2.

23. Quoted in Ken Walker, "A New Day for Women Preachers," *Charisma*, November 1998, 54.

24. Joyce Meyer, lecture given at Life in the Word convention, Tulsa, June 13–15, 2002; Ken Walker, "The Preacher Who Tells It Like It Is," *Charisma*, November 1998, 48, 50–55; Melton, Lucas, and Stone, *Prime-Time Religion*, 227–28; Joyce Meyer, *Prepare to Prosper: Moving from the Land of Lack to the Land of Plenty* (Tulsa: Harrison House, 1997); Joyce Meyer, "Where the Mind Goes, the Man Follows," *Life in the Word*, July 2001, 2–4.

25. Joyce Meyer, *Help Me—I'm Married!* (Tulsa: Harrison House, 2000), 13–20; Bill Smith and Carolyn Tuft, "Meyer Traces Her Fervor to Turbulent Early Years," *St. Louis Post-Dispatch*, November 16, 2003; Walker, "The Preacher Who Tells It Like It Is"; Joyce Meyer, "Wilderness Mentality," audio recording, 1990, Life in the Word Series, Holy Spirit Research Center, Oral Roberts University, Tulsa; Joyce Meyer, *The Root of Rejection: Escape the Bondage of Rejection and Experience the Freedom of God's Acceptance* (Tulsa: Harrison House, 1994); Joyce Meyer, "Getting Ready for the Glory: Wilderness Mentalities Part 2," *Believer's Voice of Victory*, May 1996, 14–16; Joyce Meyer, "How to Succeed at Being Yourself," *Life in the Word*, July 2001, 12–13; Joyce Meyer, "Make a Fresh Start," *Life in the Word*, August 2001, 2–4.

26. Ken Walker, "Joyce Meyer's Biggest Fan," *Charisma*, November 1998, 52–53; Joyce Meyer, *Help Me I'm Depressed: Overcoming Emotional Battles with the Power of God's Word!* (Tulsa: Harrison House, 1998): 92–93; Joyce Meyer, *When God When: Learning to Trust God's Timing* (Tulsa: Harrison House, 1994), 30–36; Melton, Lucas, and Stone, *Prime-Time Religion*, 227–28; Walker, "The Preacher Who Tells It Like It Is"; Joyce Meyer, "The Danger of Self-Exaltation," *Life in the Word*, June 1997, 7.

27. Walker, "The Preacher Who Tells It Like It Is," 54.

28. Meyer, "The Danger of Self-Exaltation," 7.

29. Walker, "Joyce Meyer's Biggest Fan," 52.

30. Walker, "The Preacher Who Tells It Like It Is"; Smith and Tuft, "Meyer Traces Her Fervor"; Joyce Meyer, "A Fresh Wind Is Blowing," *Life in the Word*, January 2004, 16–18; Lee, *T. D. Jakes*, 65.

31. Walker, "The Preacher Who Tells It Like It Is"; Radio and Television Ministries, fact sheets obtained by author at Life in the Word convention, Tulsa, June 13–15, 2002; Meyer, *Help Me I'm Depressed*, 119; Meyer, "A Fresh Wind Is Blowing," 16–18; Melton, Lucas, and Stone, *Prime-Time Religion*, 227–28; "Teaching Tape Messages Are Transforming Millions," *Life in the Word*, June 2002, 8; "Author Joyce Meyer Leaves Charismatic Publisher," *Charisma*, September 2002, 15.

32. Carolyn Tuft and Bill Smith, "Money Pitch Is a Hit with Followers," *St. Louis Post-Dispatch*, November 17, 2003.

33. Carolyn Tuft and Bill Smith, "From Fenton to Fortune in the Name of God," *St. Louis Post-Dispatch*, November 16, 2003.

34. Bill Smith and Carolyn Tuft, "Meyer Traces Her Fervor to Turbulent Early Years," *St. Louis Post-Dispatch*, November 16, 2003; Carolyn Tuft and Bill Smith, "IRS Requires Pay, Perks for Evangelists to Be 'Reasonable,'" *St. Louis Post-Dispatch*, November 16, 2003; Carolyn Tuft, "Jefferson County, Meyer Joust Over Tax Exemption," *St. Louis Post-Dispatch*, November 16, 2003; Tuft and Smith, "Money Pitch Is a Hit with Followers"; "Joyce Meyer Ministries: The Big Squeeze," *St. Louis Post-Dispatch*, May 7, 2005.

35. Corrie Cutrer, "Joyce Meyer Responds to Critics, Shifts Income Source," *ChristianityToday.com*, January 19, 2004, http://www.christianitytoday.com/ct/2004/103/13.0.html (accessed June 7, 2005); Joyce Meyer Ministries: Financial Accountability, http://www.joycemeyer.org/AboutUs/FinancialAccountability/default.htm?print=true (accessed October 30, 2006); MinistryWatch, http://www.ministrywatch.com/mw2.1/F_R&A.asp (accessed October 31, 2006); "To Our Readers, an Apology," *St. Louis Post-Dispatch*, June 19, 2005, http://www.stltoday.com/stltoday/news/special/joycemeyer.nsf/o/3230A355F7AB972B862570260050AE09?OpenDocument (accessed October 30, 2006).

36. Vicki Jamison-Peterson, *El Shaddai: The God of More Than Enough!* (Tulsa: Vicki Jamison-Peterson Ministries, 1983), 5–10, quote on 9.

37. Vicki Jamison-Peterson, *How You Can Have Joy*, rev. ed. (Tulsa: Vicki Jamison-

Peterson Ministries, 1985), 13; Vicki Jamison, "The Healing Power of the Mind," *It's a New Day*, September 1976, 2–3; Vicki Jamison, "Wonderful! The Name of Jesus," *It's a New Day*, May 1976, 2.

38. Sharon Burton, "The Name of Jesus," *It's a New Day*, May 1976, 1, 4; quote in Jamison-Peterson, *El Shaddai*, 86; Vicki Jamison, "Great Things He Hath Done," *It's a New Day*, special edition, Spring 1977, 1–4.

39. Lawless, *God's Peculiar People*; see also Wacker, *Heaven Below*, chap. 3.

40. Vicki Jamison, "Music to Remember," *It's a New Day*, January 1977, 3; Jamison-Peterson, *How You Can Have Joy*, 72–76; Doyne E. Lamb's testimony, *It's a New Day*, January 1976, 1; Vicki Jamison, "How You Can . . . Know and Do the Will of God," *It's a New Day*, July 1981, 1–3; Vicki Jamison, "I Believe with all My Heart," *It's a New Day* [ca. 1974], 2, 4; "Vicki Jamison and Jim Bakker in Studio of PTL," *It's a New Day*, March 1976, 1; Jamison-Peterson, *How You Can Have Joy*, 107–8; Vicki Jamison, "God's Dreams Only Get Bigger," *It's a New Day*, August 1981, 2–4.

41. "Report from Television," *It's a New Day* [ca. 1975], 3.

42. Jamison, "God's Dreams Only Get Bigger," 2–4.

43. Jamison, "Great Things He Hath Done," 1–4; "Vicki Jamison and Jim Bakker in Studio of PTL"; "TV Ministry in Los Angeles," *It's a New Day*, July 1976, 1; Vicki Jamison, "Acting Like the Father," *It's a New Day*, July 1978, 1–2; "Farmington, New Mexico: Three Days of Blessing!" *It's a New Day*, December 1977, 3; Burton, "The Name of Jesus," 1, 4; Jamison, "God's Dreams Only Get Bigger," 2–4.

44. "Dedication Day," *It's a New Day*, June 1977, 1; "Spiritual Climate Warms in the Northeast," *It's a New Day*, July 1977, 1, 4; "Burlington, Vermont Will Never Be the Same Again!" reprint of an article in *Newport (Vt.) Daily Express*, October 17, 1977, in *It's a New Day*, January 1978, 1; Vicki Jamison to her ministry partners, September 1977, copy in author's possession; "Radio—Update: The Radio Ministry Is on the Air," *It's a New Day*, January 1978, 4.

45. Quote in Jamison-Peterson, *El Shaddai*, 28; Vicki Jamison, "In Memoriam," *It's a New Day*, June 1982, 4–5; Vicki Jamison, "Spiritual Roots," *It's a New Day*, May 1979, 1–3; "Special Report from the Philippines," *It's a New Day*, May 1980, 3; Vicki Jamison, "God's Plan for Your Life Is Always Perfect," *It's a New Day*, April–June 1983, 2–3.

46. Quote in "Proceed with Caution: A Miracle's in Progress," *It's a New Day*, January–March 1983, 4; Vicki Jamison, "'Abraham's Vision Can Be Yours,'" *It's a New Day*, January–March 1983, 2–3, 12–13; "Moments to Remember," *It's a New Day*, July–September 1983, 4–7; Jamison, "God's Dreams Only Get Bigger," 2–4.

47. "Ministry Update," *Vicki Jamison-Peterson Ministries*, January 1984, 3.

48. "Ministry Update," *Vicki Jamison-Peterson Ministries*, January 1984, 3; Vicki Jamison-Peterson, "Roadmap to Faith," *Vicki Jamison-Peterson Ministries*, January 1984, 1–2; wedding announcement for Vicki Jamison and Carl R. Peterson, M.D., *Vicki Jamison-Peterson Ministries*, January 1984, 2; Jamison, "God's Plan for Your Life Is Always Perfect," 2–3; Vicki Jamison-Peterson biography, www.vjpm.org (accessed April 17, 2002).

49. Anne Gimenez, *The Emerging Christian Woman: She Brings Unity and Vitality to the Body of Christ* (Altamonte Springs, Fla.: Creation House, 1986), 38–41, 58–63; Burgess and McGee, *Dictionary of Pentecostal and Charismatic Movements,* s.v. "Gimenez, Anne"; Elva Cobb Martin, "What Makes the Rock Church Rock," *Charisma,* May 1986, 62–63, 65–68; Steve Lawson, "The Debut of the Rock Christian Network," *Charisma,* May 1986, 68; "Rock Church Will Close Its Satellite TV Network," *Richmond Times-Dispatch,* March 21, 1988; Peterson, "Electric Sisters," 130–32.

50. Anne Gimenez, "Taking a Lead from Esther," *Charisma,* June 1986, 30–32, 34.

51. Carolyn Curtis, "'Washington for Jesus' to Make Comeback," *Charisma,* January 1996, 16–17; Burgess and McGee, *Dictionary of Pentecostal and Charismatic Movements,* s.v. "Gimenez, Anne"; Melton, Lucas, and Stone, *Prime-Time Religion,* 113–14; Steve Lawson, "Gimenez to Address Leaders Conference," *Charisma,* March 1986, 105; E. C. Martin, "What Makes the Rock Church Rock," 62–63, 65–68; Gimenez, "Taking a Lead from Esther," 30–32, 34; Anne Gimenez as senior pastor, http://www.ritc.info/faculty2.htm (accessed February 26, 2003); Anne Gimenez as senior pastor, http://home.hiwaay.net/~contendr/1999/12–15–1999.html (accessed February 26, 2003).

52. "Changing COLORS, Changing BOUNDARIES," *Ebony,* December 2004, 155; About Paula, http://www.paulawhite.org/about.htm (accessed June 8, 2005); "'My Story Is a Story of Restoration,'" *Washington Post,* December 16, 2004.

53. Paula White Ministries, http://www.paulawhite.org/ (accessed June 8, 2005); MegaFest Atlanta, http://www.mega-fest.com/viewSpeaker.php?id=68 (accessed June 8, 2005); The Church: History, http://www.withoutwalls.org/church.htm (accessed June 8, 2005); Broadcast Schedule, http://www.paulawhite.org/tvschedule.htm (accessed June 8, 2005).

54. Michelle Bearden, "Power Pastors Give, Get a Lot," *Tampa Tribune,* August 14, 2002.

55. Michael Sasso, "Preachers of Profit," *Tampa Tribune,* May 14, 2006; Dr. Colbert's Divine Health and Nutritional Products, http://www.drcolbert.com/ (accessed June 20, 2006); Don Colbert M.D. Bible Cure Medical Books, Tapes, CDs Products, http://www.faithcenteredresources.com/authors/don-colbert-featured-products.asp (accessed June 20, 2006).

56. Billye Brim biography, http://www.billyebrim.com/ (accessed July 28, 2001); Billye Brim, "The *POWER* in the BLOOD of JESUS," *Glorious Connections,* Spring 1994, 2; Billye Brim, report on Migdal Arbel, LTD, Prayer Mountain in the Galilee, June 2000, sent to author by Billye Brim Ministries, summer 2002; Billye Brim, "The Jews, the Nations, the Church," *Glorious Connections,* September 1989, n.p.; Billye Brim, "The Purpose of Prayer Mountain in the Ozarks," promotional brochure sent to author by Billye Brim Ministries, summer 2002; Billye Brim, "God's Glorious Connections," *Glorious Connections,* November 1986, n.p.

57. Billye Brim, "He's Coming Again!!!!!!!" *Glorious Connections,* Winter 1991, 2; Billye Brim, "Prophecy Watch," *The Glory Watch,* Summer 1999, 1–2; Billye Brim, "Questions and Answers," *The Glory Watch,* February 2001, 6; Billye Brim, "In the Days of These

Kings," *Glorious Connections,* February 1993, 3; Billye Brim, "Don't Touch Jerusalem!: The Apple of God's Eye, This Nation Should Be on the Lord's Side," *The Glory Watch,* Spring 2002, 4–6, 19. At the time, Pat Robertson was probably the foremost authority among charismatics on dispensational prophecy. See Harrell, *Pat Robertson,* 143–51, 190. Since then, others, such as San Antonio pastor John Hagee and independent evangelist Perry Stone, have become recognized authorities on this subject among Pentecostals and charismatics.

58. The Vision for Prayer Mountain and Prayer Mountain in the Ozarks, http://www.billyebrim.com/ (accessed July 28, 2001); Pastor Lee Morgans, "Prayer Mountain Update," *Glorious Connections,* Spring 1996, n.p.; Kevin Berg, "Taking Stock of the Matter: Financial Update," *Prayer Mountain Gazette,* Fall 2001, 7; Kevin Berg, "The Prayer Tower: The Spirit and Heart of It All," *Prayer Mountain Gazette,* Fall 2001, 7; Brim, "The Purpose of Prayer Mountain in the Ozarks."

59. "The Voice of One Witness," *Glorious Connections,* Spring 1996, 3; Brim, "The Purpose of Prayer Mountain in the Ozarks"; Special Partner Edition, *The Glory Watch,* Spring 2002; Billye Brim, "Using the Name and the Blood to Bring Up Children," *Glorious Connections,* Spring 1995, 1–3; Chip Brim, "Champions for Christ," *The Glory Watch,* Summer 1999, 4; Itineraries for Shelli Brim Oaks and Chip Brim, *The Glory Watch,* February 2001, 8; Kylie K. Oaks, "Prayerful Agents Carry Out Covert Spiritual Operations!" *Prayer Mountain Gazette,* Fall 2001, 2; Brim, "The Purpose of Prayer Mountain in the Ozarks."

60. Kate McVeigh, "The Favor Factor: God's Favor Changed Me," *The Voice of Faith,* March–April 1997, 1–2; "Changed from the Inside Out," *The Word of Faith,* January 1998, 12–14; "RHEMA Grads Making a Difference at Home and Abroad," *The Word of Faith,* September 1989, 12; Kate McVeigh, *Conquering Intimidation: How to Overcome the Fear that Paralyzes Your Potential* (Tulsa: Faith Library Publications, 2000), 29, 43–44, 79, 85–87; Kate McVeigh, *The Favor Factor: Releasing God's Supernatural Influence to Work for You* (Tulsa: Harrison House, 1997), 13–16; Kate McVeigh, *The Overcomer's Scripture Keys from A to Z: Scriptures for Winning over Life's Problems* (Warren, Mich.: Kate McVeigh Ministries, 1999), [ix].

61. McVeigh, "The Favor Factor," 1–2; quote in "Changed from the Inside Out," 14; "RHEMA Grads Making a Difference," 12; McVeigh, *Conquering Intimidation,* 29, 43–44, 79, 85–87; McVeigh, *The Favor Factor,* 13–16; McVeigh, *The Overcomer's Scripture Keys,* [ix]; Kate McVeigh, "Ministry Update from Kate . . . We're Moving," *The Voice of Faith,* Summer 2000, 1–2.

62. "Tenth Anniversary Edition," *The Voice of Faith,* July–August 1997, 1; McVeigh, *Conquering Intimidation,* 17–18; "RHEMA Grads Making a Difference," 12; "Changed from the Inside Out," 12–14; "Ministry Update," *The Voice of Faith,* January–March 1997, 1–2; "Ministry Update," *The Voice of Faith,* September–October 1998, 1; The Voice of Faith TV Broadcast, http://www.katemcveigh.org/Tvnews (accessed February 10, 2003); Kate McVeigh, "Airplane Update," *The Voice of Faith,* May–June 1998, 3; Kate McVeigh, "Ministry Update from Kate . . . We're Moving," *The Voice of Faith,* Summer 2000, 1–2;

ministry growth, *The Voice of Faith,* January–February 2000, 3; advertisement for her annual Winter Word Luncheon in Warren, Michigan, *The Voice of Faith,* December 1997–February 1998, 3; "1998 Radio Rallies," *The Voice of Faith,* December 1997–February 1998, 2; "Kindle the Flame Women's Conference," *The Word of Faith,* February 2001, [21–22].

63. Juanita Bynum Ministries, http://www.nosheets.com/nonsplash.shtml (accessed April 20, 2001); Valerie G. Lowe, "New York Preacher Juanita Bynum Paves Way for Women in Ministry," *Charisma,* June 1999, 25–27; Juanita Bynum, *No More Sheets Devotional* (Lanham, Md.: Pneuma Life Publishing, 1998), 10; Juanita Bynum, *The Planted Seed: The Immutable Laws of Sowing and Reaping* (Lanham, Md.: Pneuma Life Publishing, 1997); Lee, *T. D. Jakes,* 149–51.

64. Lindsay Roberts, *Thirty-six Hours with an Angel* (Tulsa: Oral Roberts Evangelistic Association, 1990), 17.

65. "An Interview with Richard Roberts," *Abundant Life,* March 1981, 19–22.

66. "Richard Roberts . . . Evangelist of God's Healing Power," *Abundant Life,* October 1982, 22–23; "Life Line Testimonies," *Abundant Life,* September–October 1986, 21–23.

67. "God's City of Faith Must Be Victorious—Millions Are Counting On It!" *Abundant Life,* October 1981, 8–9; photo on cover of *Abundant Life,* December 1981.

68. L. Roberts, *Thirty-six Hours with an Angel,* 42.

69. Quote in Richard Roberts, "Personal Crusade Report: Saginaw, Michigan," *Abundant Life,* December 1982, 15; "Interview with Richard and Lindsay Roberts," *Abundant Life,* November 1982, 19; L. Roberts, *Thirty-six Hours with an Angel,* 41–45.

70. L. Roberts, *Thirty-six Hours with an Angel,* 41–42.

71. Ibid., 1–16; Lindsay Roberts, "The God of the Big, the Little, and Everything In-Between!" *Miracles Now,* March–May 2001, 14–15; Lindsay Roberts, "My Greatest Harvest," *Make Your Day Count,* October–December 2001, 34; Lindsay Roberts, "Someone to Watch Over You," *Make Your Day Count,* April–June 2003, 4; *Miracles Now,* October–2002, 22; Harrell, *Oral Roberts,* 347–48.

72. Lindsay Roberts, "Christmas Thoughts," *Abundant Life,* November–December 1984, 9; "You Have a Choice . . . So Don't Panic!" *Abundant Life,* January–February 1990, 14–15; *Miracles Now,* September–October 1997, 3; "Stop It! That's Enough!" *Miracles Now,* March–April 1998, 12; *Make Your Day Count,* April–June 2001, 2.

73. Lindsay Roberts, "A Little Word," *Make Your Day Count,* April–June 2001, 4.

74. L. Roberts, "Does God Want You to Be All That You Can Be?" 14–15; Lindsay Roberts, "Wailing in Wisdom," *Make Your Day Count,* July–September 2003, 4.

75. Make Your Day Count, http://www.makeyourdaycount.com (accessed February 25, 2003); Patricia Salem, "Who Said Anything about Money? I Have Faith for This!" *Make Your Day Count,* April–June 2002, 28–29.

76. Advertisement for OREA television programs, *Miracles Now,* January–February 2000, 15.

77. Richard Roberts, memo to ORU and OREA staff, May 7, 2004, photocopy in possession of author.

78. Lindsay Roberts biography, http://www.orm.cc/bio_lr.html (accessed February 25, 2003); Make Your Day Count, http://www.makeyourdaycount.com (accessed February 25, 2003); Harrell, *Oral Roberts*, 345–47; Richard Roberts, interview by David Edwin Harrell Jr., March 30, 2001, Tulsa, Oklahoma, audiotape in author's possession; "Whole Person Healing School," *The ORU Office of Ministerial Relations Report*, ICBM Special Edition, Spring 2002, 2; L. Roberts, *Thirty-six Hours with an Angel*.

79. See the following items in *The Word of Faith:* "Lynette Hagin Named Director of RHEMA," August 1982, 9; Lynette Hagin, "The Four 'F's of Bearing Fruit," March 1998, 26–28; "Kindle the Flame Women's Conference," [21–22]; "For a Time Such as This," January 2003, 16–17; Lynette Hagin, "Prayer: Our Spiritual Oxygen," March 2004, 14–15.

Chapter 4

1. Deborah B. Pullen, "Her Price Is Far above Rubies," *Charisma*, May 1985, 27; quote in George Brown Tindall and David E. Shi, *America: A Narrative History*, 4th ed. (New York: Norton, 1996), 1379.

2. Frederick K. C. Price, *Faith, Foolishness, or Presumption* (Tulsa: Harrison House, 1979), 10.

3. *The Word of Faith*, October 1985, 12; Fred Price, "Keeping the Faith," *Charisma*, October 1988, 61; Price, *Faith, Foolishness, or Presumption*, 9.

4. Sherry Andrews, "Black Pentecostals: Who Are They?" *Charisma*, September 1978, 52–55.

5. Stephen Strang, "The Fight against Racism," *Charisma*, June 1989, 9; Leonard Lovett, "Racism and Reconciliation," *Charisma*, April 1993, 14–15; Joe Maxwell, "Healing the Rift between the Races," *Charisma*, April 1993, 18–24; "Healing Old Wounds in Memphis," *Charisma*, April 1993, 21; Vinson Synan, "Pentecostal Leaders Mend Racial Rift," *Charisma*, January 1994, 92.

6. Mary Patillo-McCoy, *Black Picket Fences: Privilege and Peril among the Black Middle Class* (Chicago: University of Chicago Press, 1999), 17–18.

7. Stephan and Abigail Thernstrom, *America in Black and White: One Nation, Indivisible* (New York: Simon and Schuster, 1997), 183.

8. Patillo-McCoy, *Black Picket Fences*, 27.

9. James E. Blackwell, *The Black Community: Diversity and Unity*, 2nd ed. (New York: Harper and Row, 1985), 124.

10. Charles T. Banner-Haley, *The Fruits of Integration: Black Middle-Class Ideology and Culture, 1960–1990* (Jackson: University Press of Mississippi, 1994), 44–45.

11. Sharon M. Collins, *Black Corporate Executives: The Making and Breaking of a Black Middle Class* (Philadelphia: Temple University Press, 1997); Daniel J. Walkowitz, *Working with Class: Social Workers and the Politics of Middle-Class Identity* (Chapel Hill: University of North Carolina Press, 1999); Patillo-McCoy fully examines these patterns in a Chicago suburb in *Black Picket Fences;* Banner-Haley, *The Fruits of Integration;* Black-

well, *The Black Community;* L. Bart Landry, "The Social and Economic Adequacy of the Black Middle Class," in *Dilemmas of the New Black Middle Class,* ed. Joseph R. Washington Jr. (self-published, 1980). Stephan and Abigail Thernstrom argue that although a disproportionate number of blacks were unemployed, lived in poverty, and received economic aid, the poor condition of African Americans was exaggerated and they were much better off than many observers believed. See *America in Black and White,* 183–84.

12. Johnnie L. Roberts, "The Race to the Top," *Newsweek,* January 28, 2002, 44–49.

13. E. Franklin Frazier, "Durham: Capital of the Black Middle Class," in *The New Negro,* ed. Alain Locke (New York: Charles and Albert Boni, 1925), 333–40.

14. David J. Dent, *In Search of Black America: Discovering the African-American Dream* (New York: Simon and Schuster, 2000), 413.

15. Robert L. Woodson, ed., *On the Road to Economic Freedom: An Agenda for Black Progress* (Washington, D.C.: Regnery Gateway, 1987), ix–xii.

16. Robert L. Woodson, "A Legacy of Entrepreneurship," in Woodson, *On the Road to Economic Freedom,* 22.

17. Woodson, *On the Road to Economic Freedom,* xi.

18. Bill Alexander, "The Black Church and Community Empowerment," in Woodson, *On the Road to Economic Freedom,* 48.

19. Frederick K. C. Price, *High Finance: God's Financial Plan: Tithes and Offerings* (Tulsa: Harrison House, 1984), 9–10.

20. "Project Change Speaks the Language of Life," *Changing Your World,* July–September 1999, 16–17; Regina M. Roberts, "Public Housing Community Gets Boost from Church Group," *Atlanta Journal-Constitution,* June 12, 1997; Shandra Hill, "Ministry Sets Out to Change World," *Atlanta Journal-Constitution,* October 9, 1997; Rochelle Carter and Sandra Eckstein, "A Lesson in Giving," *Atlanta Journal-Constitution,* February 15, 2001.

21. Jadell Forman, "Taking Religion to the Masses: T. D. Jakes," *Texas Monthly,* September 1998, 120–21.

22. Kelly Starling, "Why People, Especially Black Women, Are Talking about Bishop T. D. Jakes," *Ebony,* January 2001, 108–14, quotes on 112.

23. Harrell, *All Things Are Possible,* 98–99.

24. Dr. Frederick K. C. Price biography, http://www.faithdome.org/content/CyberChurch/Monthly_Messages/_Holding/DrpBio.html [hereafter cited as Price online biography] (accessed August 21, 2002); David Hazard, "Fred Price: 'I'm Just Me,'" *Bridge Builder,* January–February 1988, 5–11; Larry G. Murphy, J. Gordon Melton, and Gary L. Ward, eds., *Encyclopedia of African American Religions* (New York: Grand Publishing, 1993), 614–15.

25. Hazard, "Fred Price."

26. Price online biography.

27. Frederick K. C. Price, *The Holy Spirit—The Missing Ingredient: My Personal Testimony* (Tulsa: Harrison House, 1978), quote on 5; Stephen Strang, "The Ever Increasing Faith of Fred Price," *Charisma,* May 1985, 20–26; Price online biography.

28. S. Strang, "The Ever Increasing Faith of Fred Price."

29. Hazard, "Fred Price," 11; Price online biography.

30. Murphy, Melton, and Ward, *Encyclopedia of African American Religions*, 14–15; S. Strang, "The Ever Increasing Faith of Fred Price"; Church History, http://www.faithdome.org/content/CyberChurch/Church_History/dr5.html (accessed August 21, 2002).

31. Frederick K. C. Price, *Race, Religion, and Racism: A Bold Encounter with Division in the Church*, vol. 1 (Los Angeles: Faith One Publishing, 1999), 85–87, quotes on 85, 86; "Fred Price Completes 10,000-Seat Dome," *Charisma*, November 1988, 27; Price, *The Holy Spirit*, 24–25.

32. Hazard, "Fred Price," 11.

33. Victoria B. Lowe, "Frederick Price: The Making of a Ministry," *Religious Broadcasting*, February 1987, 28; Pinn, *The Black Church*, 135–36; Price online biography.

34. Price online biography; quote in V. B. Lowe, "Frederick Price," 28; Hazard, "Fred Price."

35. Thigpen, "The New Black Charismatics," 58–67, quote on 59; David Daniels III, "African-American Pentecostalism in the Twentieth Century," in Synan, *The Century of the Holy Spirit*, 265–91.

36. Hazard, "Fred Price."

37. Price online biography; Horatio Alger Association, General Information, http://www.horatioalger.com/geninf/PressRel/Html/02NewMem.htm (accessed September 11, 2003).

38. Hazard, "Fred Price," 11.

39. Price, *Race, Religion, and Racism*, 31.

40. Ibid., 53–61.

41. Billy Bruce, "Fred Price Triggers Debate over Racism," *Charisma*, April 1998, 16–17; Price, *Race, Religion, and Racism*, xiii, 6–7, 41–54.

42. Price, *Race, Religion, and Racism*, 34.

43. Ibid., 23.

44. Ibid., 16.

45. Ibid., 40.

46. Ibid., 35.

47. Ibid., 15–16.

48. Ed Donnally, "He's Still Not Afraid to Confront," *Charisma*, August 2000, 66–69.

49. Bruce, "Fred Price Triggers Debate over Racism," 16–17, quote on 17.

50. Kenneth Hagin Jr., "Take the High Road," *The Word of Faith*, July 1998, 2.

51. Quote in Kenneth Hagin Jr., "What Goes in Is What Comes Out!" *The Word of Faith*, August 1998, 2; "Overcoming Offense," *The Word of Faith*, April 2001, 2.

52. Price, *Race, Religion, and Racism*, 66.

53. One high-profile example was the 1994 Memphis Miracle meeting, where the all-white Pentecostal Fellowship of North America dissolved itself, apologized for its

history of racism, and formed the interracial Pentecostal/Charismatic Churches of North America. See Murphy, Melton, and Ward, *Encyclopedia of African American Religions,* 339.

54. The best scholarly accounts of T. D. Jakes to date are Lee's *T. D. Jakes* and Hubert Morken's "Bishop T. D. Jakes: A Ministry for Empowerment," in *Religious Leaders and Faith-Based Politics: Ten Profiles,* ed. Jo Renee Formicola and Hubert Morken (Lanham, Md.: Rowman and Littlefield, 2001), 25–52.

55. Bishop T. D. Jakes biography, http://www.thepottershouse.org/BJ_about.html [hereafter cited as Jakes online biography] (accessed June 14, 2003); Ken Walker, "Thunder from Heaven," *Charisma,* November 1996, 37–43; Pam Lambert and Michelle McCalope, "Soul Support," *People Weekly,* November 9, 1998, 121–23; "Preacher Offers Solace to Shattered Souls," America's Best: Society and Culture, http://www.cnn.com/SPECIALS/2001americasbest/TIME/society/culture/pro.tdjakes.htm (accessed September 11, 2001); Starling, "Why People Are Talking about Bishop T. D. Jakes"; Forman, "Taking Religion to the Masses."

56. Starling, "Why People Are Talking about Bishop T. D. Jakes," 110.

57. Jakes online biography; Walker, "Thunder from Heaven"; Ken Walker, "T. D. Jakes Builds Integrated Church," *Charisma,* May 1994, 61–62; quote in "Preacher Offers Solace to Shattered Souls"; Jim Jones, "Swift Growth Shapes Potter's House," *Christianity Today,* January 12, 1998, 56; Lauren F. Winner and Douglas LeBlanc, "T. D. Jakes Feels Your Pain," *Christianity Today,* February 7, 2000, 50–59; Forman, "Taking Religion to the Masses"; Lambert and McCalope, "Soul Support," 121–23; Melton, Lucas, and Stone, *Prime-Time Religion,* 161.

58. Walker, "T. D. Jakes Builds Integrated Church," 61–62.

59. Forman, "Taking Religion to the Masses," 120–21.

60. T. D. Jakes, *Woman, Thou Art Loosed!* (1993; Shippensburg, Pa.: Treasure House, 2001), 15–16.

61. Winner and LeBlanc, "T. D. Jakes Feels Your Pain," 55.

62. Jakes, *Woman, Thou Art Loosed!* 50–51.

63. "Preacher Offers Solace to Shattered Souls"; Forman, "Taking Religion to the Masses"; Walker, "T. D. Jakes Builds Integrated Church," 61–62; Van Biema, "Bishop Unbound," 86; Jimmy Stewart, "T. D. Jakes Breaks into R&B Charts," *Charisma,* March 1999, 17; Starling, "Why People Are Talking about Bishop T. D. Jakes"; Woman, Thou Art Loosed (2004), http://www.imdb.com/title/tt0399901/ (accessed June 29, 2005).

64. Lauren F. Winner, "84,000 Join Jakes in Georgia," *Christianity Today,* September 6, 1999, 23; Winner and LeBlanc, "T. D. Jakes Feels Your Pain," 50–59; Julia Duin, "Provocative Pentecostal," *Insight on the News,* September 14, 1998, 41.

65. Maureen Jenkins, "In Profile: T. D. Jakes," *Publishers Weekly,* May 25, 1998, S14–S16; Lynn Garrett, "A Star Rises," *Publishers Weekly,* March 9, 1998, 33; Winner and LeBlanc, "T. D. Jakes Feels Your Pain," 50–59; Forman, "Taking Religion to the Masses."

66. Lee, *T. D. Jakes,* 147–49, quote on 148.

67. T. D. Jakes Ministries, T.V. Ministry, http://www.tdjakes.org/tvministry (accessed April 4, 2001); Forman, "Taking Religion to the Masses"; Duin, "Provocative Pentecostal," 41; "Watch T. D. Jakes on these Television Stations . . . ," *Get Ready,* December 2000, [4]; Jones, "Swift Growth Shapes Potter's House," 56; Van Biema, "Spirit Raiser"; Lee, *T. D. Jakes,* 33–60.

68. Bishop T. D. Jakes timeline, http://www.thepottershouse.org/BJ_timeline.html (accessed June 14, 2003).

69. Walker, "T. D. Jakes Builds Integrated Church," 61–62; Ken Ward Jr., "Successful Books, TV Exposure Allow Kanawha Minister to Live in Style," *Charleston Gazette,* April 5, 1995; "Express Line," *Charleston Gazette,* April 8, 1995; R. A. Clise, "Jakes an Example of God's Blessings," *Charleston Gazette,* April 8, 1995; Franklin Murphy Sr., "Media Bullies Successful Blacks," *Charleston Gazette,* April 8, 1995; Ruth Glassburn Jones, "Minister Makes Many Sacrifices," *Charleston Gazette,* April 8, 1995; "Express Line," *Charleston Gazette,* May 1, 1995; "Express Line," *Charleston Gazette,* April 14, 1995; Lawrence Messina, "Televangelist Tries to Evict Couple from Home," *Charleston Gazette,* May 12, 1995; Lee, *T. D. Jakes,* 144; Bob Schwarz, "Jakes Pulling Up Stakes," *Charleston Gazette,* June 4, 1996; Megan Fields, "Goodbye, So Long and Farewell," *Charleston Gazette,* July 7, 1996; "Jakes' Mansion, Second Home Go on Sale," *Charleston Gazette,* July 7, 1996.

70. Walker, "Thunder from Heaven"; Forman, "Taking Religion to the Masses"; Jones, "Swift Growth Shapes Potter's House," 56; Schwarz, "Jakes Pulling Up Stakes." In 1996, W. V. Grant, a healing evangelist who worked extensively with Gordon Lindsay's Voice of Healing organization in the 1950s, pleaded guilty to filing false tax returns, and he served sixteen months in a federal prison in Oklahoma. He was also exposed as a fraudulent faith healer in the 1980s, which led to a serious decline in his national television ministry. See Harrell, *All Things Are Possible,* 172–74; "News Briefs," *Charisma,* June 1996, 30; "News Briefs," *Charisma,* December 1996, 30; "T. D. Jakes Taking Over for Jailed Tax Cheater," *Charleston Gazette,* July 24, 1996; Erickson, *Religious Radio and Television,* 89.

71. Quoted in Starling, "Why People Are Talking About Bishop T. D. Jakes," 112; "T. D. Jakes Celebrates Anniversary," *Charisma,* September 1997, 15; Duin, "Provocative Pentecostal," 41.

72. Walker, "Thunder from Heaven."

73. Jones, "Swift Growth Shapes Potter's House," 56; Lambert and McCalope, "Soul Support," 121–23; Starling, "Why People Are Talking about Bishop T. D. Jakes"; The Potter's House, http://www.thepottershouse.org/PH_about.html (accessed June 14, 2003); T. D. Jakes, lecture given at the Atlanta Crusade 2002, April 27, 2002.

74. The Potter's House Event Center, http://www.thepottershouse.org/PH_eventcntr.html# (accessed June 14, 2003); quote in Starling, "Why People Are Talking about Bishop T. D. Jakes," 110; Cheryl Thomas, "Getting Serious about the Father's Business: Online," *Get Ready,* December 2000, [8].

75. The Potter's House, http://www.thepottershouse.org/PH_about.html (accessed June 14, 2003); quote from Walker, "Thunder from Heaven," 43.

76. Starling, "Why People Are Talking about Bishop T. D. Jakes," 114.

77. Winner and LeBlanc, "T. D. Jakes Feels Your Pain," 59.

78. Forman, "Taking Religion to the Masses"; Winner and LeBlanc, "T. D. Jakes Feels Your Pain," 50–59.

79. Valerie G. Lowe, "Jakes Launches Mentoring Ministry," *Charisma,* August 1998, 30; Winner and LeBlanc, "T. D. Jakes Feels Your Pain," 50–59.

80. First Lady Serita Jakes, http://www.thepottershouse.org/BJ_serita.html (accessed June 14, 2003); "Don't Miss It!" AlabamaCBF listserv, October 24, 2001; Lambert and McCalope, "Soul Support," 121–23; "When the Bishop Speaks, People Listen," *Charisma,* November 1996, 39.

81. T. D. Jakes Ministries, ManPower Conference, http://www.tdjakes.org/manpower/ (accessed April 4, 2001); George J. Wallace, "T. D. Jakes Offers Alternative to Farrakhan Rally," *Charisma,* December 1995, 17–18.

82. Jakes lecture.

83. Jacqueline Jakes Sedgwick, "Maximized Manhood: Manpower 2000," *Get Ready,* December 2000, [5–7].

84. G. J. Wallace, "T. D. Jakes Offers Alternative," 17–18.

85. "Mega Fest Atlanta 2005," http://www.mega-fest.com/about.php (accessed June 10, 2005).

86. Quote in Jakes lecture; Valerie G. Lowe, "Stand Up and Be Counted," *Charisma,* December 1999, 70–74, 76.

87. John Drake, "Strength in Numbers: ManPower Conference Draws Thousands for Prayer, Fellowship," *Dallas Morning News,* July 14, 2001.

88. Jakes lecture.

89. Quote from Van Biema, "Bishop Unbound," 86; "Time Magazine Names Jakes Top 'Spiritual Innovator,'" *Charisma,* February 2001, 40; V. G. Lowe, "Stand Up and Be Counted"; "The Healer's Due," *The Economist,* May 31, 1997, 28; Winner and LeBlanc, "T. D. Jakes Feels Your Pain," 50–59; Starling, "Why People Are Talking about Bishop T. D. Jakes."

90. Van Biema, "Spirit Raiser."

91. "Preacher Offers Solace to Shattered Souls."

92. Lee, *T. D. Jakes,* 4, 6.

93. Dr. Creflo A. Dollar, "The 'Nothing Missing, Nothing Broken' Lifestyle: Understanding God's Will and Our Covenant of Peace," *Changing Your World,* November 2001, 5; Creflo Dollar Ministries, http://www.creflodollarministries.com/bio_t/ (accessed October 30, 2002); "Remember When," *Changing Your World,* August 2001, 25; Dr. Creflo A. Dollar, "How It All Began," *Changing Your World,* August 2001, 6–9; Dr. Creflo A. Dollar, "Choose Your Destiny!" *Changing Your World,* December 2001, 7.

94. C. A. Dollar, "How It All Began," 6–9.

95. Creflo Dollar Ministries, http://www.creflodollarministries.com/bio_t/ (accessed October 30, 2002).

96. C. A. Dollar, "How It All Began," 7.

97. C. A. Dollar, "The 'Nothing Missing, Nothing Broken' Lifestyle," 4–6; Taffi L. Dollar, "Under Construction: Building Your Future Worry Free," *Changing Your World,* August 2001, 26–27; Dr. Creflo A. Dollar Jr., "Freedom from the Quicksand of Debt," *Changing Your World,* September 2001, 4–6.

98. C. A. Dollar, "How It All Began," 9.

99. "Remember When," 25.

100. C. A. Dollar, "How It All Began," 6–9.

101. The *Atlanta Journal-Constitution* documents Dollar's struggles with his College Park neighbors as his ministry grew and his facilities expanded. See Barbara Ann Moore, "$6.5 Million Sanctuary-in-the-Round: Church Plans Dome Home: But World Changers' Neighbors Worry," October 10, 1992; Barbara Ann Moore, "Megachurch, Residents Square Off: Neighborhood Opposes Expansion," November 26, 1992; Ken Foskett, "'Mega' Church a Cross for Fulton to Bear: County to Consider Religious Freedom, Community Needs," February 3, 1993; Kent Kimes, "Dome of Contention: Residents Resist Church Plan: World Changers Wants to Expand Its Building," October 12, 1995; "College Park Church's Fight with Neighbors, County Grows," October 26, 1995; "Neighborhood vs. Church: Commission Postpones Request for Expansion," November 9, 1995; "Megachurch Wins Expansion Approval after Protest Folds," December 14, 1995; "Neighborhood Leader Draws Fire for Backing Church Expansion," December 21, 1995; "World Changers Make a Sort of Peace with Dome's Opponents," January 4, 1996; Kay S. Pedrotti, "Ministry Gets Planners' Nod for New Site Rezoning," April 24, 1997; Sandra Eckstein, "Neighbors Fear the Impact of Megachurch's Expansion," May 17, 2000; John McCosh, "Parking Ticket: Church Expansion Curbed Zoning: A Megachurch Was Pushed and Pulled over New Facility, and Fulton Planners Voted No," May 18, 2000; Sandra Eckstein, "Fulton Panel Kills Church Complex," June 8, 2000; "Rezoning Denied for Large Church," June 15, 2000; Charles Yoo, "Church Gets More Parking," November 20, 2001.

102. "From the Family," *Changing Your World,* August 2001, 18.

103. Creflo Dollar, *Understanding God's Purpose for the Anointing* (College Park, Ga.: World Changers Ministries, 1992).

104. Creflo Dollar, "Burden-Removing, Yoke-Destroying Power: The Anointing," *Believer's Voice of Victory,* July–August 1996, 9.

105. "Project Change Speaks the Language of Life," 16–17.

106. Creflo Dollar Ministries, http://www.creflodollarministries.org/international_t.html (accessed November 6, 2002); "Beacons of Light," *Changing Your World,* August 2001, 22; CDM staff, conversations with author, Atlanta, June 7, 2002; WCCI Timeline provided by CDM staff on June 7, 2002; Veleta Bowen, conversation with author, Atlanta, June 7, 2002.

107. WCCI Timeline; and the following items in *Changing Your World:* "Radio

Broadcasts," January–March 1999, 16–17; "Radio Broadcasts," April–June 1999, 17; "Changing Your World Broadcast Schedule," January 2000, 21–22; "Changing Your World Broadcast Schedule," March 2000, 14–15; "Changing Your World Weekly Broadcast Schedule," August 2000, 12; "Daily Broadcast Schedule," April 2001, 12–13; "Weekly Broadcast Schedule," November 2001, 8–9.

108. WCCI Timeline; CDM staff, conversations with author, Atlanta, June 7, 2002; and the following items in *Changing Your World:* "Television Broadcasts," January–March 1999, 16–17; "Television Broadcasts," April–June 1999, 16–17; "Changing Your World Broadcast Schedule," January 2000, 21–22; "Changing Your World Broadcast Schedule," March 2000, 14–15; "Changing Your World Weekly Broadcast Schedule," August 2000, 12; "Daily Broadcast Schedule," April 2001, 12–13; "Weekly Broadcast Schedule," November 2001, 8–9.

109. Arrow Records, http://www.arrowrecords.org (accessed November 6, 2002); CDM staff, conversations with author, Atlanta, June 7, 2002.

110. See the following articles in the *Atlanta Journal-Constitution:* Ralph Ellis, "Holyfield Minister Must Tell about Ties," August 28, 1999; "Pastor Fields Gift, Holyfield Queries," December 22, 1999; "Appeal Averts Jail for Holyfield Minister," March 2, 2000; "Sheriff Orders Arrest of Holyfield Minister," March 2, 2000; "Appeal Halts Search for Holyfield's Pastor," March 3, 2000. "Holyfield Settlement Will Keep Dollar in Circulation," March 11, 2000.

111. See the following articles in the *Atlanta Journal-Constitution:* Jack Warnet and Gita M. Smith, "Ethics Ruling: Fulton Officers Must Return $1,000," December 17, 1999; Ralph Ellis, "Pastor Fields Gift, Holyfield Queries," December 22, 1999; Alfred Charles, "Fulton Police Unit to Get Charity Role," December 23, 1999; "Ex-Fulton Chief Hasn't Returned Money to Church," February 29, 2000; Jim Dyer, "Most Officers Return $1,000 Gifts," September 23, 2000; D. L. Bennett, "Three Fulton Cops Didn't Repay Pastor," September 26, 2000.

112. Thigpen, "The New Black Charismatics"; Hawkins, "Shoutin' It from the Housetops," 22–29; Gaines, "Revive Us, Precious Lord." Milton C. Sernett traces the origins of this convergence of mainline African American religion with Pentecostalism to the Great Migration of southern blacks northward to urban areas during and after World War I. He argues that the modern scholarly and popular stereotype of the "core" African American cultural tradition of expressive worship and social activism developed during the 1920s and 1930s when black middle-class urban churches were yoked to the "distinctively 'black' (variously defined) cultural forms" of southern Pentecostal worship (6). See *Bound for the Promised Land: African American Religion and the Great Migration* (Durham, N.C.: Duke University Press, 1997).

Chapter 5

1. Eddie L. Long, lecture given at ManPower Conference 2002, Charlotte, North Carolina, August 9, 2002.

2. Quoted in Pinn, *The Black Church,* 28.

3. Ibid., 30.

4. Ibid., xii–xiii, 18–35. See also Conn, *The American City,* 184–86.

5. "New Members Handbook," Word of Faith International Christian Center [WOFICC] (Southfield, Mich.: WOFICC, 2002), 5–9; Steve Beard, "Pastor Keith Butler: Motor-Town Councilman," *Charisma,* June 1992, 14–19; "Expanding the Vision," *Vision,* July–August 1995, 2; "Good Friday Service," *Liberty,* May 1988, 1; Martha Fleming and Andrea Simpson, "The Greatest Love Story Every Told," *Vision,* May–June 1995, 4; "Word of Faith Detroit Closes on Duns Scotus Property," *Vision,* October–December 1996, 2; "Church Happenings: A Word from the Pastor," *Vision,* January–March 1997, 10; Grace Martin, "The Jewel of the City," *Vision,* October–December 1996, 8–9; announcement for ground-breaking ceremony, *Vision,* Fall 1997, 3.

6. "New Members Handbook," 5–9; WOFICC television and radio broadcast schedule, http://www.wordoffaith-icc.org/wof_broadcasts/wof_broadcasts/ (accessed November 11, 2002); "Set Your Dial for the Living Word Television Broadcast," *Vision,* July–August 1995, 15; schedule for radio and television broadcasts, *Vision,* January–March 1997, 15.

7. WOFCC-Philadelphia, http://www.wofccphilly.com/bio/ (accessed November 11, 2002); "Expanding the Vision," 2; Fleming and Simpson, "The Greatest Love Story Ever Told," 4; "Church Happenings: Word of Faith Opens in Jackson, Mississippi," *Vision,* October–December 1995, 10; "Quick Takes," *Vision,* October–December 1995, 11; "Word of Faith Is Marching On," *Vision,* October–December 1996, 2; "Forget '96: 1997 Will Be Like Heaven," *Vision,* January–March 1997, 2; WOFICC satellite churches, http://www.wordoffaith-icc.org/satellite_churches/satellite_churches/ (accessed November 11, 2002).

8. "Pakistan Calls on the Name of Jesus," *Vision,* May–June 1995, 10–11; "Spotlight on Missions: Word of Faith International Is Growing!" *Vision,* January–March 1997, 8–9; "The Consecration and Investiture of Pastor Keith A. Butler, Sr. to the Office of Bishop," *Vision,* Fall 1997, 10–11.

9. Word of Faith Bible Training Center, http://www.wordoffaith-icc.org/aducation/bibl_training_center/ (accessed November 13, 2002); Word of Faith Layperson's Bible School, http://www.wordoffaith-icc.org/aducation/layperson_bible_school/ (accessed November 13, 2002); Rodney Pearson, "Church Happenings: Graduation Day for School of Ministry Students," *Vision,* July–August 1995, 12; Patti Sanford, "Church Happenings: To God Be the Glory," *Vision,* July–August 1995, 12.

10. "Detroit Experiences a Word Explosion," *Vision,* October–December 1995, 2; announcement for the Living Word Convention in June 1997, *Vision,* January–March 1997, 6.

11. "Ministerial Association Is Formed," *Vision,* July–August 1995, 2; "Consecration and Investiture of Pastor Keith A. Butler, Sr.," 10–11.

12. "Church Happenings: Christian Business Association," *Vision,* October–

December 1996, 7; Word of Faith Kingdom Business Association, http://www. wordoffaith-icc.org/education/education/ (accessed November 13, 2002).

13. Keith A. Butler, "Is There a Separation between Church and State?" *Liberty*, September 1987, 3–4; S. J. O'Neal, "School Based Health Clinics vs. English, Math, Science," *Liberty*, June 1987, 3–4; S. J. O'Neal, "VICTORY for Our Children's Sake!" *Liberty*, September 1987, 1; quote in Beard, "Pastor Keith Butler," 18.

14. Beard, "Pastor Keith Butler," 18, 15, 19.

15. "Charismatic Pastor 'Prayed Hard' before Running for U.S. Senate," *Charisma NOW*, http://www.charismanow.com (accessed April 19, 2005); pundits quoted in Dan Gilgoff and Kenneth T. Walsh, "Republican and Black," *U.S. News and World Report*, February 27, 2006, 31; George Will, "A Conservative Black Candidate Is Making Ohio's Governor Race," *Chicago Sun-Times*, February 19, 2006; Clarence Page, "Year of the Black in GOP," *Chicago Tribune*, May 7, 2006.

16. Pastor biographies, http://www.wordoffaith-icc.org/home_page_links/pastoral_ bios (accessed November 13, 2002); Beard, "Pastor Keith Butler," 14–19.

17. Deborah Butler, "Molding Our Children toward Responsible Adulthood," *Liberty*, September 1987, 2; Deborah Butler, "Women of Virtue: A Personal Note from Deborah Butler," *Liberty*, June 1987, 3; Deborah Butler, "Women Empowered by God to Dominate in '98," *Vision*, Spring 1998, 8–9.

18. C. Pearson, *I've Got a Feelin'*, n.p.; Thigpen, "The New Black Charismatics"; Lee, *T. D. Jakes*, 40.

19. V. G. Lowe, "Carlton Pearson Aims at Racial Unity," 40.

20. Hazard, "A Narrow Way"; C. Pearson, *I've Got a Feelin'*, n.p.

21. Natalie Nichols, "Pearson Helps Heal Racial Divisions," *Charisma*, August 1993, 66.

22. Hazard, "A Narrow Way"; C. Pearson, *I've Got a Feelin'*, n.p.; HDEC Church History, http://www.higherd.org (accessed April 5, 2002).

23. Carlton Pearson, "The Spirit of Azusa," *Charisma*, January 1992, 16; "Interview with Carlton Pearson," *Bridge Builder*, March–April 1987, 11–12.

24. Thigpen, "The New Black Charismatics," 62.

25. Valerie G. Lowe, "COGIC Leaders Face Growth Challenge," *Charisma*, October 1999, 18–19; HDEC Pastor Biography, http://www.higherd.org (accessed April 5, 2002).

26. Advertisement for Azusa Conference 1993, *Charisma*, May 1993, n.p.; Lee, *T. D. Jakes*, 38–44.

27. Carlton Pearson, "Letters: Carlton Pearson Responds to Criticism," *Charisma*, August 2002, 12.

28. Natalie Nichols Gillespie, "People and Events: Controversy Clouds Pearson's Ministry," *Charisma*, October 2002, 24–25; John Blake, "Honoring Many Paths," *Atlanta Journal-Constitution*, December 17, 2005; "Pearson's 'Gospel of Inclusion' Stirs Controversy," *Charisma*, May 2002, 15.

29. "Pearson's 'Gospel of Inclusion' Stirs Controversy," 15.

30. Gillespie, "People and Events," 24–25; Julia Duin, "Keeping the Faith," *Washington Times,* March 19, 2003; "'Inclusionism' Deemed Heresy," *Washington Times,* April 21, 2004; Adelle M. Banks, "Minister Called Heretic for Views on Christianity," *Washington Post,* May 1, 2004.

31. John Blake, "Long View at New Birth," *Atlanta Journal-Constitution,* July 10, 1999; Biographical sketch, http://www.bellmins.com/biography/ (accessed November 21, 2002); Church history, http://www.newbirth.org/ (accessed April 20, 2001); Marcia Ford, "Baptist Spreads Renewal in Atlanta," *Charisma,* August 1994, 50–51.

32. Richard Daigle, "Shouting It from the Housetops!" *Charisma,* August 1999, 44.

33. Ford, "Baptist Spreads Renewal in Atlanta," 50–51.

34. Blake, "Long View at New Birth"; Biographical sketch, http://www.bellmins.com/biography/ (accessed November 21, 2002); Church history, http://www.newbirth.org/ (accessed April 20, 2001); Ford, "Baptist Spreads Renewal in Atlanta," 50–51; Daigle, "Shouting It from the Housetops!" 39–42, 44.

35. Daigle, "Shouting It from the Housetops!"; Ford, "Baptist Spreads Renewal in Atlanta," 51.

36. Blake, "Long View at New Birth"; Daigle, "Shouting It from the Housetops!" 39–42, 44.

37. Daigle, "Shouting It from the Housetops!"; Valerie G. Lowe, "Atlanta School Erupts in Revival," *Charisma,* December 1997, 40.

38. Quote in Daigle, "Shouting It from the Housetops!" 40; Bishop Eddie L. Long, "God and the Ballot Box," *Charisma,* October 2000, 14.

39. See the following articles in the *Atlanta Journal-Constitution:* quotes in John Blake, "March Divides King Followers," December 11, 2004; Add Seymour Jr., Kelly Simmons, and Don Plummer, "March Pushes Moral Agenda," December 12, 2004; Add Seymour Jr., "Long Doesn't Run from Controversy," December 12, 2004.

40. Harrell, *All Things Are Possible,* 234–35.

41. Melton, Lucas, and Stone, *Prime-Time Religion,* 278–80; Erickson, *Religious Radio and Television,* 151; Sam Nix, telephone conversation with author, May 1, 2002.

42. Michael Horton, "The Agony of Deceit," in Horton, *The Agony of Deceit,* 24.

43. Art Lindsley, "Settling for Mud Pies," in Horton, *The Agony of Deceit,* 57.

44. Quentin Schultze, "TV and Evangelism: Unequally Yoked?" in Horton, *The Agony of Deceit,* 196.

45. Harrison, *Righteous Riches,* 14.

46. Ever Increasing Word Ministries, http://www.eiwm.org/about.html (accessed December 23, 2002); Bruce Boyet, telephone conversation with author, June 3, 2002.

47. Ever Increasing Word Ministries, http://www.eiwm.org/speaking.html (accessed April 5, 2002).

48. Dr. Leroy Thompson, *Money, Thou Art Loosed!* (Darrow, La.: Ever Increasing Word Ministries, 1999), 5.

49. Ibid., 11.

50. Leroy Thompson, lecture given at New Life Interfaith Ministry, Bessemer, Alabama, August 2, 2002.

51. Quote in Gaines, "Revive Us, Precious Lord," 39; Peter K. Johnson, "People and Events: Vanguard of Pentecostal Revival," *Charisma,* August 1991, 15–16.

52. Hawkins, "Shoutin' It from the Housetops," 22–29; quote in Gaines, "Revive Us, Precious Lord," 38.

Conclusion

1. O. Roberts, *Expect a Miracle,* 231–32.

2. Osborn interview.

3. Harrell, *All Things Are Possible,* 237.

4. Griffith provides an overview of the modern therapeutic culture in *God's Daughters,* 33–39.

5. Harrell, *All Things Are Possible,* 229.

6. Harrison, *Righteous Riches,* 132.

7. Ibid., 134–37.

Bibliographic Essay

The most reliable source of information about these ministries is periodical literature. As I noted in the introduction, *Charisma and Christian Life* magazine was the single best source for gauging the mood of the charismatic movement. Founded in 1975 by Stephen Strang, *Charisma* addressed nearly all of the important issues facing the charismatic and Pentecostal movements at the end of the twentieth century. It also served as a clearinghouse for up-and-coming evangelists, providing them with much-needed publicity early in their careers. Although it was not the magazine's stated intention, *Charisma* provided the same type of exposure for independent charismatic evangelists in the late twentieth century that Gordon Lindsay's *The Voice of Healing* magazine provided healing evangelists in the previous generation. Nearly all of the ministers in this study published magazines or newsletters that provided valuable information about the growth of their ministries. Books and pamphlets published by these evangelists also proved to be invaluable resources. Though most often written to promote the message of prosperity or emotional and physical healing, they nearly always contained important biographical information about the ministers and offered a glimpse into their lives and ministries. Newspaper reports and popular periodicals such as *Christianity Today*, *Redbook*, and *Life* offered a more balanced and critical view of these ministries.

Historians have largely overlooked these evangelists, and few scholarly works have been written about them, even in fields other than history. The best account of the emergence of the independent charismatic movement is David Edwin Harrell Jr.'s *All Things Are Possible: The Healing and Charismatic Revivals in Modern America* (Indiana University Press, 1975), which describes the healing revival of the 1950s and the charismatic revival of the

1960s and early 1970s. Vinson Synan's edited volume *The Century of the Holy Spirit* (Thomas Nelson, 2001) provides a popular overview of the Pentecostal and charismatic movements in the twentieth century. It includes essays by Susan C. Hyatt and David Daniels III on the role of women and African Americans in these movements, but their broad scope allows for only cursory coverage of the charismatic movement in the last thirty years. Other works on early Pentecostalism, such as Robert Mapes Anderson's *Vision of the Disinherited* (Oxford University Press, 1979), Vinson Synan's *The Holiness-Pentecostal Tradition*, 2nd ed. (1971; Eerdmans, 1997), Harvey Cox's *Fire from Heaven* (Addison-Wesley, 1995), and Grant Wacker's *Heaven Below* (Harvard University Press, 2001), set the stage for the story of these modern charismatics.

Several biographies of varying quality provide insight into the leadership of the Pentecostal and charismatic movements. David Harrell has written the definitive scholarly biographies of Oral Roberts and Pat Robertson, two of the most visible and influential charismatic leaders. Edith L. Blumhofer and Daniel Mark Epstein have explained with great insight the important contributions of Aimee Semple McPherson to American Protestantism. Wayne Warner, Jamie Buckingham, Roberts Liardon, and Helen Kooiman Hosier have offered less analytical "insider" perspectives on Kathryn Kuhlman. R. G. Robins's *A. J. Tomlinson* (Oxford University Press, 2004), Shayne Lee's *T. D. Jakes: America's New Preacher* (New York University Press, 2005), and Grant Wacker and James R. Goff's edited volume *Portraits of a Generation* (University of Arkansas Press, 2002) are welcome additions to the body of scholarship of these movements. C. Douglas Weaver's biography of healing evangelist William Branham, first published in 1987, was reprinted and released by Mercer University Press in 2000.

Numerous polemical theological critiques of the Word of Faith movement have been published. Hank Hannegraff's *Christianity in Crisis* (Harvest House, 1997), David Hunt and T. A. McMahon's *The Seduction of Christianity* (Harvest House, 1985), D. R. McConnell's *A Different Gospel* (Hendrickson, 1988), John Ankerberg and John Weldon's *The Facts on the Faith Movement* (Harvest House, 1993), and Michael Horton's edited volume *The Agony of Deceit* (Moody Press, 1990) have gained the largest amount of popular attention. Derek E. Vreeland's paper presented at the 2001 annual meeting of the Society for Pentecostal Studies, titled "Restructuring Word of Faith Theology: A Defense, Analysis and Refinement of the Theology of the Word of Faith Movement," provides one of the most objective critiques by a member of the charismatic movement. Other observers, including sociologists Milmon Harrison and Shayne Lee, have provided insightful critiques of the effects of the Word of Faith movement on American society.

Sociologists, ethnographers, and theologians have contributed a great deal to our understanding of African Americans in the twentieth century, especially in relation to the Pentecostal and charismatic movements. E. Franklin Frazier in *The New Negro* (Charles and Albert Boni, 1925) and *The New Negro Thirty Years Afterward* (Harvard University Press, 1955) conducted some of the earliest research on the rise of the black middle class, which became the benchmark for later interpretations. James E. Blackwell's *The Black Community* (Harper and Row, 1985), Charles T. Banner-Haley's *The Fruits of Integration* (University Press of Mississippi, 1994), Stephan and Abigail Thernstrom's *America in Black and White* (Simon and Schuster, 1997), Sharon M. Collins's *Black Corporate Executives* (Temple University Press, 1997), and Mary Patillo-McCoy's *Black Picket Fences* (University of Chicago Press, 1999) trace the rise of the black middle class and provide the context for understanding its relationship to the modern charismatic movement. Milton C. Sernett, in *Bound for the Promised Land* (Duke University Press, 1997), examines the convergence of traditional mainline African American religion with Pentecostalism and the rise of a black urban middle class. Milmon F. Harrison, in *Righteous Riches: The Word of Faith Movement in Contemporary African American Religion* (Oxford University Press, 2005), offers the best sociological account of how the prosperity message affected modern black churches. Karen L. Kossie's Ph.D. dissertation, "The Move Is On: African-American Pentecostal-Charismatics in the Southwest" (Rice University, 1998), and Cheryl J. Sanders's *Saints in Exile: The Holiness-Pentecostal Experience in African American Religion and Culture* (Oxford University Press, 1996) provide information about the experience of African Americans in these movements. Anthony B. Pinn also provides analysis of African American religion in *The Black Church in the Post–Civil Rights Era* (Orbis Books, 2002).

A vast body of literature exists on the modern women's movement and its effects on American society. An excellent overview of the feminist movement in the late twentieth century is Ruth Rosen's *The World Split Open* (Viking Penguin, 2000). Other influential works include Judith Hole and Ellen Levine's *Rebirth of Feminism* (Quadrangle, 1971), Mary Carden's *The New Feminist Movement* (McKay, 1975), William Chafe's *The Paradox of Change* (Oxford University Press, 1991), Flora Davis's *Moving the Mountain* (Simon and Schuster, 1991), Kathleen C. Berkeley's *The Women's Liberation*

Movement in America (Greenwood Press, 1999), and Amy Erdman Farrell's *Yours in Sisterhood* (University of North Carolina Press, 1998). Margaret Caffrey, in *American Families* (Greenwood Press, 1991), examines the changing dynamics of the contemporary American family that emerged in the 1920s, which led to the tension that many fundamentalist Christians felt when trying to cope with the dramatic social changes of the post–World War II era.

Janet Wilson James's collection of essays *Women in American Religion* (1978; University of Pennsylvania Press, 1980) provides a broad overview of women's roles in American religion. In Thomas Tweed's edited volume *Retelling U.S. Religious History* (University of California Press, 1997), Ann Braude establishes women—not men—as the main characters in her narrative of American religious history, titled "Women's History *Is* American Religious History." In the summer 1995 issue of the journal *Religion and American Culture,* David G. Hackett discusses the history of gender and American religion in his article "Gender and Religion in American Culture, 1870–1930." Other scholars, including Margaret Lamberts Bendroth in *Fundamentalism and Gender* (Yale University Press, 1993), R. Marie Griffith in *God's Daughters* (University of California Press, 1997), Brenda E. Brasher in *Godly Women* (Rutgers University Press, 1998), and Julie Ingersoll in *Evangelical Christian Women* (New York University Press, 2003), focus more narrowly on the role of women in conservative evangelical movements.

Although little has been written about the rise of female ministers in the charismatic movement, a few studies have addressed the roles women have played in Pentecostal denominations. Charles H. Barfoot and Gerald T. Sheppard published some of the earliest research on this topic with a September 1980 article in the journal *Review of Religious Research* titled "Prophetic vs. Priestly Religion: The Changing Role of Women Clergy in Pentecostal Churches." Edith L. Blumhofer's spring 1995 article "Women in American Pentecostalism" in the Pentecostal journal *Pneuma* contributed fresh insight as well. Blumhofer's two-volume denominational history, *The Assemblies of God* (Gospel Publishing House, 1989), her *Restoring the Faith* (University of Illinois Press, 1993), and Mary Elizabeth Jones Jackson's 1997 Ph.D. dissertation, "The Role of Women in Ministry in the Assemblies of God" (University of Texas at Arlington), examine the role of male and female ministers in that denomination. In his 1997 Ph.D. dissertation, "Limiting Liberty: The Church of God and Women Ministers, 1886–1996" (Vanderbilt University), David G. Roebuck argues that although women played prominent roles as evangelists, prophets, and, occasionally, pastors in the denomination's early years, the male leadership of the Church of God (Cleveland, Tennessee) was never comfortable with women in the upper echelons of the denominational hierarchy. He rejects the common assertion that there was a "golden age" of sexual equality in the early twentieth century and demonstrates how denominational leaders limited the roles of women in the Church of God. In *God's Peculiar People* (University Press of Kentucky, 1988), folklorist Elaine J. Lawless examines the oral tradition among "oneness" Pentecostals in southern Indiana and maintains that their practice of allowing women to testify, prophesy, and preach gave women a modicum of control over their audiences and influence in their churches. The experiential nature of Pentecostal and charismatic worship services provided a great deal of freedom for women to participate publicly in the life of the congregation. Susan C. Hyatt's aforementioned essay in *The Century of the Holy Spirit* outlines the contributions of women to the Pentecostal and charismatic movements in the twentieth century, contending that female leadership diminished as Pentecostalism stabilized and institutionalized.

Index